NEW HISTORY IN CONTEXT 1

M.E. Collins

Peter Gallagher

Jim Byrne

John Keogh

General Editor: M.E. Collins

THE EDUCATIONAL COMPANY

First published 1995

The Educational Company of Ireland

Ballymount Road

Walkinstown

Dublin 12

Editorial Consultant: Roberta Reeners

Design and Artwork: Design Image

Cover: Design Image

Origination: Impress Communications Group

Printed in the Republic of Ireland by Smurfit Webb Press

Acknowledgments

The publishers wish to thank the following for assistance with photographic material and for permission to reproduce copyright material:

Charlotte Fabian, Rod Tuach, Ancient Art and Architecture, The Mary Evans Picture Library, Bord Failte/The Irish Tourist Board, The Office of Public Works, The National Museum.

Approved Quality System

The paper used in this book comes from Managed Forests in Northern Europe For every tree felled, at least one new tree is planted

0 1 2 3 4 5 6 7 8 9

CONTENTS

🏛 SECTION 8

THE PLANTATIONS

SPECIAL STUDY ◀

🏛 SECTION 9

THE AGE OF REVOLUTION

SPECIAL STUDY ◀

🏛 SECTION 10

THE INDUSTRIAL REVOLUTION

SPECIAL STUDY ◀

SECTION

1

THE WORK OF THE HISTORIAN

CHAPTER

1

Looking at the Past

What is history?

History is the story of the people who lived in the past and the events which took place in the past.

History could be the story of **ancient** times from thousands of years ago. Or it could be **modern** history, which may have happened only yesterday.

When we study history, we are trying to find out about these people and events. We must ask questions like this.

- How did they dress?
- What kinds of houses did they live in?
- What food did they eat? How did they cook it? Did they get it by hunting, farming or trading?
- Did they go to war? Why? What kinds of weapons did they use?
- Did they believe in a god? What kind of god did they believe in?

Historians

The people who try to find the answers to these questions are called **historians**. There are many ways in which historians find out about the past. They start by asking questions like the ones above. To get answers to these questions, the historian must learn certain skills.

During the Junior Certificate course, you will learn about and practise some of the skills which a good historian uses.

What is the past?

The past could be yesterday. It could be millions of years ago. But realistically, we can only find out about the lives of people who have lived during the last 10,000 to 12,000 years.

Dates

This is still a lot of time. To make sense of it, historians have ways of labelling and grouping years. The basic label is a **date**.

We use many dates in our everyday lives. For example, what is today's date? What year is it? Do you know the date on which you were born? On what dates were your parents born? When did your school or club win a big sporting event? In what year did an Irish athlete win a gold medal?

All of these dates are named by giving the day, the month and the year – Tuesday 17 March 1987.

THE CHRISTIAN CALENDAR

A date like this comes from a way of counting time which was invented in Europe. The people who introduced it were Christians. They believed that modern time began with an event which was very important to them – the birth of Jesus Christ. They called that year *Anno Domini*, which means "the year of Our Lord".

BEFORE CHRIST

For Christians, the year in which Christ was born marked the dividing line in history. They labelled the years before his birth with the letters **BC**, meaning **before Christ**. So the first year before the birth of Christ is 1 BC. One hundred years before is 100 BC. One thousand years before is 1000 BC.

ANNO DOMINI

The years after Christ's birth are **AD,** for *Anno Domini*. The year in which Christ was born is 1 AD. One hundred years after is 100 AD. One thousand years after is 1000 AD. The year in which you were born was 19— AD (you fill in the blanks), which means you were born that many years after the birth of Christ.

CENTURIES

Historians like to group years together to make them easier to handle. A group of ten years is called a **decade**. A group of 100 years is a **century**.

This is the twentieth century. This may seem odd, because it begins with the number 19. The diagram below will show why centuries are labelled in this way.

This system of dates is very important for historians. Unless you are familiar with it, you will have great difficulty learning to be a historian.

COMPLETE THESE TABLES. GO UP TO 2000 IN EACH CASE. THIS SHOWS YOU WHY THE YEAR 1990 IS IN THE **TWENTIETH CENTURY**, NOT THE NINETEENTH.

Activity

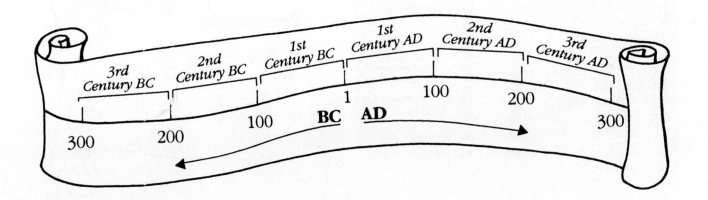

Activities

1. HERE ARE SOME DATES FOR YOU TO PRACTISE. FOR EACH DATE, TELL WHICH **CENTURY AD** IT BELONGS TO. WRITE THE ANSWERS IN YOUR COPYBOOK.

753 AD	385 AD
632 AD	1334 AD
564 AD	1198 AD
1189 AD	1867 AD
1014 AD	1639 AD
1572 AD	

2. THE WAY WE COUNT TIME WAS INVENTED BY CHRISTIANS. BUT OTHER RELIGIONS ALSO HAVE THEIR OWN CALENDARS. TRY TO FIND OUT ABOUT THE JEWISH AND MUSLIM CALENDARS. THEN TRANSLATE THIS YEAR IN THE CHRISTIAN CALENDAR INTO ITS JEWISH OR MUSLIM EQUIVALENT.

Ages, eras and periods

Historians also group centuries together into times when particular things were taking place. These groups of centuries are called **ages**, **eras** or **periods**. For example, the time during which people made their tools from stone is called the **Stone Age**. This timeline shows some of the main periods you will study in Junior Certificate History.

This stone calendar was carved by the Mayan people who once lived around Central America. It was made between 500-900 AD.

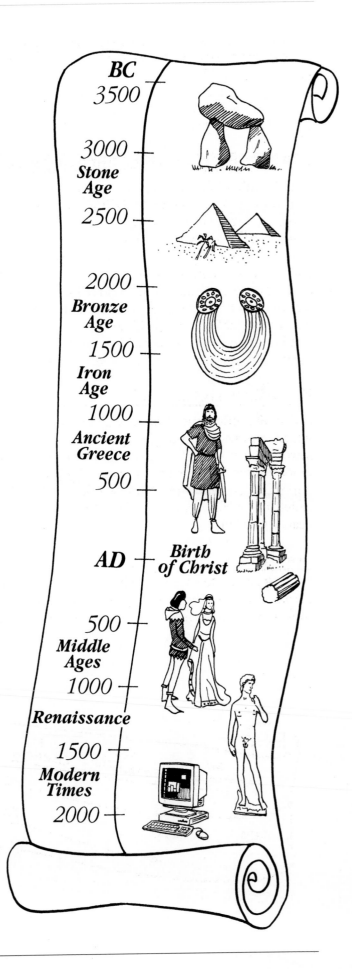

BC
3500
3000
Stone Age
2500
2000
Bronze Age
1500
Iron Age
1000
Ancient Greece
500
AD — Birth of Christ
500
Middle Ages
1000
Renaissance
1500
Modern Times
2000

CHAPTER 2

The Sources of History

🏛 How to find out about the past

If your teacher asked you to write an essay about life in Ireland two thousand years ago, what would you do? You would probably get out a history book and look for information about ancient Ireland.

🏛 SECONDARY SOURCES (HISTORY BOOKS)

Historians also look for information in history books. They call history books **secondary sources**. That means that they were **written by another historian about the past.** The book you are reading now is an example of a secondary source.

🏛 PRIMARY SOURCES (THINGS FROM THE PAST)

But how did the historian who wrote the history books find out about ancient Ireland? How did he or she know what to write? Where did the information come from? This is the real business of the historian – finding out things about the past which no one has found before.

Historians hunt for clues that come **directly from the people they are studying**. They call these clues **primary sources**. Historians put these primary sources together. They study them, think about them and try to come up with sensible answers.

No historian feels that he or she knows anything about the past until they have studied both the primary sources and the secondary sources (the history books). The primary sources are the **evidence** which the historian uses to make an informed statement about the past.

▲ *These primary sources show a burial mound at Dowth, Rembrandt's painting of his mother, Kilkenny Castle, and Pope John Paul II's visit to Ireland.*

⌂ YOUR OWN PRIMARY SOURCES

Let's look at a simple example of a primary source. How old are you? Write down your age in your workbook.

Historians would not be satisfied with that answer. They would say: "How do you *know* how old you are? What *evidence* do you have? What are your *sources* for saying you are that age?"

To answer the historians, you would have to produce your evidence. Here are some of the sources you might use.

- ☑ A **birth certificate**
- ☑ A **newspaper announcement** of your birth
- ☑ Information from your **parents**
- ☑ A **photograph** of you as a baby with the date written in

▲ *A baby photograph is an important source of information about your life.*

These sources would convince any historian that you are right about your age. Perhaps you could add more sources from other parts of your life – a report from your primary school, a picture of you in a newspaper. From primary sources like these, historians have the evidence they need to start building a history of your past life.

⌂ Historical sources

Birth certificates and newspaper announcements are examples of **personal sources**. Historians can use a much wider range of sources. Here are some examples.

⌂ PICTORIAL SOURCES

It is always interesting to know what people looked like. We can find out from sources such as paintings and carvings. In some places, **pictorial sources** like these can go back a long way.

Three thousand years ago in ancient Egypt, people painted pictures about their lives on the walls of tombs. But Egypt is an exception. In Ireland, there are no pictures or paintings of real people until about five hundred years ago.

◄ *This Egyptian wall painting tells the story of a bride and groom. The priest on the left is sprinkling them with holy water.*

▲ *This photograph from the Lawrence Collection shows Patrick St in Cork at the beginning of the 20th century.*

⌂ FILMS AND PHOTOGRAPHS

Photographs and films are great sources of information about what people looked like in the past. The camera was invented in the 1830s and we have photographs dating from around 1840. Movie cameras were invented in the 1890s, so we only have moving pictures dating back a century. Modern developments such as videos can now give us instant images.

⚏ ORAL SOURCES

When you wanted to find out how old you were, you asked your parents. Their answer is an **oral source**.

An oral source is something someone **tells** us about the past. You could find out about what life in Ireland was like fifty or sixty years ago by asking older people like your grandparents. If you record what they say, you will have a very valuable permanent record on tape which will still be there long after a person has died.

Like photographs, oral sources do not go back very far. You probably won't meet many people who can remember back more than ninety years. And since voice recording began around 1880, the oldest recordings only go back about 100 years.

⚏ WRITTEN SOURCES

The most important sources of historical information come from writing. **Written sources** are so important that historians divide history into two parts.

- ◤ **pre-history**: before people developed a system of writing
- ◤ **history**: after people learned to use writing

The great advantage of written sources is that people speak to us through the written word. They tell us their names. They tell us about their beliefs. They let us know about their most intimate secrets, ideas and feelings.

Historians can build up pictures of people and events from the words people write. We will be looking at many written sources in this book.

⚏ THE START OF WRITING

Writing is a fairly new development. The earliest known writing appeared around 3000 BC in a region called Mesopotamia (near modern Iran). From there, writing slowly spread throughout Asia and Europe.

The Greeks (Section 3) were the first Europeans to develop a system of writing. They began to write about 500 BC. At about the same time, the Jewish people in Palestine began to write down the Old Testament of the Bible. The written word first appeared in Ireland about a thousand years later, in 400 or 500 AD. So you can see that the line between history and pre-history is different in different places.

◤ *This is a sample of the earliest known writing. It is about 5000 years old. It is called "cuneiform" and comes from Mesopotamia.*

Here are some important written sources.
letters
diaries
account books
certificates
newspapers
inscriptions on tombs
the Bible
coins
maps
books of memoirs

◤ QUESTIONS ◤

1. What is a **historical source**?
2. Explain the difference between a **primary source** and a **secondary source**.
3. Give one example of each of the following: (a) an **oral** source; (b) a **pictorial** source; (c) a **written** source.
4. Which of these sources do historians value most? Explain your answer.
5. What do historians mean by **pre-history**?

CHAPTER 3

Archaeology

Artefacts

When people have not developed a system of writing, we can only find out about them from the things they **made** rather than from the things they **wrote**. Things which people make are called **artefacts**. When we study people who could not write, or who did not write very much, their artefacts are our main sources of information.

Here are some of the artefacts that we use as sources.

tools
furniture
houses
toys
clothes
jewellery
pottery
weapons
coins

This carved figure was found in a bog in Co. Cavan.

Archaeologists

Historians who study artefacts are **archaeologists.** They also try to answer questions about the past, but they do it in a special way. Here is how archaeologists go about their work.

AN EXCAVATION

First, archaeologists find a place where people once lived. They call it their **site**. They **excavate** (dig) in the ground at the site, looking for things left behind by the people who once lived there.

Archaeologists look for all sorts of things – bits of pottery, the foundations of houses, the bones of animals, tools, coins, even seeds. From these, they carefully build up a picture of the lives of the people who lived in that place hundreds or even thousands of years ago.

An archaeological excavation in progress at the Ceide Fields in Co. Mayo.

How do archaeologists know where to look? Various things can lead them to a site.

LOOK IN THE OBVIOUS PLACE

Some archaeological sites are obvious because an old building stands on the spot. The photograph below shows one example of an obvious place – the pyramids of Egypt. We know the pyramids were built about 4000 years ago.

In Ireland, there are many sites like this, such as Newgrange in Co. Meath (page 16).

The pyramid and sphinx at Giza in Egypt – an obvious place to look!

FOLLOW UP A STORY

Sometimes, stories or legends about a place will make archaeologists curious. In Greece, there were many stories about the wars between the Greeks and the Trojans. These tales encouraged archaeologists to look for the places in which these legendary people lived. You will read about this in Section 3.

In Ireland, Emain Macha in Co. Armagh is associated with the stories about the hero Cú Culainn. Today, this place is called Navan Fort. Archaeologists excavated the site and made many exciting discoveries.

More recent stories come from the time of the Spanish Armada. The Armada was a huge fleet of Spanish ships which was wrecked by fierce gales off the west coast of Ireland in 1588. In recent years, underwater archaeologists have found and excavated some of these wrecks.

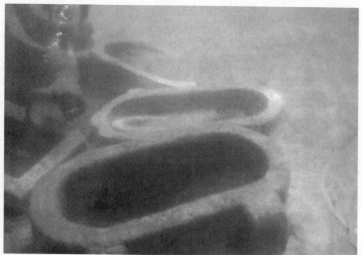

▲ *Underwater archaeology is now possible with modern equipment. The picture shows some cargo from a Roman shipwreck.*

LOOK FROM THE AIR

Aerial photographs can help archaeologists to find a promising site. From these pictures, archaeologists may see things they might have missed while walking.

Look at the photograph at the right. The fort might not have been so obvious from the ground, but the aerial photograph picks it up clearly.

RESCUE ARCHAEOLOGY

A lot of modern archaeology begins with an emergency. When builders are planning a new development, they often ask archaeologists to look at the site first, in case they destroy something important. This is called **rescue archaeology**, and it can lead to wonderful finds. Here are two recent examples.

◢ **Mount Sandel**: When some new houses were being built in Co. Derry, the archaeologists discovered a place where people had lived 9000 years ago. So far, this is the oldest human settlement ever discovered in Ireland.

◢ **Wood Quay**: When Dublin Corporation wanted to build new offices at Wood Quay, they asked archaeologists to have a look at the site. From their excavations, they discovered a great deal of new information about the life of Dubliners who had lived at Wood Quay over a thousand years ago.

A LUCKY FIND

Luck often plays a part in archaeology. In 1974, workmen digging a well in China discovered some life-sized statues of warriors and their horses. This led archaeologists to one of the most spectacular finds of modern times, the burial place of an ancient Chinese emperor.

In Ireland, several important sites were found when the gas pipeline was being laid between Cork and Dublin. Sometimes, a farmer ploughing land

▲ *This aerial photograph gives a clear view of the mound at Rathcroghan, Co. Roscommon. It is said to be the place where the kings of Connacht were crowned.*

turns up an ancient grave or the foundations of a house. At Corlea in Co. Longford, turf-cutters in a bog uncovered an ancient roadway made of planks of wood.

◀ *A lucky find – the famous Chinese Warriors were discovered in 1974. They were placed in an emperor's tomb in 210 BC.*

How archaeologists work

PREPARING FOR AN EXCAVATION

Once archaeologists have found a possible site, they prepare to excavate it. They organise a team of assistants to help with the **dig**.

The first step is to make a detailed plan of the site. On it, archaeologists mark the main features. They then divide the site into squares and give each square a number or a letter. Then when a find is made, they know exactly which part of the site it came from.

DIGGING

When excavation begins in one of the squares, the team looks for tiny things – seeds, bones, bits of pottery. They must work slowly and carefully because they do not want to destroy any valuable evidence.

Once the top soil has been removed, they no longer use spades or shovels. Instead, they use trowels or even brushes to ease the soil away. Sometimes they put the soil through a sieve to find tiny seeds or bits of bone. Some of the soil may even be examined under a microscope to find minute grains of **pollen** (plant dust).

RECORDING THEIR FINDS

When something is found, it is photographed exactly where it lies. It is then carefully removed, cleaned and labelled. Every detail is written on the label – exactly where it was found, its size and shape, and what was above or below it. It is then stored away to be studied properly when the excavation is over.

◀ *An archaeologist studies the finds taken from a dig in the Middle East.*

LOOKING AT THE SOIL

Archaeologists carefully study the soil in which they are digging. Here are some of the things they are looking for.

▧ When timber posts rot away, they leave small round, dark patches in the soil. Archaeologists call them **post holes**. Ancient people often used wooden posts in the walls of their houses, so post holes in the soil could mean that an ancient wooden house once stood on the site. If the post holes are in a circle, it was a round house. If they form a rectangle, then it was a rectangular house.

▧ A square dark patch with traces of ashes may mean a fireplace. Sometimes, small post holes near a fireplace suggest that a pot was hung over the fire on a wooden stand.

Dating the finds

ORGANISING THE EVIDENCE

At the end of a successful dig, archaeologists will have found a great deal of evidence. They may spend years examining it to find out what it can tell them. There are many questions they have to ask. They often look for help from other scientists to find the answers.

🏛 How old is it?

When they excavate a site, archaeologists first ask:
- ◢ **When** did people live here?
- ◢ **How old** are the things we have found?

🏛 Getting a Date

Occasionally, it is easy to say how old things are. Archaeologists may find a coin with someone's picture on it or an inscription on a tomb which gives them a clue. But this is exceptional. Usually, archaeologists have to use other ways to find the date of an object. Here are three of the most important ways of working out the age of a site or artefact.

Comparing Objects

Up to fifty years ago, archaeologists had only one way of working out dates. They compared the objects they found with similar objects found on other sites whose age they knew. The easiest artefacts to date are pottery. If a particular type of pot was found in two places, it seemed likely that people had lived in these places at roughly the same time.

This method of dating was not very reliable, however. Since the 1960s archaeologists have found better ones. The first is **carbon dating**.

Carbon Dating

Carbon dating began in America. Scientists discovered that all living plants and animals absorb a radioactive carbon called **carbon 14** into their cells from the atmosphere. When they die, the carbon 14 decays at a fixed rate. After 5730 years, half of it is gone. By measuring how much carbon 14 is left in a bone or a piece of wood, it is possible to work out how old it is.

Carbon dating was first tried out on tombs in Egypt where the age of the artefacts was already known. It gave a roughly accurate date for the things being tested. But these dates were only approximate, and no one was sure whether carbon dating would work for Ireland. Irish archaeologists wanted to develop a method that would give them a more exact date.

Dendrochronology

Around 1970, archaeologists in Belfast began to work on a new method of dating. It is called **dendrochronology**. This means using wood (*dendro*) to work out dates (*chronology*). The wood they used was oak.

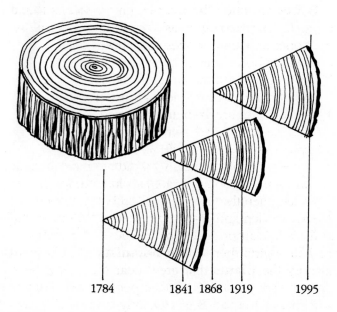

1784   1841 1868 1919   1995

◢ *Dendrochronology is a method of dating which uses the patterns in tree rings.*

Oak trees have grown in Ireland for 8000 years. People used oak to build houses, boats and bridges. Like all trees, an oak forms rings as it grows. The rings may be wide or narrow, depending on the weather. Over the hundreds of years that an oak can live, the rings form a pattern. All oaks growing in the same years will have the same pattern.

Archaeologists believed that by matching these patterns, they could work out when a particular piece of oak had been growing. If they knew that, they could tell when the building it was used in was built. The sketch above shows how this works.

Many ancient oaks are buried in Irish bogs. When they are found, their ring patterns are added to the record. By 1984, archaeologists had traced a set of oak patterns back to 5289 BC (with one or two short gaps). This is the second oldest dendrochronological record in the world. Because of it, the archaeologists who found the timber roadway at Corlea in Co. Longford (page 9) can say that the timber used to make it was cut between "the autumn of 148 BC and the spring of 147 BC".

Carbon dating and dendrochronology have helped Irish archaeologists to answer their most important questions: How old is this site? When did people live here?

🏛 Information from Bones and Plants

As well as working out the date, archaeologists ask many other questions about the sites they have excavated. They call on other scientists to help them.

Bones are often the most common objects found on a site. Archaeologists ask **zoologists** to examine the bones and answer questions about them.

☑ Are the bones animal or human?

☑ If the bones are human, how did the people die? What diseases or injuries did they have?

☑ If the bones are from animals, what kind of animals are they? If there are only bones from wild animals, the people who lived on the site were probably hunters who did not farm. If there are bones of domestic animals like sheep or cattle, then the people were probably farmers.

Seed, pollen and grain are sometimes found in the soil or embedded in pieces of pottery. Archaeologists then call in **botanists** to help them identify the **plants** that grew near the site. Wheat, oats or barley indicate that the people were farmers who planted crops. Seeds entirely from wild plants suggest that the people did not farm the land.

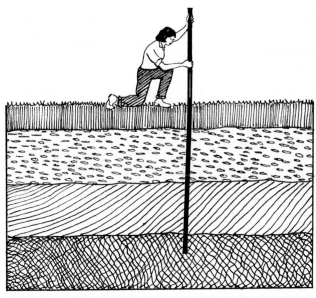

▧ *Taking a pollen sample*

THE POLLEN RECORD

Archaeologists can learn a lot from **pollen**, a very fine plant dust. All plants give off pollen, and botanists know which kind of pollen comes from which plant. With this information, archaeologists will know what plants were growing nearby when the site was occupied. This can also give them information about both the climate at the time and the food the people had.

Pollen in bogs is especially useful to archaeologists. Bogs are formed when layers of mosses and other types of plant material build up. Each layer covers the one beneath, trapping any pollen blown in by the wind. Archaeologists use a special method of getting pollen samples from bogs. The sketch above shows how it works.

A long hollow tube is pushed into the bog. When it is pulled out, it contains a piece of each layer of the bog. A botanist then looks at the pollen in each layer. The findings may look like this.

Layer C (the most recent layer) contained only pollen from trees – birch, ash, oak and elm.

Layer B had pollen from oats and barley, with very little tree pollen.

Layer A (the oldest layer) had pollen from trees like ash, oak and elder.

What does this pollen evidence show? From the pollen record in Layer A, the oldest layer, this site was first covered with forests. Then farmers came. Layer B suggests that they cut down the forest and planted crops. Layer C, the most recent layer, contained only tree pollen. This suggests that the

farmers left the site for some reason, and the forest returned.

Why did the farmers leave? Archaeologists can only guess. Did the climate change? Did the people emigrate to a better place? Much more evidence is needed before these questions can be answered.

☑ QUESTIONS ☑

1. What is an **artefact**?
2. What kind of historian finds out about the people of the past by studying their artefacts?
3. Explain in your own words how archaeologists do their work.
4. What is an **excavation**? Give **three** reasons why an archaeologist might decide to excavate a particular place.
5. Describe the main steps in an archaeological excavation.
6. Name **two** ways in which archaeologists date the artefacts found at an excavation. Describe how **one** of these works.
7. What can an archaeologist learn about the past from: (a) the **pollen record**; and (b) **bones**?

IS THERE ANY PLACE NEAR YOU WHERE AN ARCHAEOLOGIST MIGHT WANT TO EXCAVATE? WRITE A PARAGRAPH ABOUT THE PLACE, GIVING REASON WHY YOU THINK IT IS WORTH EXCAVATING.

Activity ▼

CHAPTER 4

The Mesolithic Period – Ireland's First People

Our earliest ancestors

In this section we will study the people who lived in ancient Ireland. Up to about 500 AD, people in Ireland did not know how to write, so we only know about them from artefacts like the tools, tombs or pottery they left behind.

When people have not developed a system of writing, there are many things we cannot find out about them. For example, we do not know what they called themselves. Archaeologists have had to invent names for them like "stone age people" or "the first farmers".

The end of the last ice age

Until about eleven thousand years ago, most of Ireland was covered by a great sheet of ice. We know that people lived in both Europe and Britain at that time. But so far, archaeologists have not found any evidence of people in Ireland during the ice age.

Around 9000 BC, the ice began to melt. At first, the seas around Ireland were shallow and a **land bridge** linked this island to Britain and the continent. Animals like deer and wild pigs were able to walk across this bridge. Perhaps the first people reached Ireland in the same way.

Later, the land sank beneath the water and the land bridge vanished. The Irish Sea was formed, making further land crossings impossible.

Discoveries at Mount Sandel

We do not know when or how the first people came to Ireland. Archaeologists have found traces of them in many places around the country. The best evidence about them comes from Mount Sandel in Co. Derry.

When Mount Sandel was excavated, the archaeologists found circles of post holes. These suggest that the people lived in round huts made from branches bent over and tied in the middle, like an Indian wigwam. The branches were then covered with something – perhaps skins or sods of earth. There was a **hearth** (fireplace) in the centre of the floor.

TOOLS AND FOOD

Archaeologists at Mount Sandel found sharp stones scattered around the site. These were probably used to make spears and arrows, They also found the bones of deer, hares, dogs, fish and small birds. A few burnt hazel nuts and some apple seeds also survived. Carbon dating showed that people had lived at Mount Sandel between about 7040 BC and about 5935 BC.

MESOLITHIC PEOPLE

This period is called the **Mesolithic period** or the **Middle Stone Age**.

Mesolithic people lived in small groups of about half a dozen adults and their children. They used simple stone tools and weapons. They moved through the forests, setting up camp on the banks of rivers or lakes. They hunted, fished and gathered berries and nuts. When they had used up the local food supply, they moved on to another spot. Archaeologists sometimes call these people **hunter-gatherers**.

USE THE INFORMATION IN THIS CHAPTER AND INFORMATION FROM BOOKS IN THE LIBRARY TO DESCRIBE THE LIFE OF A PERSON DURING THE MESOLITHIC PERIOD. YOU SHOULD REFER TO:

Finding Out

- [ ] THEIR HOUSE
- [ ] THEIR TOOLS
- [ ] THEIR FOOD AND HOW THEY GOT IT
- [ ] THEIR CLOTHES.

Using evidence from Mount Sandel, an artist was able to create this impression of a group of Mesolithic people.

The Neolithic Period – The First Farmers and Tomb-builders

Ireland's first farmers

For about 3000 years, hunter-gatherers had the island of Ireland to themselves. Then, around 4000 BC, a new group of people arrived. They may have come from Britain in dug-out canoes, although it is possible that some came directly from the continent.

These people knew how to farm. They brought domesticated animals like cattle, pigs, sheep and goats with them as well as the seeds of wheat and barley.

They cut down trees in the forest to make clearings. They planted crops there and let their animals graze. Because they had a regular food supply from farming, there were far more of them and they stayed put in one place.

The Neolithic Period: 4000 BC – 2000 BC

The period of the first farmers is called the **Neolithic Period** or the **New Stone Age**. It began in Ireland around 4000 BC and lasted for about 2000 years.

Since Neolithic farmers stayed in one place, it is easier to find traces of their houses and fields. They made things which have lasted, like pottery and jewellery. They also left memorials in the form of great stone monuments (pages 15-17).

THE CÉIDE FIELDS

The best information about the Neolithic farmers comes from the **Céide Fields** in Co. Mayo. People digging turf in this area often found old stone walls buried in the bog, but it was only when archaeologists excavated the site that they realised how old the walls were.

Neolithic farmers built these walls 5000 years ago. The walls enclose fields where the farmers herded their sheep or cattle. In one place, archaeologists even found the marks made by a stone age plough.

These 5000-year-old walls, hidden beneath a bog, led to the excavations at the Céide Fields.

NEOLITHIC FARMHOUSES

Several neolithic farmhouses have been found in Ireland. The best are at Tankardstown and at Lough Gur, both in Co. Limerick.

There were two houses at Tankardstown. Both were rectangular and built of planks. The smaller house measured 6.5m by 5m. The bigger house was 15m by 7.5m and had three rooms.

At Lough Gur, there were several houses. The walls were made of hazel rods, woven together like a basket. Mud was then daubed on the basket-work to keep out the draughts. This method of building is called **wattle and daub**.

TOOLS AND WEAPONS

Neolithic farmers used stone axes to cut trees and a kind of stone plough to dig the earth before planting seed. Although they got much of their food from farming, they still hunted wild pigs and deer in the forest, using stone-tipped arrows and spears.

The walls of Neolithic houses were made by weaving hazel rods together, as the photograph shows. The basket-work was then covered with mud. This is called "wattle and daub".

POTTERY

Neolithic farmers were the first people in Ireland to make pottery. They made bowls by hand, using rolls of clay. Then they fired the bowls in bonfires which were heated to 800°C. Some pots were used to hold the ashes of people whose bodies had been **cremated** (burnt).

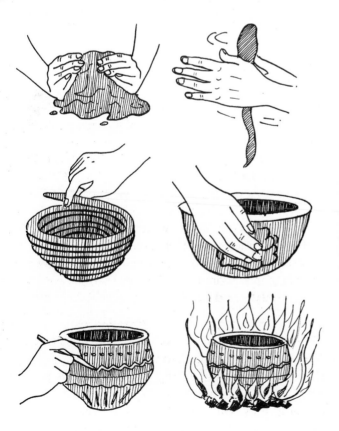

Neolithic pottery was made using rolls of clay.

☑ QUESTIONS ☑

1. What does the word **Neolithic** mean?
2. Give **two** ways in which Neolithic people were different from those who lived before them.
3. Name one site in Ireland where Neolithic farmers lived. Describe the kind of houses that archaeologists found there.
4. Select one kind of artefact (tools, pottery) from the Neolithic period and describe it.

Megalithic tombs

Neolithic farmers have left us some very spectacular monuments. These are the great stone tombs that can be seen all over Ireland. Archaeologists call them **megalithic** (meaning "big stone") **tombs**.

There are four kinds of megalithic tombs: court cairns, wedge tombs, portal tombs and passage graves.

COURT CAIRNS

Court cairns were the earliest megalithic tombs. (A cairn is a mound of stones.) There are at least 400 of them in Ireland, mainly in the northern half of the country. Similar tombs are found all over Europe.

A court cairn at Creevykeel, Co. Sligo

Court cairns have two parts. In front is the **court**, an open area surrounded by stones. Archaeologists think that some ceremony connected with the dead may have been held in this court area.

Behind the court is the cairn. This is a mound which covers a stone passage opening into a chamber. The cremated bodies were buried here, with the ashes in pottery bowls.

WEDGE TOMBS

These are similar to court cairns, but without the court. They consist of a covered passage that is higher at the entrance and gets lower towards the end. Wedge tombs get their name from their wedge shape.

There are over 460 wedge tombs in Ireland. There are none in Britain, although some have been found in Brittany in France. Because of this, archaeologists wonder whether the idea of wedge tombs came to Ireland from there.

A wedge tomb at Haroldstown Co. Carlow

PORTAL TOMBS OR DOLMENS

There are over 160 portal tombs or dolmens in Ireland. Dolmens are very spectacular and consist of four huge stones. Three stones stand on the ground and support the fourth, a massive "roof stone" (or "cap stone") which can weigh many tonnes.

The Poulnabrone dolmen in the Burren, Co. Clare

PASSAGE TOMBS

Passage tombs are the greatest of Ireland's megalithic tombs. Over two hundred of them are scattered around the countryside. They are mounds, sometimes as big as a small hill, covering a long passage which leads into a chamber at the centre.

A general view of Newgrange, showing the white stones used to decorate the outside

The most famous passage tombs are in the Boyne Valley at Newgrange, Knowth and Dowth. Since the 1960s, archaeologists have excavated these tombs and have made many important and fascinating discoveries.

Excavating Newgrange

At Newgrange, the biggest of the passage tombs, archaeologists carefully took the mound apart, stone by stone. Here are some of the things they found.

- Some objects from the tomb have a carbon date of 2675 to 2485 BC. That makes Newgrange older than the pyramids of Egypt or Stonehenge in England.
- When the mound was taken apart, thousands of shiny white stones were found. They came from the Wicklow Mountains about 65km (40 miles) away, so they must have been carried there by the builders. When the archaeologists put the tomb back together, they put these white stones on the outside.
- The tomb at Newgrange was made of huge stones, many of which were decorated with spirals and diamond designs. The most decorative of all is the massive kerb stone which lies across the entrance. No one knows what the decorations mean, although some people think they can see faces in the designs.

The passage into the central chamber in Newgrange. How do you think the great stones were put in place?

An archaeologist noticed that the entrance faced south-east and decided to try an experiment. On 21 December, the shortest day of the year, he went into the chamber and waited for the sun to rise. As it came above the horizon, a thin beam of light shone into the roof box. Slowly the light crept along the passage until it reached the chamber where he stood. Then, just as slowly, the light retreated, leaving him alone in the darkness. This amazing experience had lasted for seventeen minutes.

The entrance stone at Newgrange, with the roof box above it.

- Inside the tomb is a long passage which opens into a cross-shaped chamber at the centre. The walls of the passage are made of large upright rocks. The roof is made of similar rocks, one placed over the other until they meet in the centre in a single cap stone. The archaeologists found that the roof sloped slightly outward and had carved channels to let the rain run off. After 4500 years, the inner chamber is still perfectly dry.
- Inside the chamber are stone basins which may have been used in ceremonies for burying the dead.
- As they examined the tomb, archaeologists found a square opening at the entrance which they called the **roof box**. Of course, they wondered what it was for. Local people told one archaeologist of a local legend which said that, on certain days, the sun shone on the decorated stone at the entrance.

The stone basin in the central chamber. We do not know what ceremonies were carried on here.

🏛 WHAT IS NEWGRANGE?

The mystery of the roof box had been solved. It had been perfectly placed so that the sun could enter the chamber only on a few days around 21 December each year. But a bigger mystery still remains. *Why did these Neolithic people build Newgrange?*

- Was it a sort of calendar to tell them when the sun was at its lowest point?
- Was it a temple or church where they worshipped the sun?
- Was it a tomb where they buried their dead or a special house for the souls of the dead?

After Newgrange was excavated, archaeologists examined other passage graves. They have found many cremated bodies, some placed in pottery bowls. They discovered jewellery made from bones and antlers. But none of the tombs had a roof box like that in Newgrange.

◢ QUESTIONS ◣

1. What does the word **megalithic** mean?
2. List the main kinds of megalithic tombs found in Ireland.
3. Name one example of a portal tomb. Describe or draw it.
4. Newgrange is the best and most famous example of a passage grave in Ireland. Select **two** features of Newgrange and write a short paragraph describing each of them.
5. No one knows what Newgrange was for. Write a paragraph saying which explanation you prefer. Give reasons for your choice.

CHAPTER 6

The Bronze Age

The discovery of metal

The people who built Newgrange used only simple stone tools. They did not know how to make things from metal. It was nearly one thousand years after the building of the passage tombs that metal objects first appeared in Ireland.

We do not know how metal arrived in Ireland. Perhaps traders brought small pieces to exchange for other goods. Perhaps people with metal weapons conquered parts of the country.

IRELAND'S FIRST COPPER MINES

The first metal objects appeared about 1700 BC. They were made of copper. There were large copper deposits in Ireland, and by 1500 BC it was being mined in places like Mount Gabriel in Co. Cork.

Bronze and the Bronze Age

Copper is a soft mineral, however. Tools or weapons made from it are more ornamental than practical. Someone discovered that if tin (which was mined in England) was added to copper, it made a much harder metal called **bronze.** Tools made from bronze are more efficient and longer-lasting than copper or even stone tools.

Bronze slowly replaced stone until people stopped using stone tools altogether. For that reason, archaeologists say that the Stone Age had ended and a new period – the **Bronze Age** – had begun. In Ireland, the Bronze Age lasted roughly from 1700 BC to 500 BC.

Archaeologists have found many bronze objects in Ireland.

A BRONZE AGE INDUSTRY

At Rathgal in Co. Wicklow, archaeologists found what they think was a bronze workshop dating from around 800 BC. They found traces of a large building, hearths where fires had been lit, and a large number of moulds for making swords, spears and axes.

GOLD FROM THE BRONZE AGE

Copper was not the only metal found in Ireland during the Bronze Age. There were also large quantities of gold which was used to make jewellery rather than tools or weapons. Some spectacular examples of Ireland's Bronze Age gold can be seen in the National Museum in Dublin.

LUNULAE

These gold objects are called **lunulae** because of their half-moon shape (*luna* means "moon" in Latin). They were probably some kind of neck ornament.

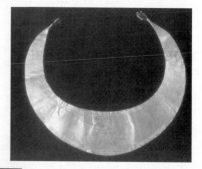

TORCS

Torcs are made by twisting strips or bars of gold. They were probably used as bracelets or neck ornaments.

DRESS FASTENERS

Archaeologists think this kind of ornament was used as a dress or cloak fastener. Do you agree?

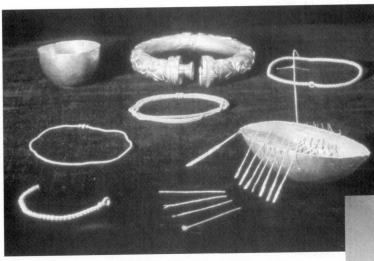

Hoards

Many of the gold ornaments in the National Museum were found buried together in **hoards**, or groups of artefacts. The Broighter Hoard contained a cup, jewellery, pins, and the wonderful little "Broighter boat".

We do not know why people buried their treasures in this way. Perhaps they were afraid that robbers would steal them. Perhaps it was the robbers themselves who had buried their loot. What do you think?

The Derrintaggart Stone Circle on the Beara Peninsula, Co. Cork

Bronze Age Farmers

Bronze Age people farmed in much the same way as their Stone Age ancestors. They kept cattle and sheep and grew crops like wheat and barley. They lived in houses made of wattle and daub.

Burials

Bronze Age people did not bury their dead in huge megalithic tombs. Instead, they used single graves called **cist graves**. They are like stone boxes in which the body is placed. Sometimes a small mound was put on top. Farmers often find cist graves when they are ploughing their fields.

Stone Circles

Although Bronze Age people did not build big tombs, they have left behind some mysterious **stone circles**. No one knows what they were for. In some of them, archaeologists have found graves with some cremated human bones. So perhaps they were places where burial ceremonies took place. But this is only a guess. What do you think the stone circles mean?

QUESTIONS

1. Explain what archaeologists mean by the Bronze Age.
2. Where did people mine copper in Ireland during the Bronze Age?
3. Pick **four** of the metal objects made in Ireland during the Bronze Age. Give their names. In the case of **two** of them, explain what they were for.
4. What kind of megalithic monument did Bronze Age people make? Describe it. What do archaeologists think it was used for?

Activity

Is there a stone monument from either the Stone Age or the Bronze Age near you? If so, try to visit it. Take photographs and measurements. Describe what you found.

CHAPTER 7

The Iron Age and the Celts

The Iron Age

Bronze weapons and axes were better than stone or copper, but neither was as strong as iron. Sometime around 1400 BC, people discovered how to make iron tools. This new period in history is called the **Iron Age**.

The Celts

Iron was first used in the Middle East and reached the north of Europe about 500 BC. At about the same time, the Greeks had developed a system of writing. Their writings tell us about an iron-using people who lived in Germany, France and Britain called the **Celts**.

There were Celts in Ireland too. We know this because when people in Ireland first began to use writing, in about 500 AD, they used a Celtic language. This is the language from which modern Irish comes.

WHEN DID THE CELTS COME TO IRELAND?

It was once believed that the Celts came to Ireland sometime between 500 and 200 BC and that they brought iron with them. Today, however, archaeologists are not sure if this is really what happened. It is possible that the Bronze Age people were Celts. But since we do not know what language they spoke, we cannot be sure.

How we know about the Iron Age

Until about 500 BC, the only evidence we have about the people living in ancient Ireland comes from archaeological remains. Archaeologists can also tell us a lot about the Celts, but we have several other sources of information about them.

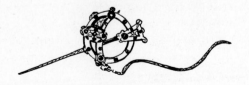

- The Greeks and Romans wrote about the Celts.
- The Celts in Ireland began to use a written language in about 500 AD. They began to write down their laws and legends. The best-known Celtic story is the *Táin Bó Cuailgne* which tells the tale of Cú Chulainn and the great war between Ulster and Connacht over the Brown Bull of Cooley. Other Celtic stories tell of Fionn mac Cumhaill and the Fianna.
- When the Celts became Christian, the early monks recorded about the main events such as battles and deaths which took place each year. These records were called the **Annals.**

The *tuath*

The Celts lived together in large groups called tribes. Each tribe had its own lands and was led by its own king. The tribe and the land it owned was called the *tuath*. There were about 150 *tuatha* in Ireland.

THE KING

The most important people in the *tuath* were the royal family. They were called the **derbfine**. The king of the tuath came from the derbfine. The Celts believed that if he was just and brave, the tuath would do well and prosper. But if he was bad, the crops would fail and the people would starve.

The king had many duties. In peace-time, he settled disputes among his people and punished wrongdoers. Here are some of the king's peace-time duties which were listed in the Celtic **Law Tracts** (book of laws).

Sunday is for drinking ale, for he is not a lawful chief who does not give ale every Sunday.
Monday is for judgment, for the good of the people.
Tuesday is for chess.

Wednesday is for seeing greyhounds coursing.
Thursday is for marriage duties.
Friday is spent at horse racing.
Saturday is for giving judgments.

The king's most important duty was to lead his warriors in battle. For this reason, he had to be physically perfect. A man who was blind or lame could never become king. If a king was disabled in battle, he had to give up his kingship.

▲ *The Celts played a game called* báire. *It was played with a ball and sticks, like hurling. The object was to get the ball into a hole in the ground, so it was also like golf.*

THE NOBLES AND THE *AOS DANA*

Apart from the royal family, the most important men in the *tuath* were the **nobles** and the ***Aos Dana***, or learned men.

▰ The **nobles** were warriors. They spent their lives with the king, fighting his enemies, hunting, playing games and feasting.

Nobles owned cattle and land, but they were not farmers. They gave cattle and land to poor farmers and received part of their crops in return. A noble protected his farmers from attack. The more farmers a noble had, the more important he was.

▰ The ***Aos Dana*** were learned men with the special skills that the *tuath* needed. They were judges, priests, poets, doctors and musicians, as well as goldsmiths and other skilled craftsmen.

People all over Ireland valued the skills of the *Aos Dana*. They could travel safely from one *tuath* to another and wherever they went, they were well treated by kings and nobles.

THE *FILE* (THE POET)

The most respected member of the *Aos Dana* was the ***file*** or poet. His job was to write poems which recorded the great deeds of the kings and nobles. He went to a special school where he learned to recite all the great Celtic stories by heart. He then worked for his king

When the king won a battle, his *file* made a poem praising the king's bravery. If the king was pleased with it, he rewarded the *file* with gifts of cows or gold. Many of these poems have come down to us and they are a very important source of information about the Celts.

Here are other members of the *Aos Dana* and the jobs they did.

▰ **Judges** – They knew the laws of the *tuath*. Even the king had to accept the decision of the judges.
▰ **Bards** – At the king's feast, the bards recited the poems that the *file* had composed.
▰ **Musicians** – They played the harp, the flute and the horn at the king's feast.
▰ **Doctors** – They made medicines from herbs and used magic spells to heal wounds and cure diseases.

CELTIC FARMERS AND SLAVES

Most Celts were neither nobles nor members of the *Aos Dana*. Most of them were the farmers or slaves who did all the hard work.

RICH FARMERS

Some farmers were very rich. They owned large herds of cattle and were given large amounts of land by the nobles. In return, they gave the nobles a share of the crops they grew and some of the animals they reared.

POOR FARMERS

Most farmers were not rich. They had only a few cattle and spent much of their time digging the earth and growing crops in the small fields around their homes. They also had to do labouring jobs for the nobles and the rich farmers.

THE SLAVES

The Celts also kept slaves. Many of them were prisoners who were captured in wars. Male slaves had to do the heavy tasks like herding and ploughing. Women slaves worked around the house. They ground corn and made bread, spun and wove cloth and looked after children.

There was a thriving slave trade in Celtic times. A female slave was worth three cows. Archaeologists found iron chains in Co. Meath. These were probably used to bind slaves together and suggest that some slaves were treated harshly.

These chains were used in Celtic Ireland. What do they tell us?

QUESTIONS

1. Which people were already living in Ireland when iron first arrived here?
2. When the Irish began to write, what language did they use?
3. List **four** sources of evidence about the Celts.
4. Explain what a *tuath* was in your own words .
5. Write three sentences about the king of a tuath.
6. Who were the *Aos Dana*? List three members of the *Aos Dana* (other than the *file*) and describe what they did.

CHAPTER 8

Life in Celtic Ireland

Where did the Celts live?

In Celtic times, Ireland was covered with thick forests. In the forests lived wolves which attacked farm animals, and robbers who stole cattle. Because of these dangers, Celtic farmers built their farmhouses in open spaces in the forests and protected them with walls or earthen banks. Sometimes, for greater safety, they lived on islands in lakes or on the tops of hills.

CELTIC FORTS

Archaeologists have found four different kinds of the dwelling places associated with the Celts.

RATHS OR RING FORTS AND CASHELS

Raths or **ring forts** were Celtic farmsteads. Archaeologists have discovered 40,000 of them all

Aerial view of the ring fort at Lough Gur, Co. Limerick

over Ireland. They can be seen more easily in aerial photographs.

A **rath** was surrounded by a ditch and a high bank made of earth. In places, the Celts built a timber fence on top of the bank. There was one opening in the bank, with a gate that could be easily closed. In the west of Ireland where there were few trees, a rath was enclosed by a stone wall. It was then called a **cashel** or **cahir**.

During the day, the farmers' cattle grazed in the surrounding fields, but at night they were brought inside the rath and the gate was closed.

Houses in a rath

Archaeologists have excavated several raths, but their best information comes from a rath at Deer Park Farms in Glenarm, Co. Antrim. At some time, the people living in the rath decided to flatten their old houses and build new ones on top. Water rose around the old houses and preserved them until the archaeologists discovered them in 1986-87.

House at Deer Park Farms

The houses at Deer Park Farms were round, with two rooms. There were beds against the walls in the bigger room and a fireplace in the middle of the floor. There was a fireplace, but no beds, in the smaller back room. Archaeologists wondered if it was used as a kitchen.

The walls of the houses were made from hazel rods woven together like a basket. But what surprised the archaeologists was that there were two sets of walls, one inside the other. The space in between would have been filled with grass or soil to give warmth and keep out draughts. This made the houses stronger and warmer than anyone had expected.

One house had a wooden door frame. Dendrochronology showed that the wood for it had been cut down in 648 AD.

In other raths around the country, archaeologists have found the foundations of houses, some of which are round, others square. But none are as well preserved as the ones at Deer Park Farms.

SOUTERRAINS

Some raths have underground passages called **souterrains**. These were either storage areas for food or places to hide in during an attack.

The entrance to a souterrain in Co. Louth

Crannógs

Crannógs were small islands built in lakes. Archaeologists have found almost 200 of them, mostly in south Ulster and the midlands where there are many lakes. Crannógs seem to have been used for many centuries, from the end of the Stone Age until about 1000 AD.

Archaeologists have learned a lot from crannógs because the water has preserved the wood, leather and cloth that might have disappeared elsewhere.

A reconstruction of a crannóg at Ferrycarrig, Co. Wexford

Hill forts

Hill forts are much bigger than raths or crannógs. There are about fifty of them around the country. They were built on hills and are surrounded by several ditches and earthen banks. Hill forts can enclose large areas. The biggest are eight hectares in size.

The Hill of Tara in Co. Meath was the legendary home of Ireland's High King. St Patrick is said to have preached there, so his statue now stands on the mound.

Many hill forts were associated with Celtic ruling families. The Hill of Tara in Co. Meath is where the High King of Ireland is said to have lived. In Co. Donegal, Grianán of Aileach was the home of the Uí Neill clan. In Leinster, the ancient capital was said to be at Dun Ailinne in Co. Kildare. In Connaught, it was at Cruachain in Co. Roscommon.

For a long time it was believed that Celtic kings lived in the hill forts with their followers. But when archaeologists excavated these forts, they found very little evidence of dwelling places. However, in Emain Macha in Co. Armagh, they found the remains of a huge wooden building. At its centre was a great oak which had been cut down in 94 BC.

Archaeologists now think that some hill forts were not dwelling places at all. Perhaps they were used for religious ceremonies or as meeting places in which assemblies of the *tuath* were held.

Promontory forts

In some places around the coast, stone walls or earthen banks were built across a headland. These are called **promontory forts**. It seems likely that people went into these forts for safety when they were attacked.

Dun Aenghus is one of the most dramatic promontory forts in Europe. It sits on a 70m cliff high above the stormy Atlantic on Inishmore in the Aran Islands.

The chevaux-de-frise *at Dun Aenghus. Thousands of stones placed upright in the ground protected the fort from unwanted visitors.*

QUESTIONS

1. Why did the Celts need to live on well-protected farms?
2. For each of the following, write a sentence explaining what it was and how it was used:
   (a) rath; (b) crannóg; (c) hill fort; (d) promontory fort
3. Using the information from the Deer Park Farms excavation, describe a house in a ring fort.
4. What was a **souterrain**? What could it have been used for?
5. Name two hill forts that you have heard of. Explain why archaeologists now think they were not used as dwelling places.

What did the Celts look like?

Irish and Roman writers help us to answer that question. Read these descriptions carefully. Then answer the questions.

HAIR

The *Táin Bó Cuailgne* tells us that Celtic warriors had

"...flowing hair, fair-yellow, golden streaming manes".

The hero Cú Chulainn had hair which was
"...dark next to the skin, blood-red in the middle, and hair like a crown of red-gold covering them".

Perhaps the *Táin* exaggerates. But here is a description of the Celts from a Roman called Strabo. Does it fit with what the *Táin* says?
"Their hair is not only naturally blond, but they use artificial means to increase this natural colour. They continually wash their hair with lime-wash and draw it back from the forehead to the crown of the head and the nape of the neck."

BIG PEOPLE

The Roman writers say that the Celts were big men who were proud of their appearance. Strabo says. . .
"They are strong and muscular and try not to become stout and fat-bellied. Any young man who becomes too fat is fined."

A Roman called Diodorus said . . .
"They gather large quantities of gold and use it to decorate themselves, not only the women but the men. For they wear bracelets on their wrists and arms and round their necks thick rings of solid gold. They also wear finger rings and even tunics sprinkled with gold.

They are terrifying in appearance with deep-sounding, harsh voices. They frequently exaggerate with the aim of praising themselves and insulting others. They are boasters and threateners, yet they are clever with a good natural ability for learning."

◢ QUESTIONS ◣

1. Read these sources carefully. From them, find and list eight things we know about the appearance of the Celts. In each case put the source of your information in brackets after the description. Here is an example to start you off:
   The Celts were big people. (Strabo)
2. Which of these sources come from Ireland and which are from other places? Which do you think would give us a more reliable account of the Celts, the Irish sources or the foreign ones? Give reasons for your answer.

Celtic clothing

CLOTH

The Celts made all their clothes themselves. The farmers reared sheep for their wool and grew the flax from which linen was made. Making the wool and flax into cloth was women's work.

The cloth was brightly coloured, possibly with a plaid pattern. The women made dyes from blackberry juice, mosses, lichens, nettles and many other sources.

MEN'S CLOTHES

The Celts wore very simple clothes. The men had a linen shirt and over it a knee-length tunic, also made of linen. The tunic was tied at the waist with a belt. The tunics of the nobles had coloured fringes and

were decorated with fine embroidery. On the continent, Celts wore knee-length trousers, but in Ireland, only poor men wore trousers.

WOMEN'S CLOTHES

Women's clothes were similar to men's, but their tunics reached down to their ankles. Both men and women wore long woollen cloaks over their tunics. These had no sleeves, but were tied at the neck with a brooch. The rich had the finest cloaks and the most elaborate brooches.

◤ QUESTIONS ◥

1. Draw and describe a Celtic man or woman.
2. Where did the Celts get their clothes?

Celtic food

The Celts grew their own crops and reared their own animals. They drank milk and made butter and cheese. In the autumn, they killed some cattle and salted or smoked the meat to preserve it through the winter months. In fact, their word for salted meat was **winter food**.

They hunted deer and wild pigs in the forest, as well as ducks and geese. They fished for trout and salmon and collected shellfish along the coast. They kept bees for honey which was used to sweeten food since they did not have sugar. Large amounts of honey were made into an alcoholic drink called **mead**.

GRINDING CORN

Celtic farmers grew oats, wheat and barley. Barley was made into ale which was their main drink. Wheat and oats were made into bread and porridge. Women ground the wheat and oats on a **quern**.

Archaeologists have found querns at many sites around the country. They were made from two stones, one fitted on top of the other. A woman poured some wheat through a hole in the top stone. It fell into the space between the two stones. Then she turned the top stone around, grinding the wheat below into flour. This had to be done every day to make bread and porridge.

COOKING

Women baked bread on hot, flat stones placed near the fire. Bread baked in this way was thin and hard,

Querns were used to grind corn into flour.

like an oat cake. Meat was probably roasted on wooden spits which were hung over the fire. Archaeologists found great bronze or iron pots, but only rich nobles could afford these. Ordinary farmers may have made stews in animal skins hung like pots over the fires.

FULACHTA FIA

Some Celtic legends tell of the heroes cooking their food out in the open in places called *fulachta fia*. Archaeologists have found many places around the country that they think might be these mysterious cooking places. They contain a rectangular pit, lined with wooden planks. Nearby is a hearth and piles of stones that have clearly been burned in the fire.

How did people cook food in a *fulacht fia*? Archaeologists tried an experiment. They dug a pit and lined it with timber. Then they filled it with water. They lit a fire beside the pit and put some big stones in it. When the stones were red-hot, they dropped them into the water, which soon boiled.

Next they wrapped a leg of mutton tightly in straw and dropped it into the boiling water. They left it in the water for the same cooking time that modern cooks would use – twenty minutes to the pound and twenty minutes over. From time to time, they added another hot stone to keep the water boiling. When they took out the meat, it was perfectly cooked! Although the water was dirty, the straw had kept the mutton clean.

Archaeologists think this way of cooking in a *fulachta fia* began during the Bronze Age and continued until 1000 AD or even later.

🏛 Carpenters and boat-builders

🏛 CARPENTERS

In every Celtic *tuath* there were skilled carpenters. They made the wooden houses in which the Celts lived and the wooden vessels from which they ate their food.

When archaeologists excavated Lagore crannóg near Dunshaughlin in Co. Meath, they found a carpenter's kit. It contained a collection of tools including a hammer, an axe, a saw, a draw-knife, a chisel, awls and nails. Parts of a fence found on the crannóg were very well made, proving that skilled carpenters worked there.

🏛 CELTIC BOATS AND BOAT-BUILDERS

Carpenters also built boats. The Roman writer Strabo described the boats used by the Celts of Brittany.

Their sails were made of leather and they pulled them up with chains instead of ropes. They make their boats with broad bottoms and high sterns and prows. The material used is oak of which they have a large supply.

The Irish probably had similar boats, as well as smaller boats like the **currachs** which are still made in the west of Ireland to this day. Long ago, the Irish told stories about a monk, St Brendan, who set out in a currach. After many adventures, he and his crew of fellow monks discovered a new world across the Atlantic. For a long time, everyone thought these stories were just legends. But in 1976, the explorer Tim Severin decided to see for himself.

Severin had a boat built of wood and skins such as St Brendan might have had. Then he and his crew set out to cross the Atlantic. They sailed to the Faroe

Islands and to Iceland and at last they arrived in Newfoundland on the east coast of Canada. Tim Severin had not proved that St Brendan *did* sail the Atlantic, but he had proved that such a journey was *possible*.

▲ This is the Staigue Fort in Co. Kerry. Look at it closely and say what kind of Celtic building it is.

Celtic Religion

The Celts were a very religious people who believed in many gods and goddesses. They thought that if the gods were pleased, the harvest would be good. But if they were angry, there would be famine and disease. Because of this, the Celts often made sacrifices to please the gods. Sometimes they even killed people to satisfy their gods. This is called **human sacrifice**.

The druids

Druids were Celtic priests and members of the *Aos Dana*. A druid studied for twenty years, learning about the gods, what prayers to say and what offerings to make. He also learned how to make magic spells and foretell the future.

This magical knowledge made a druid very powerful. He was in charge of the great religious festivals. At these, he offered sacrifices to the gods and foretold the future of his people. The druids sometimes acted as judges as well as teachers for the children of the nobles.

The Turoe Stone in Co. Galway was probably made between 300-200 BC. It may have been used in druidic ceremonies.

Religious festivals

The Celts had four great festivals in the year.

- **Imbolg (early February)** – This was held in honour of the goddess Brigid at the start of the lambing season.
- **Beltaine (May Day)** – This was held in honour of the god Bel at the beginning of summer when cattle were driven out to the hills to graze. People lit bonfires on the hills and drove the cattle through the fires to protect them from the diseases which evil spirits could bring.
- **Lughnasa (late July or early August)** – This was in honour of the god Lug and marked the start of the harvest season.
- **Samhain (the start of November)** – This festival was held to honour all the spirits of the underworld. It also marked the beginning of winter and the end of the year.

Celtic festivals were held in clearings in the forest. These were magic places where there was usually a holy well or a stream nearby. Sometimes there was a magic oak tree which the druids worshipped. Larger festivals may have been held at hill forts such as Tara and Emain Macha.

Historians think all the people of the *tuath* went to the festivals and exchanged goods and gossip. Strangers came to sell things like salt, which the Celts needed but which they could not make themselves. There were sports and entertainments in which men ran races and wrestled with one another. People watched horse races and hurling matches. Musicians played, bards recited the latest poems and kings held great feasts to show off their wealth.

🏛 BURIALS

The Celts believed that their souls lived on after they died. They went to **Tír na nOg** where people never grew old. They burned the bodies of their dead and buried them in small mounds surrounded by a ditch.

Because the bodies were cremated, it is hard for archaeologists to tell a great deal about them. Sometimes they have found fragments of jewellery and glass beads mixed with the ashes. Does this mean that the bodies were dressed in their finery before being burned so that they would look well in the next life?

🏛 STONE MONUMENTS

The Celts left many stone monuments around the country. We are not always sure what they were for. Some may have been grave stones, while others may have had something to do with religion. The Turoe Stone on page 28 is one of them.

🏛 OGHAM STONES

In the fifth century AD, shortly before Christian ideas reached Ireland, the Celts developed a kind of writing. It is called **ogham**. It was mainly used on gravestones and gave the names of the kings who were buried underneath.

Ireland's earliest writing – an ogham stone in Co. Kerry.

◪ QUESTIONS ◪

1. Who were the druids? Write a short paragraph about the training and work of the druids.
2. List the four main Celtic festivals and give the date on which each one was celebrated. What religious festivals do we have today that fall around the same times? Do they have anything in common with the Celtic festivals? Give reasons for your answer.
3. What is the Irish name for the place where souls went after death?

The ogham alphabet

Looking at the evidence ▼ ▼

PICK ONE OF THE MONUMENTS LEFT BY THE CELTS AND DESCRIBE ITS APPEARANCE AND PROBABLE USE.

Activity

WHAT IS **OGHAM**? USING THE OGHAM ALPHABET, WRITE YOUR OWN NAME.

CHAPTER 10

The Celts and Christianity

Christianity and writing

In the fifth century AD (between 401 AD and 500 AD), two very important things happened in Ireland. The Celts became Christians and they learned how to write. For the first time, we can learn about the Celts from their own words.

IRELAND'S FIRST CHRISTIANS

Both Christianity and writing came to Ireland from Britain, which was then part of the Roman Empire. We do not know when the first Christians arrived here, but we do know there were some here in 431 AD. In that year, a Frenchman called Prosper of Aquitaine wrote this.

"Blessed by Pope Celestine, Palladius was sent as the first bishop of the Irish, who believe in Christ."

Unfortunately, this is all we know about Palladius. Did he ever reach Ireland? If so, what part of the country did he work in?

And who were these first Irish Christians? Some of them were probably merchants from Britain who had settled here, or Irish people who had learned about Christ while living in Britain. Others may have been slaves who were captured in Britain by Irish pirates who raided the coast. That is the story of the most famous Christian to come to Ireland at that time – Patrick.

The story of Patrick

Other bishops followed Palladius to Ireland, but the only one we know much about is Patrick. We know about him because he wrote two books which we can still read.

His first book is called *A Letter to the Soldiers of King Coroticus*. Coroticus was a British king whose soldiers had raided Ireland. They took into slavery some people whom Patrick had converted to Christianity. Patrick wrote to the king, protesting about this.

Patrick's second book is more important. It is called *The Confession*. In it, Patrick explains to some British bishops why he brought Christianity to Ireland. This is the story Patrick tells about himself in *The Confession*.

Patrick was born in Britain. His family were Christians. When Patrick was a boy, he was captured by Irish pirates and brought to Ireland. He was sold as a slave and sent to herd sheep on a remote mountain. One night in a dream, a voice told him to escape. Patrick went to the coast where a boat took him home.

But at home he had more dreams. He heard the voices of the Irish calling him to come back and teach them about Christ. Patrick decided to become a priest. Then he returned to Ireland as a missionary to preach the gospel. He spent the rest of his life converting the Irish to Christianity.

These are the facts we know about Patrick. But there are many things he did not tell us in *The Confession*.

◤ Where in Britain did he come from?
◤ When did he come back to Ireland?
◤ How did the Irish receive him?

Since the answers to these and other questions are not in *The Confession*, it is not likely that we will ever find out.

The legend of Patrick

After his death, Patrick became a legend. The names of other bishops who preached to the Irish were forgotten and Patrick got the credit for any work they had done. Monks made copies of *The Confession*, but added bits to it to make us think that Patrick had travelled all over Ireland. In fact, he had worked mainly in the north and lived in Armagh.

All sorts of stories were told about Patrick. One says that he banished all the snakes from Ireland.

30

(Of course we know now that there were never any snakes here in the first place.) Other stories suggest that he had magic powers.

These stories were not true. But as Irish people stopped believing in the old gods, they transferred the stories they used to tell about those gods to Patrick and to other Christian saints.

◥ QUESTIONS ◤

1. Were there any Christians in Ireland before Patrick? Explain how we know.
2. We know about Patrick because he left two books. What were they? Write three short paragraphs, giving the main facts we know about Patrick's life. Use your own words.

Finding out

THERE ARE A GREAT MANY STORIES TOLD ABOUT PATRICK'S LIFE. THESE OFTEN SAY THAT HE VISITED A PLACE AND BLESSED A WELL OR FOUNDED A CHURCH. IS THERE A STORY ABOUT PATRICK WHICH IS TOLD IN YOUR AREA? IF SO, FIND OUT WHAT IT IS AND WRITE IT DOWN. IF NOT, FIND ANY STORY ABOUT PATRICK AND WRITE IT. IS THIS STORY TRUE? GIVE REASONS FOR YOUR ANSWER.

Looking at the evidence

PATRICK IS THE NATIONAL SAINT OF IRELAND AND A FAMOUS CHARACTER IN OUR HISTORY. DOES HE DESERVE TO BE? GIVE REASONS FOR YOUR ANSWER. ▼

CHAPTER 11

Celtic Monks and Monasteries

🏠 Early monasteries

About a hundred years before Patrick came to Ireland, some Christians in the Middle East went to lonely places where they lived alone, far from all distractions. They prayed, fasted and worshipped God. These men were called **hermits**.

Sometimes several hermits came together to live in a small group. They owned no property, and prayed regularly. By living like this they hoped to please God. These men were **monks** and the places where they lived were **monasteries**.

🏠 The first Irish monastery

About the time that Patrick was working in Ireland, St Ninian set up a monastery in Scotland. An Irishman called Enda visited Ninian's monastery and, in 490 AD, set up his own monastery on one of the Aran islands. He and the monks who followed him had a hard life on this small island out in the rough Atlantic. But they did not mind. They believed that a hard life brought them closer to God.

🏠 SCEILG MHICHÍL

Other monks went to an even more remote place. It was Sceilg Mhichíl, a cliff rising 150 metres above the Atlantic Ocean off the coast of Kerry. The monks built tiny stone huts to shelter them from the fierce Atlantic storms. If you visit Sceilg Mhichíl today, you can still see the huts that the monks built.

There was no soil on Sceilg Mhichíl, so the monks brought earth from the mainland in baskets. They put it in sheltered gaps between the rocks to grow a few vegetables and enough grass to feed some goats. They also caught fish and gathered eggs from the seabirds.

Sceilg Mhichíl is a tiny island in the Atlantic. Monks built stone huts there which are still standing today.

Only a few monasteries were built in such remote places. Most were built near the raths of an important king. Clonmacnoise, Derry and Kells are examples of this kind of monastery.

Convents

Nuns also established a few convents. The most famous nun, St Brigid, set up a convent in Kildare near an ancient Celtic religious site. In the seventh century, a monk described Kildare as "a vast city".

LIFE IN AN EARLY IRISH MONASTERY

The drawing of an early Irish monastery shows that it was like the raths of the Irish farmers. It was surrounded by a circular bank or stone wall. Inside there were many buildings. These were very small and made of wood, because the early monks did not know how to build with stone. The wooden

The ruins of one of the tiny stone churches at Clonmacnoise, Co. Westmeath

buildings have all disappeared, though archaeologists can still find traces of them in excavations.

St Kevin's Church and the round tower at Glendalough, Co. Wicklow

Later, some churches were made of stone, and a few of them are still standing today. One of the best-preserved stone churches is St Kevin's Church at Glendalough in Co. Wicklow.

Around the tenth century, the monks built **round towers**. They were used as bell towers or as watch towers in case the monastery was threatened.

Monks at Glendalough lived in wattle and daub huts which stood around the churches. But in the west, where trees were scarce, the monks built stone huts. These survive today and are called **beehive huts**.

An artist's impression of an early Irish monastery

Stone work in early Irish monasteries

Some early monasteries eventually grew into small towns with many activities taking place inside or nearby. Craftsmen like carpenters, stone masons and metal smiths went to work for the monks.

HIGH CROSSES

Before Ireland became Christian, masons had decorated stones to mark the burial places of their chiefs. The monks carried on this tradition, but they put up crosses, the symbol of their religion. These High Crosses are among the finest works of art produced in early Irish monasteries.

The earliest crosses were very simple, but over the centuries they became larger and much more decorative. Later crosses were covered with carvings showing scenes from the Bible. Standing beside the cross, a monk would teach students or the local people about the Christian faith. He used the pictures on the cross to help him explain his message.

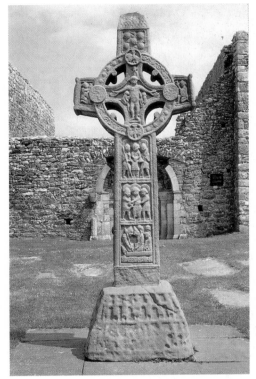

A High Cross at Clonmacnoise

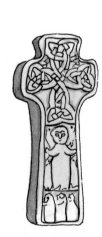   

7th Century   8th Century   9th Century   10th Century

Metal work

The monks employed gold and silver smiths to make precious objects for their churches.

CHALICES

Chalices are cups used during Mass. The best known examples are the Ardagh Chalice and the Derrynaflan Chalice. Both are in the National Museum in Dublin.

The Derrynaflan Chalice

RELIQUARIES

Book shrines like this held a monastery's precious manuscripts.

Relics are objects connected with the holy men and women. The monks asked their metal workers to make special shrines called **reliquaries** to hold these relics. **Book shrines**: The most precious objects in a monastery were the books. They contained the word of God and had taken years to make by hand. Many of them were beautiful works of art, so they were carefully guarded and often kept in **book shrines** decorated with jewels, gold and silver.

■ QUESTIONS ■

1. What were High Crosses used for?
2. What is a chalice? Name two chalices made in early Irish monasteries and say where you could see them today.
3. Name two other kinds of metal objects made in an early Irish monastery. Describe why they were made and how they were used.

FIND OUT THE NAME OF A HIGH CROSS NOT MENTIONED IN THE BOOK AND GET SOME PICTURES OF IT. FROM THESE, TRY TO WORK OUT WHAT CENTURY IT WAS MADE IN. THE ILLUSTRATIONS ON PAGE 33 WILL HELP YOU.

Finding out

Learning and art in Irish monasteries

SCHOOLS AND SCHOLARS

Irish monasteries were important places of learning. Young people came from all over Ireland and Europe to study in the monastic schools. They learned to read and write Latin which was the language used in the Christian church.

Writing was an important skill. Students learned to write by cutting letters into a wax tablet with a pointed stick. When they made a mistake, they smoothed over the wax and wrote the letter again.

MAKING MANUSCRIPTS

At the time of the early Irish monasteries, the printing press had not yet been invented. So all books had to be copied by hand. Such books are called **manuscripts**, which means *hand-written*. It took a long time to copy a book like the Bible, so even a rich monastery had very few books.

Manuscripts were written on **vellum** which was made from calf-skins, or **parchment** made from the skin of sheep. It took a long time to stretch and scrape the skins to make them suitable for writing. A large book needed the skins of many animals, which added to the cost of a manuscript.

Books were written in the **scriptorium**. Only the best writers were allowed to work on the precious religious books. The monks wrote with quills made from feathers. They also used brushes to paint decorations and knives to scrape away mistakes.

Ink was made from roots and vegetable juices. The ink was held in a cow's horn stuck on a stand in the ground. Coloured inks were used for decoration. Some came from metal ores – green came from copper and red came from lead. They also used dyes from plants and even a paper-thin gold called gold leaf.

Illuminated manuscripts

The most important books in a monastery were the Gospels and the mass books that the monks used during church services. Each monastery made its own books and valued them highly.

The earliest books were very plain, with little decoration or colour. Later books, like the Book of Kells, were full of complicated and colourful decoration. Books illustrated in this way are called **illuminated manuscripts**. It is hard to imagine how such books could be made by men who had no bright lights or magnifying glasses.

All the illuminated manuscripts we have today are religious books. They can be seen in libraries in Ireland, Britain and continental Europe.

IMPORTANT IRISH MANUSCRIPTS

THE CATHACH

This was written around 600 AD. It is the oldest Irish manuscript, so it is quite plain. For centuries it was owned by the O'Donnell clan who always carried it into battle as a good-luck charm. That is how it got its nickname of *Cathach* or "Battle Book'. Today, it is kept in the library of the Royal Irish Academy in Dublin.

THE BOOK OF DURROW

This book was made about 100 years after the Cathach, probably at the monastery of Durrow. It is now in the library of Trinity College in Dublin. In *The Book of Durrow*, the first letters in each chapter are very decorative. As in many manuscripts, the four **evangelists** – the men who wrote the gospels – are represented by the following figures.

Matthew – human figure
Mark – lion
Luke – griffin
John – eagle

THE BOOK OF KELLS

This is the most famous Irish manuscript. It was made in the early ninth century and was kept at the monastery of Kells in Co. Meath. Many people regard *The Book of Kells* as the most beautiful manuscript in the world. Today it can be seen in Trinity College in Dublin.

ATTACKS ON THE IRISH MONASTERIES

At first the Irish monasteries flourished in peace. But as they became richer, they attracted envy. Irish kings began to raid them for their treasure. Later, the Vikings from Scandinavia came too. They burned the monasteries, took the gold and silver, killed the older monks and carried the younger ones back to Scandinavia with them as slaves.

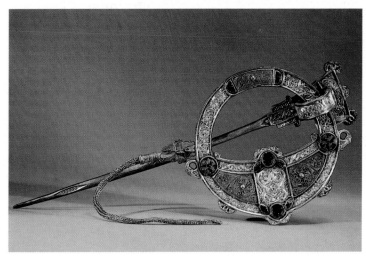

Treasures like the Tara Brooch were made in Ireland around the 8th century AD

A page from St Matthew's Gospel in the Book of Kells

CHAPTER 12

How do we know about Ancient Greece?

The ancient Greeks lived in south-east Europe towards the end of the Bronze Age. Because they had developed a system of writing, it is still possible to read the things they wrote. Many of our modern ideas began with these people who lived long ago. The first European historians, scientists and dramatists were Greeks. We get our idea of democracy from them as well.

The map of Greece shows some of the main places that will be mentioned in this section.

The evidence

The Greeks have left us plenty of evidence about their lives. Using this, archaeologists and historians have a good idea of how the Greeks lived.

Study this map of Greece. Locate the places mentioned in the text as you read this section.

WRITTEN EVIDENCE

From an early date, the Greeks had developed a way of writing. Our word **alphabet** comes from the first two letters in the Greek alphabet – *alpha* (α) and *beta* (β). Greek letters are not like our own. For example, the Greek word for city is *polis*, but they would have written it πολισ.

> USE AN ENCYCLOPAEDIA OR DICTIONARY TO LOOK UP THE GREEK ALPHABET. WRITE YOUR NAME AND ADDRESS USING THE GREEK ALPHABET. YOU MAY ALSO WANT TO WRITE A SHORT NOTE OR MESSAGE USING THE GREEK ALPHABET.
>
> *Activity* ▼▼

The written evidence about ancient Greece comes in many forms. There are poems, histories, discussions, inscriptions on buildings and tombs, and words written on pieces of pottery.

We know about events in Greek history from historians like Herodotus. Poets like Homer tell us the legends and stories of the Greeks. Philosophers like Plato and Aristotle tell us what the Greeks thought about things. Playwrights like Euripides and Aeschylus wrote plays.

VASE PAINTINGS

The Greeks loved decorated vases. These were covered with pictures from daily life and legends.

A vase from the fifth century BC shows people harvesting the olive crop.

SCULPTURE

Sculpture was very common in Greece. Sculptors created beautiful statues, particularly of their gods, heroes and athletes.

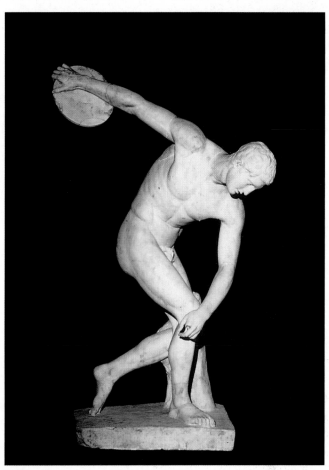

How might this statue of a discus thrower be useful to someone who is studying ancient Greece?

ARCHAEOLOGY

Archaeology is one of the best ways of reconstructing the past. To this day, Greece has many archaeological remains which are still being studied.

> **QUESTION**
>
> Four ways of finding out about Greece are mentioned in this chapter. What are they? Which way do you think is the most useful? Give reasons for your answer.

CHAPTER 13

Schliemann and the Archaeology of Troy

Homer and the siege of Troy

About 750 BC, the Greek poet Homer wrote two long poems called the *Iliad* and the *Odyssey*. This is the story the *Iliad* tells.

In Turkey there was once a great city called Troy. Priam was the King of Troy and Paris was one of his sons.

Paris was asked by three goddesses to say which of them was the most beautiful. One of these goddesses was Aphrodite. To make sure she was chosen, Aphrodite promised Paris the love of the most beautiful woman in the world. This was Helen, who was already the wife of King Menelaus of Sparta. Of course Aphrodite won the contest and made Helen fall in love with Paris. Together, Helen and Paris ran away from Sparta and made their way back to Troy.

The angry Menelaus wanted to get Helen back and punish Paris. He persuaded other Greek leaders to join him in a war against Troy. The leader of the Greek army that set sail for Troy was King Agamemnon of Mycenae. The greatest Greek hero was Achilles.

For ten years, the Greeks laid siege to the city of Troy. They finally managed to capture the city using a trick which we now call the Trojan Horse. The Trojans woke up one morning to find that their Greek enemies had gone, leaving behind a wonderful wooden horse. The Trojans thought it was a gift, so they brought it into the city and celebrated. During the night, Greek warriors who were hiding in the horse silently left it. They opened the gates of the city and let their fellow countrymen in.

The sleeping Trojans were not prepared for this trick. Their city was soon in flames and the war was lost. Paris was killed and Helen was finally brought back to Greece.

The Greek hero, Achilles, in battle with Hector, the Trojan hero

King Menelaus takes his wife, Helen, back to Greece.

DO YOU KNOW ANY OTHER GREEK LEGENDS? ONES LIKE *JASON AND THE GOLDEN FLEECE* ARE VERY WELL KNOWN. READ A FEW GREEK LEGENDS. THEN WRITE A SHORT STORY ABOUT ONE OF THEM.

Activity

Looking at the evidence ▼

WHAT DO YOU THINK IS MEANT BY THE SAYING "BEWARE OF GREEKS BEARING GIFTS"? USE THE EVIDENCE IN THIS CHAPTER TO SUPPORT YOU ANSWER.

Schliemann found this gold mask at Mycenae. Homer had said that Mycenae was "rich in gold". This convinced Schliemann that the mask showed the face of Agamemnon.

Schliemann finds Troy

▪ *Heinrich Schliemann*

Just over a hundred years ago, a German called Heinrich Schliemann read Homer's poems. He believed every word he read and decided to prove Troy was not just a legend and that it really had existed.

Schliemann was not an archaeologist. But he was a rich man, so he was able to organise an expensive expedition to modern Turkey. At Hissarlik in 1870, he found a hill that fit Homer's description and which local people had always linked with Troy.

▪ *A view of Mycenae, the legendary home of King Agamemnon*

To the surprise of professional archaeologists, Schliemann found the remains of several cities, one on top of the other. He also found jewels and gold which, he said, came from the time of the Trojan War.

Schliemann next started digging at Mycenae, which legend says was the home of King Agamemnon. He found a palace with great walls, and graves containing beautiful gold masks. So much gold was found that Schliemann said he must have found the palace and grave of Agamemnon.

WHAT HAD SCHLIEMANN FOUND?

Today, we have learned much more about Troy and Mycenae, so we know that Schliemann was wrong about many things.

Archaeologists eventually discovered nine cities on the site of Troy. As one city was destroyed, another was built on top of it. Homer's Troy was probably the seventh city from the bottom. Since Schliemann had found his treasures much further down, they could not have come from the time of the Trojan War.

The Lion Gate. Its huge, thick walls convinced Schliemann that he had discovered the palace of Agamemnon.

The same was true at Mycenae. The gold objects which Schliemann had found actually belonged to people who had lived five hundred years before the Trojan War.

Although Schliemann got many things wrong, he still got some things right.

☑ He discovered the site of Troy and began its excavation.

☑ He found evidence about ancient Greece at Troy and Mycenae.

☑ He proved that there was some truth in the stories of Homer.

1. Why did Schliemann go to Turkey in 1870?
2. What did Schliemann discover at the places which he thought were Troy and Mycenae?
3. Schliemann was not a professional archaeologist. In his day, modern methods of archaeology (pages 7-11) had not yet been developed. Schliemann did many things badly.

☑ He used pick axes and other heavy tools to dig things up.

☑ He dug a deep trench across the site at Hissarlik.

☑ He did not keep records of where things were found.

For each of these points, explain what a modern archaeologist would do. Why would they say that Schliemann had done things badly? Remember to refer to the information

CHAPTER

14

Gods, Burials and Games

A religious people

The Greeks worshipped many gods and goddesses. Different gods looked after different things. The Greeks believed that their gods lived in the clouds at the top of Mount Olympus.

▲ Mount Olympus, the home of the Greek gods and goddesses

Greek citizens built homes for the gods in their cities. These were called **temples**. In the temples, the Greeks sometimes killed an animal or bird as an offering to the gods.

Here is a list of some of their main gods and goddesses, along with their special responsibilities.

Zeus	The father of the gods, who was also in charge of thunder and lightning
Aphrodite	The goddess of love and beauty
Apollo	The god of the sun and music
Athene	Daughter of Zeus, goddess of the city of Athens
Poseidon	God of the sea

The theatre

Like the Olympic Games, Greek theatre started as part of religious festivals. Stories called **dramas** were told through song, dance and words.

Actors performed on the **stage**. A **chorus** chanted comments on the action from the **orchestra**. Actors wore masks with mouthpieces which helped carry their voices to everyone in the large open-air theatre.

Dramas went on all day during a festival – **tragedies** were performed in the morning and **comedies** in the afternoon.

The theatre at Epidauros was built in the fourth century BC.

Finding out

1. FIND OUT MORE ABOUT THE GREEK GODS AND GODDESSES. MAKE A LIST OF THEM AND TELL WHAT SPECIAL JOB EACH ONE HAD.
2. THE ROMANS ALSO BELIEVED IN MANY GODS AND GODDESSES. FIND THE ROMAN NAME FOR EACH OF THE GREEK GODS AND GODDESSES YOU HAVE LISTED.

BURYING THE DEAD

The Greeks believed that when a person died, the soul was led to the River Styx by the messenger-god Hermes. Charon the boatman ferried the souls across the river to the underworld, Hades. The lucky ones were taken to the Islands of the Blessed.

Greek burial customs were simple. The corpse was wrapped in a shroud and then, after a funeral procession, it was placed in a grave which was marked with a headstone. Dead warriors were often burned on a funeral pyre, particularly during wartime.

The Olympic Games

The Greeks held the Olympic Games to honour their gods. Athletes came from all over Greece to take part in this religious festival which was held at Olympia. The games were held every four years and only men could take part.

A sculpture showing Greek wrestlers

An umpire judges two wrestlers

Two athletes, with a javelin (left) and a discus (right)

Greek vases provide many examples of the types of sports which took place.

QUESTIONS

1. In your opinion, who was the most important Greek god or goddess? Give reasons for your answer.
2. What beliefs had the Greeks about the next life?
3. Greek dramas took place in the open air during the day. Modern performances usually take place indoors at night. Can you give reasons for these differences?

Finding out

1. FIND OUT MORE ABOUT THE ANCIENT OLYMPIC GAMES.
2. WHEN DID THE MODERN OLYMPIC GAMES START? FIND OUT MORE ABOUT THE MODERN OLYMPICS AND WRITE A REPORT ON YOUR FINDINGS.
3. WHAT IS THE DIFFERENCE BETWEEN A TRAGEDY AND A COMEDY? NAME SOME GREEK TRAGEDIES AND COMEDIES. WRITE A SENTENCE OR TWO TELLING WHAT EACH OF THESE PLAYS IS ABOUT.

Daily Life in Fifth-century Athens

Athens in the time of Pericles

Pericles, a wise ruler

A man called Pericles was the ruler of Athens in the second half of the fifth century BC. He was a wise ruler, so the city became rich and powerful. Under Pericles, many beautiful buildings were built which can still be seen in Athens today.

Because Athens was often threatened by war, Pericles enclosed the city with strong walls. The **Long Walls** connected Athens to its port, Piraeus, eight kilometres away.

The acropolis

Most Greek cities had a central hill or fortress called an **acropolis**. The one in Athens dominates the city, even today.

THE PARTHENON

On a hill called the acropolis in Athens, Pericles built a beautiful temple to the goddess Athene. It was called the **Parthenon**, and it took eleven years to build. Inside was a huge statue of Athene made of gold and ivory.

The Parthenon was built to honour Athene. Its ruins can be seen on the acropolis in Athens today.

The carvings shown here are no longer in Athens. About two hundred years ago, a British nobleman, Lord Elgin, tore them out and brought them to London. These ancient carvings are called the **Elgin Marbles** and are now in the British Museum.

A group of horsemen - part of the Elgin Marbles

The Greek government has recently asked Britain to return the Elgin Marbles. Do you think they should be sent back to Athens? Give reasons for your opinion.

THE AGORA

Below the acropolis was the **agora**, a very busy marketplace. This is where merchants made deals, people argued about politics, and shops sold food, wine, fish or vases. Only men and slaves went shopping. Women were rarely allowed out on the streets.

Behind many of the shops, craftsmen like potters and smiths had their workrooms.

THE POTTERS

Potters made dishes for food, statues of Athene to sell to visitors, vases and many other things. About 150 potters worked in Athens at the time of Pericles.

On their vases, Greek potters painted designs showing scenes from Greek life. Vases are often used in this book as sources of evidence about life in ancient Greece.

THE SMITHS

Smiths produced knives, swords, pins to hold dresses and other metal objects.

Buildings and houses

Many buildings around the agora were large and elegant. Some were temples to the gods. Others were sports halls called **gymnasia** (singular = **gymnasium**) where men could train for the army. There were also theatres for entertainment.

Private homes were very simple. Poorer people lived in huts with walls made of wood or thin bricks. There was no glass for windows. Small openings were covered with shutters to keep out the summer heat and the winter cold. The houses were dark and cramped inside, but because of the Mediterranean climate, the Greeks were able to live out-of-doors much of the time.

Wealthy Greeks lived in houses like these. Compared with the Parthenon, such homes were quite simple.

Soldiers in Athens

Every citizen of Athens had to spend two years in the army or navy. A soldier had to provide his own armour and weapons. Rich men could afford to have horses and a chariot, but most soldiers fought on foot. A fully-armed foot-soldier was called a **hoplite**.

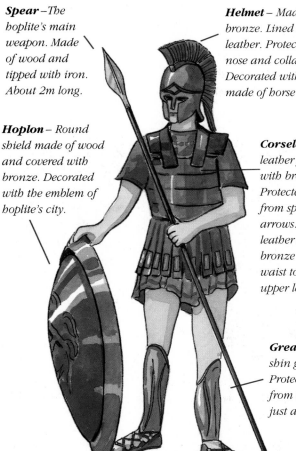

Spear – The hoplite's main weapon. Made of wood and tipped with iron. About 2m long.

Hoplon – Round shield made of wood and covered with bronze. Decorated with the emblem of hoplite's city.

Helmet – Made of bronze. Lined with leather. Protected head, nose and collar bone. Decorated with plume made of horse hair.

Corselet – Heavy leather jacket covered with bronze strips. Protected the body from spears and arrows. Strips of leather studded with bronze hung from the waist to protect the upper leg.

Greaves – Bronze shin guards. Protected the leg from the ankle to just above the knee.

Sandals – Covered with bronze to protect the feet.

A hoplite

Greek clothing

Both rich and poor in Athens wore the same styles of dress, but the rich used better-quality cloth. Women wore a woollen dress called a **peplos**. It was long and fastened at the shoulder with pins. The wool was woven by the women in their own homes.

A linen dress called a **chiton** was also popular. It could be tied without using pins and was cooler

Two hoplites in battle. Describe the scene in detail.

than the peplos. The chiton was worn by both men and women. Men also wore a cloak called a **himation** which was draped around the body.

Greek women wearing a peplos (left) and a chiton (right)

Women in Athens

Greek girls stayed at home with their mothers. They learned to spin and weave wool and linen into cloth and to run the home.

In many houses, slaves did the hard work like cooking and cleaning. They also did the shopping because women were not supposed to go out into the streets.

Athenians believed that women should stay out of sight. Here is what a Roman visitor wrote about them.

"No Roman thinks it embarrassing to take his wife to a dinner party. In his home, the wife holds the first place and entertains the husband's guests.

Things are different in Greece, where the wife is never present at dinner unless it is a family party. She spends all her time in a remote part of the house called the women's quarter..."

Women could not be citizens or own property. In fact, the only career a woman could have was as a priestess in the temple.

Education

Only Greek boys went to school. Early each morning, a family slave brought the boy to school and waited for him all day. Classes were often held in the open air and there were no desks. Boys sat on wooden benches with wax tablets on their knees. Using a stick called a **stylus**, they cut letters into the wax. When they had finished writing, the wax could be smoothed over and used again.

There were no books in Athens, only rolls of **papyrus**, an early kind of paper made from reeds. When a student wanted to read a page, he unwound a roll from one stick to another.

A Greek school boy's equipment. Tell what each of these things was used for.

▨ QUESTIONS ▨

1. Describe the city of Athens at the time of Pericles.
2. Why was the Parthenon built?
3. Describe a typical scene in the agora.
4. What evidence do we have about the tradesmen of Athens?
5. What was the position of women in Athens? Is this different from Ireland today? Explain your answer.
6. Was Greek clothing suited to the climate? Give reasons for your answer.
7. Was the life of a Greek school boy different from your own? Explain your answer.

MAKE YOUR OWN LABELLED DRAWING OF A HOPLITE.

Activity

CHAPTER 16

The Middle Ages

Around the year 800 AD, a new period in European history began. We call this period the **Middle Ages**, because it lies *between* the time of the ancient world of Greece, Rome and Celtic Ireland *and* modern times which began with the Renaissance (Section 5). Historians use the word **medieval** to describe the people and events of the Middle Ages.

In Ireland, the old Celtic way of life (Section 2) lasted for a long time. The medieval period did not begin here until outsiders brought new ideas and customs to the country.

The Vikings

The first of these outsiders were the **Vikings** who came from Scandinavia. Early Viking visitors were often pirates who raided Irish monasteries and stole their treasures. Archaeologists have found some Irish treasures in Scandinavia.

But later Vikings were peaceful traders. They brought goods from Britain and Europe to Ireland and sold them to the Irish. They set up trading posts which soon grew into towns. Waterford, Dublin, Cork and Limerick were all started by Viking traders. These were the first real cities in Ireland.

Archaeologists have excavated the centres of these cities and found plenty of Viking remains.

As time passed, the Vikings settled down in Ireland. They intermarried with the Irish and became involved in their wars. By 1100, the Vikings were very like the Irish among whom they lived.

A Viking bowl and spoon found at Wood Quay in Dublin. What could archaeologists learn from these artefacts?

A MONK IN AN EARLY IRISH MONASTERY
WROTE THIS POEM.
> WILD IS THE WIND TONIGHT
> TOSSING THE SEA'S WHITE HAIR.
> I FEAR NO FIERCE VIKINGS
> SAILING THE IRISH SEA.

EXPLAIN IN YOUR OWN WORDS WHAT YOU
THINK THE MONK IS WRITING ABOUT.

▲ *The feudal pyramid. Talk about what this drawing tells you about the feudal system.*

The Normans

The next invaders who came to Ireland were the **Normans** who originally came from Normandy in northern France. In 1066, the Norman leader, William the Conqueror, invaded England. Following his victory in the Battle of Hastings (page 49) he declared himself king.

A hundred years later, in 1169, the Normans came to Ireland. William's descendant, King Henry II, called himself **Lord of Ireland** and his Norman lords conquered much of the country. This began the link between England and Ireland which has lasted to this day.

The Normans brought the medieval way of life to Ireland. One of the things they introduced was the **feudal system**. It worked like this.

THE KING

Whenever the Normans conquered a country, they assumed that all the land belonged to the king. He divided it among his **lords**.

THE LORDS

The lords were **earls** or **barons**, **bishops** or **abbots**. Each lord got a large area of land from the king. In return for the land, he had to promise the king that he would:
- keep his laws and obey his orders;
- pay for a certain number of soldiers who would fight for the king when he needed them.

THE KNIGHTS

Each lord built a castle on his land and divided it among his followers. They were soldiers called **knights**. Each knight got an area of land called a **manor**. In return for the manor, a knight promised to obey his lord and to fight with him at times of war.

THE PEASANTS

The **peasants** were the farmers who worked on the manor. They paid rents and taxes to the knights, the lords and the king. The whole feudal system depended on their work.

◢ QUESTIONS ◣

1. Name three Irish towns established by the Vikings.
2. Which people brought medieval ways of life to Ireland?
3. Draw a labelled diagram to show how the feudal system worked.

Medieval Soldiers

Wars were very common in the Middle Ages, so kings and lords kept armies to defend themselves. There were three kinds of soldiers in these armies: **knights**, **archers** and **foot soldiers**.

Knights

A museum display of a medieval knight on horseback. Both the knight and his horse are wearing armour. Describe what you see.

A knight was the most important soldier in a medieval army. He rode on horseback and was dressed in heavy **armour**.

In the early Middle Ages, the knight's armour was made of **chain mail** – iron rings knitted together. On his head he wore a helmet with a nose guard to protect his face. This armour was very heavy and a knight had to be extremely fit to wear it.

Later, knights wore **plate armour**, with helmets that covered their faces and heads completely. It was so heavy that a knight needed a crane to lift him onto his horse.

No one could recognise a knight behind his helmet, so he wore a **coat of arms** on his shield to show who he was. A coat of arms was like a family trademark. Even today, some families have coats of arms.

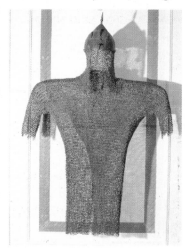

A suit of chain mail

A knight's weapons

The knight's main weapon was a long spear called a **lance.** In a battle, he charged at the enemy with the lance. When it broke, he used other weapons. These were his **sword**, his **battle axe** and his **mace**, an iron ball with deadly spikes.

Training to be a knight

A knight's armour, horse and weapons were all expensive, so only the sons of rich lords could become knights. It took thirteen years for a boy to become a knight.

THE PAGE

When a lord's son was seven, his father sent him to be a **page** in another lord's castle. There he learned to ride a horse and use a sword. The page learned good manners by serving the lady of the castle and waiting at table. He also learned to dance, sing and play the lute (an instrument like a guitar).

THE SQUIRE

When the boy was fourteen, he became a **squire**. He learned to use a knight's weapons and to fight on horseback. He helped his lord with his armour and went with him into battle. If his lord was wounded, it was the squire's duty to help him to safety.

KNIGHTHOOD

When he was twenty-one, the squire finally became a knight. He spent the night before this important ceremony in church, praying that God would help him to be a good knight. In the morning, his family helped him into his armour. He then knelt before his lord, who touched him on the shoulder with his sword and said, "Arise, Sir Knight".

A medieval drawing showing a knight kneeling before his king

The code of chivalry

A good knight was supposed to observe the **code of chivalry**. This said that a knight must always tell the truth and protect women and children. Although all knights did not observe the code at all times, it still set out an ideal of how a soldier should behave. Today, we still have that ideal in the word **chivalrous.** In the Middle Ages, people admired chivalrous knights. There were many stories about these men and their gallant deeds. There were legends about St George who rescued young girls from dragons, and about King Arthur and his knights of the Round Table.

Finding out

1. LOOK UP THE WORDS **CHIVALRY** AND **CHIVALROUS** IN YOUR DICTIONARY AND TELL WHAT THEY MEAN.
2. FIND OUT ABOUT SOME OF THESE MEDIEVAL LEGENDS, SUCH AS ST GEORGE AND THE DRAGON AND KING ARTHUR AND THE KNIGHTS OF THE ROUND TABLE.

Tournaments

When there were no wars to fight, medieval knights kept fit by fighting in **tournaments**. These were mock battles which were usually held near a castle. People came from miles around to see the knights and to bet on their favourites. There were two kinds of contests.

A 16th century picture of two knights jousting

- In the **joust**, two knights in full armour rode towards each other at top speed. Each was trying to knock the other off his horse. The winner was given the loser's armour.
- In the **tourney**, groups of knights fought a mock battle with blunt swords and lances. Many knights were injured in the tourney.

Archers

Before gun-powder was invented, all armies had **archers** who fought with bows and arrows. There were two kinds of bow. English archers preferred **long bows** because they were light to carry and quick to re-load. French archers preferred the **crossbow**. These were heavier and slower, but they could fire a bow much farther.

Medieval archers and foot soldiers. Describe their clothing and weapons.

Foot soldiers

Most medieval soldiers were **foot soldiers**. They wore padded tunics and sometimes a helmet made of leather or iron. Their weapons were swords and daggers. Some foot soldiers also carried a light wooden shield padded with leather.

Looking at the Evidence

THE BAYEUX TAPESTRY

An important source of information about medieval soldiers is the **Bayeux Tapestry**. This huge piece of embroidery is 70 metres long and 50cm high. It was made in France around 1080 AD and tells the story of the Norman invasion of England in words and pictures.

Here are three scenes from the Tapestry. Look at them closely and see what they tell us about medieval life.

Picture 1: This picture shows a medieval king seated on the throne. Two lords stand at his right and a bishop on his left. Can you see the king's name?

Picture 2: This picture shows a medieval ship. Can you find (a) how many sails it had and (b) how it was steered?

Picture 3: This picture shows knights. (a) What kind of armour are they wearing? (b) Describe their helmets. (c) What weapons can you find?

Using the evidence from the Bayeaux Tapestry:
- Describe or draw a medieval lord.
- Describe or draw a medieval knight.
- Describe a journey from England to Ireland in Medieval times.

IMAGINE YOU ARE A MEDIEVAL KNIGHT AND WRITE AN ACCOUNT OF YOUR LIFE. YOU SHOULD INCLUDE: (A) TRAINING TO BE A KNIGHT; (B) THE DAY YOU WERE KNIGHTED; (C) FIGHTING IN A TOURNAMENT AND IN A BATTLE.

YOU SHOULD ONLY INCLUDE INFORMATION FOR WHICH YOU HAVE EVIDENCE, EITHER FROM THIS BOOK OR ANOTHER REFERENCE BOOK.

Activity

Picture 1

Picture 2

Picture 3

Life in a Medieval Castle

Motte and bailey castles

When the Normans conquered an area, they quickly built a simple castle. They started by building a high, steep mound called a **motte**.

On top of the motte, a **wooden tower** was built. The lord posted soldiers in the tower to keep a look-out for the enemy. A wooden fence was put up around the tower.

Below the motte was a flat area called the **bailey**. It too was enclosed by a wooden fence. Inside the bailey were houses and sheds where the lord, his family and his soldiers lived. The bailey was linked to the motte by a wooden **drawbridge**.

If the solders saw an enemy approaching, everyone retreated to the motte and pulled up the drawbridge. It was hard for an enemy to capture the motte with its steep sides. The best way was to set fire to the wooden tower with flaming arrows.

MOTTES IN IRELAND

The Normans built many motte and bailey castles in Ireland. Today, all the wooden buildings are gone, but the high mottes can still be seen.

Mottes like this can be seen around the Irish countryside. Are there any near your home or school?

▲ *An artist's reconstruction of a motte and bailey castle*

▲ *Study this drawing of a stone castle. Describe each part of the castle, telling where it is located and what its use is.*

Stone castles

A wooden castle could be burned quite easily, so kings and rich lords soon replaced them with stone castles. The layout of castles varied from time to time and from place to place, but most of them had some of the features shown in the drawing.

Read these descriptions of the parts of the castle and find them in the picture.

The main building in the castle was the **keep**, which was usually three or four storeys high. The walls were three metres thick at the base and two metres thick at the top. The windows were narrow slits through which archers could fire their arrows. On each corner were **towers** with narrow, winding stairs inside.

The **kitchen** was outside the keep, since a fire there might set the whole castle alight. The **garden** supplied fresh food and the **well** provided fresh water. Both of these were vital if the castle was attacked.

Around the keep there were usually two **courtyards**. These were normally very busy places, with smiths shoeing the horses or making swords, masons mending the walls, and archers practising their shots.

▲ *A portcullis guards a French castle. Why would this give a castle extra protection?*

The castle was enclosed by high walls and a **moat**. The moat was often a stream which was diverted to flow around the walls. Along the walls there were **turrets** which stuck out at right angles. From these, the **sentries** could see in all directions, which made a sneak attack more difficult.

The enemy could easily break through the **gate**, so it had extra defences. There was a **gatehouse** with strong turrets, a **drawbridge** over the moat and a **portcullis**, which was an iron gate that could be raised or lowered from the gatehouse.

A BUSY PLACE

A big castle was like a small town, filled with busy people. The lord and his family lived there with their attendants. These included a priest to say Mass, a clerk to write letters and servants to wait on them.

The lord's knights, archers and foot soldiers guarded the castle. Grooms minded the horses. Smiths shod the horses and mended the weapons and the armour. Carpenters and masons kept the castle in good repair.

The people of the castle needed food, especially if there was a siege. So there was also a garden and gardeners, some cattle with herdsmen to tend to them, and cooks to prepare the food for everyone.

Ross Castle in Co. Kerry

Study this modern drawing of a keep and describe the places mentioned in the text.

Life in the castle

INSIDE THE KEEP

The keep was the castle's main building. The best rooms, where the lord and lady lived, were on the top floor. It was usually cold there because the windows had no glass, only shutters. The walls were covered with **tapestries** (carpets) for colour and warmth. The beds had curtains around them to keep out the draughts.

During the day, the lady sat in the **solar**. This was a small room in the south turret which got lots of sun. This was where she sewed tapestries, listened to musicians and chatted to her attendants.

The main room in the keep was the **great hall**. During the day, the lord carried on his business there, and at night soldiers and servants slept there on the rush-covered floor. Below the great hall were the **dungeons** in which food was stored and where prisoners were held in chains.

A BANQUET IN THE GREAT HALL

If the lord had important guests, he gave a banquet in the great hall. The most important guests sat at the high table at the end of the hall. The rest sat at tables along the walls.

Vast quantities of food were prepared in the kitchen and carried to the hall. Plates were laden with bread and vegetables. There was meat of every kind – pork, beef, venison, goose, pheasant, even swans, gulls and thrushes. Great cakes made of almond paste were shaped like ships and castles.

The food was brightly coloured – yellow from saffron, black from charcoal, red from blood and green from mint and parsley. It was also spiced with pepper, nutmeg and cloves. It was not very fresh because they had no means of preserving it, so the spices made it taste better. Spices were very expensive then, so only kings and lords could afford them.

The food was served on large slices of stale bread called **trenchers**. People used knives, spoons and fingers to eat it. (There were no forks.) Anyone who did not want to eat the trencher threw it to the dogs which searched for scraps on the floor. The people at the high table drank wine, while the rest had ale.

While they ate, entertainers kept the lord's guests amused. Acrobats and jugglers showed their skills and the lord's jester told jokes. Musicians played on flutes and harps. They sang songs of the brave deeds of knights and their love for fair ladies. This is a verse from a love song of the time.

Song, to greet my fair one, fly
Asking not a thing
But with prudent sighs tell why
I am languishing.
Beseech her never to forget
My loyal heart on her is set.
Her vassal, I will her adore
Or die, if that would please her more.

KEEPING THE PEACE

The lord's soldiers kept peace in the neighbourhood. They arrested robbers and brought them before the lord in the great hall. If they were found guilty, they were thrown into the dungeon or even executed.

CASTLES BECOME TOWNS

Because life was usually safe and peaceful around the castle, people wanted to live nearby. Traders knew that robbers would not dare to attack them and peasants brought food to sell to the inhabitants. Slowly, villages and towns grew up near castles. An Irish example is Kilkenny, where the town grew beside the castle of the powerful Norman family, the Butlers. Many other Irish towns started in the same way.

Defending the castle

PREPARING FOR A SIEGE

In a war, the lord had to defend his castle from his enemies. He prepared carefully. He doubled the number of sentries on the walls and ordered them to watch for the enemy. He hired extra soldiers, got the masons to strengthen the walls and told the smiths to make more weapons. The lord even sent people out to gather stones and rocks which could be hurled over the walls at the attackers. He stored extra food and checked that the well in the courtyard was open and clean.

When at last the enemy approached, local farming families came inside the walls, bringing their animals with them. The lord gave them weapons so they could fight alongside the soldiers. Then the drawbridge was raised, the portcullis was lowered and the people in the castle got ready to defend themselves.

A SIEGE

It was not easy to capture a well-prepared stone castle. The best way was to lay **siege** to it. That meant surrounding it with an army and letting nothing in or out. The idea was to starve the people inside into surrendering.

AN ATTACK

But a siege could last a long time because the people in the castle were well prepared, with supplies of food and water. And while the castle held out, the leaders of the attacking army had to feed and pay their soldiers. So they usually tried to speed things up by launching an **attack** on the castle. There were several ways to do this.

- The enemy could climb over the walls using long ladders and **siege towers**. But the defenders could easily push the ladders back and shoot arrows and stones at the siege towers.
- The enemy could try to knock down the walls with a **battering ram**. The weakest part of the castle was the gate, but it was well defended by the drawbridge and the portcullis. The moat made it hard to reach the walls, but the enemy could fill it with stones and branches and get at the walls that way.

Wherever they attacked, the enemy had to work under a constant hail of arrows and stones from the defenders up on the walls. Sometimes they even poured boiling water or oil down on the invaders.

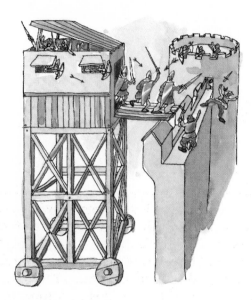

Catapults like these could cause a great deal of damage.

A siege tower

▟ The enemy could hurl big stones from a giant **catapult**. But these were hard to aim and had little effect on the walls. However, catapults could do great damage inside the castle and upset the defenders, who never knew where the next stone would land.

▟ One of the best ways to attack the castle was to dig a tunnel called a **mine** under the walls. The mine was started well back from the castle, out of sight of the defenders. When it reached the walls, a big cave was hollowed out which was filled with wood and animal fat and set alight. The heat of the fire would crack the walls and bring them down.

The defenders dreaded these mines more than anything else. So they kept bowls of water on the castle walls, and if the water quivered, they knew a mine was being dug. The defenders then built their own **counter-mine** to try to cut across the enemy's. But that only worked if they guessed its route correctly. Their best hope was that the tunnel would cave in on top of the miners, as it often did.

Attackers use a battering ram while the castle's defenders hurl down rock from above.

Most of the time, the defenders were able to hold out and in the end, the attackers had to give up and go home. Until gun-powder was invented in the 1400s, it was very hard to capture a medieval castle.

▟ QUESTIONS ▟

1. In the drawing of the castle on page 51, thirteen parts are shown. In your workbook, write the name of each part and say in your own words what it was used for. Begin like this:
   1. Keep: The big square tower where the lord lived
2. Dozens of people lived in a castle. List five of them and say what each did.
3. Explain how castles sometimes became towns. Name **two** towns in Ireland which grew up in this way.

Activities

1. DRAW A MOTTE AND BAILEY CASTLE AND CLEARLY LABEL THE VARIOUS PARTS. WHAT WAS ITS MAIN WEAKNESS?
2. IMAGINE YOU ARE LEADING AN ATTACK ON A MEDIEVAL STONE CASTLE. USING INFORMATION IN THIS BOOK AND FROM LIBRARY BOOKS, PLAN HOW TO CAPTURE IT. DRAW SOME OF THE SIEGE WEAPONS YOU WOULD USE.
   NOW, IMAGINE THAT YOU ARE THE LORD OF THE CASTLE. HOW WOULD YOU STOP THE VARIOUS ATTACKS?
   YOUR CLASS MIGHT WANT TO DIVIDE INTO GROUPS TO SEE WHO CAN PLAN THE BEST ATTACK OR DEFENCE.
3. IMAGINE YOU ARE A LORD OR LADY OF A MEDIEVAL CASTLE. WRITE AN ACCOUNT OF YOUR LIFE. YOU SHOULD INCLUDE: (A) A DESCRIPTION OF THE CASTLE AND OF YOUR ROOMS; (B) THE THINGS YOU DID DURING THE DAY; (C) A BANQUET; (D) A SIEGE.

Life in a Medieval Manor

What was a manor?

In the Middle Ages, most people were **peasants** (farmers). They lived in small villages and farmed the land around them. A village, along with its land, was called a **manor**.

THE MANOR HOUSE

The biggest house in the village was the **manor house**. It was built of stone with a thatched roof and belonged to the **lord of the manor**.

Inside, one large room, the **hall**, took up most of the first floor. This is where the lord, his family and their servants lived. At night, the lord's family slept in a small private room, but everyone else slept on the floor in the hall.

Below the hall were the **stables** for the animals. Around the manor house there was an **enclosure** with barns and more stables.

THE PRIEST AND THE PARISH CHURCH

Near the manor house was the parish church, with the priest's house beside it. The priest said Mass for the people each Sunday. He also baptised, married and buried them. In return, the people had to give him a tenth of their crops. This was called the **tithe**.

THE HOUSES OF THE PEASANTS

The peasants lived in the small houses scattered around the village. These were simple huts about 8m long and 4m wide. The peasants built the huts themselves, using the wood they had collected in the forest. The walls were made of mud or of wattle and daub (see page 14), and the roofs were thatched.

The huts were dark and smoky inside because there were no chimneys or windows. A fire burned in the middle of the floor. Stools were the only furniture. The family slept on rushes piled on the earth floor. They could not afford candles, so they got up at dawn and went to bed at sunset.

THE FOREST

The forest which surrounded the manor was very important to the peasants. From it they got timber to build their houses. They also used wood to make farm implements like ploughs and spades and household goods like stools or plates. The forest also supplied them with fuel to cook their food and keep them warm through the winter. To supplement the food they grew themselves, they gathered nuts and berries in the forest as well.

The land of the manor

There were two kinds of land on the manor.
- The grassland where the peasants grazed their animals was called the **commons**.
- The **farmland** is where crops were grown. It was divided into three huge fields and each field was divided into long, narrow strips.

THE LORD AND THE PEASANTS

All the land of the manor belonged to the lord. He kept part of it to farm himself. This was called his **demesne**. The rest he divided among the peasants.

Each family was allowed to keep some animals on the commons, to sow crops on strips of land in each of the three big fields, and to collect wood in the forest. But the peasants had to pay for all this. They had to give their lord money, or part of the crops they grew, or some of their animals. And they had to work on his demesne without pay for a certain number of days each year.

FARMING

Peasants had to work very hard on the land. Medieval manuscripts tell us a great deal about the work they did.

PLOUGHING THE LAND

In spring, the peasants ploughed the land to get it ready for the crops. This account of a ploughman's day was written around 1100 AD by an English monk called Aelfric.

*"I work very hard. I go out at dawn and I drive the **oxen** to the field and **yoke** them to the plough. I dare not stay at home for fear of my lord. Every day I plough a full acre or more. I have a boy who drives the oxen with a **goad**, and even now, he is hoarse from cold and shouting. I fill the ox-bins with hay and I clear out the dung. It is very hard work because I am not free."*

USE THE PICTURE AND THE DOCUMENT TO ANSWER THESE QUESTIONS.

1. FROM THE PICTURE, DESCRIBE HOW A MEDIEVAL PEASANT DRESSED.
2. LOOK UP **YOKE**, **GOAD** AND **OXEN** IN YOUR DICTIONARY. WHICH ONES CAN YOU SEE IN THE PICTURE?
3. THE DOCUMENT WRITTEN WAS BY A MONK, NOT A PEASANT. DO YOU THINK WE CAN TRUST IT TO GIVE A FAIR IDEA OF A PLOUGHMAN'S LIFE? EXPLAIN YOUR ANSWER.

Looking at the evidence

▲ *This drawing from a medieval manuscript shows a peasant ploughing the land with his oxen.*

▲ *Study this modern drawing of a manor and locate the* ▼ *things mentioned in the text.*

FARM LANDS

SOWING AND REAPING

When the land was ploughed, the peasants scattered seed on the earth. The children and dogs were kept busy scaring off the crows.

In autumn, the ripe crops were harvested. Men and women worked together to cut the grain using a curved knife called a **sickle**.

In this medieval drawing, men reap the grain with sickles while the women rake and stack the hay.

GOING TO THE MILL

The grain was taken to the mill where it was ground into flour. The mill often belonged to the lord and the peasants had to pay to use it. The mill wheels were turned by water or wind.

FOOD

The peasants produced most of their own food. Their main food was bread made from wheat, barley or rye which was often mixed with beans. They had milk, butter and cheese, but could only afford meat as a special treat.

Their only vegetables were onions and cabbage, but they ate nuts, berries and herbs which they gathered in the forest. Their main drink was ale which they brewed themselves. They usually had two meals a day, the first at sunrise, the second in mid-afternoon.

CLOTHES

The peasants had to make their own clothes. They sheared the wool from their sheep, spun it into thread and then wove it into cloth. They grew flax and made it into linen. They dyed the cloth using dyes made from berries and mosses. They made leather from animal skins and turned it into shoes and coats.

THE THREAT OF FAMINE

You may think that medieval peasants were well off, but that was not so. They had vegetables, milk and eggs in summer and autumn, but without

COMMONS

refrigeration or tins, these could not be kept for long. In winter, the food often ran out and by the spring they were usually hungry.

If the harvest was good, they had just enough to survive until the next one. But if it was bad, they faced a famine when many of them died. Historians think that there was a bad harvest every seven years in the Middle Ages.

FAMILY WORK

Because life was hard, a peasant family had to work together as a team if they were to survive.

Men usually did the heavy farming work like ploughing and shearing sheep. Women baked and cooked, spun and wove the cloth, made clothes and dyed them, milked the cattle and sheep, and made butter

Everyone in the village had to help with the harvest.

and cheese. But at harvest time, when every hand was needed to bring in the precious food, women and men worked side by side in the fields gathering in the crops.

Almost as soon as children could walk, they helped too. They scared the crows off the seed, pulled weeds, protected the animals from wolves and foxes, and collected firewood, nuts and berries in the forest. There were no schools, so they learned by watching their parents.

THE MANOR COURT

The lord of the manor kept order in the village. If one peasant stole from another, or if two of them quarrelled about something, they were brought before the **manor court**. This consisted of the lord and some of the villagers. They listened to the evidence and decided whether a person was guilty or innocent.

FREEMEN AND SERFS

On the manor, some peasants were **freemen**. They owned their own land, though they had to pay a

rent to the lord. They could come and go as they pleased.

But other peasants were not free. They were called **serfs** or **villeins**. They belonged to the lord. They had to work without pay on his demesne and they could not get married or leave the land without his permission.

ESCAPE TO ANOTHER LIFE

Many serfs wanted to be free. But if they ran away, the lord had the right to bring them back and punish them. However, if a serf got to a town and hid there for a year and a day, he won his freedom.

Looking at the evidence

LOOK AT THE DOCUMENT ON PAGE 56. IS THE PLOUGHMAN A FREEMAN OR A SERF?

QUESTIONS

1. Describe or draw a manor house.
2. There were three kinds of land around a manor. What were they and what did the peasants get from each?
3. Explain each of the following: lord of the manor, tithe, demesne, freeman, serf.
4. What did the peasants have to do for their lord in return for the right to farm the manor land?

Activities

1. LOOK AT THE ILLUSTRATIONS IN THIS CHAPTER. USING THE INFORMATION IN THEM, DRAW OR DESCRIBE THE CLOTHES WORN BY MEDIEVAL MEN AND WOMEN.
2. IMAGINE YOU WERE A MEDIEVAL PEASANT (MAN OR WOMAN). DESCRIBE YOUR LIFE. YOU SHOULD INCLUDE: (A) IF YOU WERE FREE OR NOT; (B) YOUR CLOTHES; (C) YOUR HOUSE; (D) YOUR FOOD; (E) THE WORK YOU HAVE TO DO THROUGHOUT THE YEAR.
   USE EVIDENCE IN THIS BOOK OR FROM OTHER SOURCES.

CHAPTER 20

Medieval Churches

Bishops and dioceses

In the Middle Ages, most of the people in Europe were Christians. They belonged to the Catholic Church whose leader was the pope in Rome. In each country, the local Christian leaders were the bishops who ruled over an area called a **diocese**.

In Ireland, people had been Christians since the time of St Patrick (see Section 2), but in the early years, monasteries and their abbots were more important than bishops. This began to change around 1100 AD when the country was divided into dioceses. The dioceses which were set up then have lasted up to the present day.

CATHEDRALS

In each diocese the bishop's headquarters was the **cathedral**. This was a special church with a chair in it for the bishop. (The word "cathedral" comes from the Latin word for "chair".)

The cathedral was usually a very large church. Bishops liked to build them in the latest styles and to get the best masons, sculptors and artists to work on them. As a result, some of the most magnificent medieval buildings were the cathedrals.

This magnificent cathedral is at Rheims in France. It is one of Europe's greatest medieval buildings.

Finding out

WHAT DIOCESE DO YOU LIVE IN? DO YOU KNOW WHERE ITS CATHEDRAL IS?

Medieval architecture

In the Middle Ages, there were two main architectural (building) styles – **Romanesque** and **Gothic**.

ROMANESQUE CHURCHES

In the tenth century, people learned how to build big stone churches. They modelled them on old Roman buildings, which is why they are called **Romanesque** (which means "in the Roman style").

Romanesque buildings had thick walls to hold up the heavy roofs. Inside, the roof was supported by massive columns with great round arches above them. Because the walls were thick, the windows had to be small, so Romanesque churches were dark and gloomy inside.

Inside a Romanesque cathedral. Look at the massive columns and the rounded arches.

GOTHIC ARCHITECTURE

Around 1140, a French monk designed and built a new style of church. He put supports called **flying buttresses** against the outside walls to carry the weight of the roof. It was now possible to have much thinner walls with bigger windows. And inside, the columns did not have to support the roof, so they could be much more slender and graceful.

This was the **Gothic** style of architecture. It quickly became fashionable all over Europe. Bishops and abbots started to build churches in the new style.

■ Gothic churches had magnificent windows made of stained (coloured) glass. The glass was made into scenes from the Bible using rich reds, purples, blues and yellows. When the sun shone, the glass sparkled like jewels. People thought that heaven must look like this.

◄ Flying buttresses carry the weight of the roof.

Slender, graceful columns inside a Gothic cathedral.

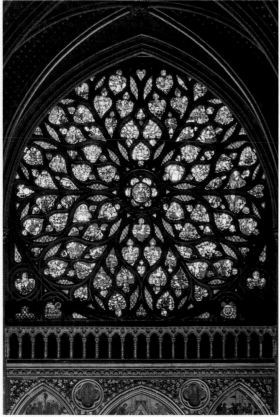

◄ Many Gothic cathedrals had magnificent "rose windows".

Some stained glass windows showed scenes from the Bible. What does this show?

Life in a Medieval Monastery

The ruins of the medieval monastery at Jerpoint Abbey. The buildings are much bigger than the Celtic monasteries you studied in Section 2.

Medieval monks and nuns

Some medieval Christians were very religious and wished to worship God in a special way. They became monks in a monastery or nuns in a convent and lived lives of prayer and penance.

THE RULE OF ST BENEDICT

A wood carving of St Benedict

Medieval monks followed the **Rule of St Benedict** (page 62). This was drawn up about 520 AD by St Benedict who founded a monastery at Monte Cassino in Italy. The Rule set out the duties of the monks, the work they must do and the prayers they must say. Monks who followed the Rule of St Benedict were called **Benedictines**.

The head of the monastery, the **abbot,** was elected by the other monks. The Rule said that the abbot must be like a father to his monks and that they were to obey him in everything.

BECOMING A MONK

When a boy entered a monastery, he was called a **novice**. He had to learn the Rule and find out if the life of a monk suited him. If the abbot decided he would be a good monk, he then took **solemn vows**. These were promises of **chastity** (he must not marry), **poverty** (he must have no possessions of his own) and **obedience** (he must obey the abbot).

His hair was cut in a **tonsure** (shaved around the crown). He then put on a simple black **habit** and became a monk.

Monks at prayer. Each monk's hair is cut in a tonsure.

MEDIEVAL MONASTERIES IN IRELAND

Medieval monasteries were very different from the early Irish monasteries (Section 2). They were much bigger and had many more stone buildings. Medieval monasteries were built in either Romanesque or Gothic styles. The Irish started building this kind of monastery shortly before the Normans arrived. There are many medieval monasteries in Ireland today but most of them are in ruins.

IS THERE A MEDIEVAL MONASTERY NEAR YOU? FIND OUT AS MUCH AS YOU CAN ABOUT IT. THEN WRITE A REPORT OF YOUR FINDINGS, INCLUDING DRAWINGS AND PHOTOGRAPHS.

Activity

A typical monastery

This is a drawing of a typical medieval monastery. Look at it closely. Then find each building that is listed below.

1. The **church** where the monks prayed
2. The **almonry** where sick people went to get help
3. The **library** where the monastery's books were kept
4. The **scriptorium** where monks wrote and illustrated **manuscripts**
5. The **dormitory** where the monks slept
6. The **infirmary** where sick monks were nursed
7. The **refectory** where the monks ate their meals
8. The **cloister** where monks walked and students attended classes
9. The **guest house** where all travellers were welcomed
10. The **abbot's house** where the abbot lived
11. The **barns** where crops from the monastery's farms were stored.
12. The **chapter house** where the monks decided the business of the monastery

The life of a medieval monk

FOLLOWING THE RULE

The Rule of St Benedict said that a monk must not speak to anyone except on business or in an emergency. This left him free to pray. Praying was the main reason for becoming a monk and the Rule gave detailed instructions about the prayers a monk had to say throughout the day.

Here is an account of a monk's day. As you read it, look up the buildings mentioned in the drawing and work out where he went.

PRAYERS IN THE NIGHT

Monks went to bed about 8.00 p.m. They all slept in one long room called the **dormitory** which was near the church. Each monk had a bed surrounded by a wooden panel that gave him some privacy. On the bed was a mattress stuffed with straw and one or two rough woollen blankets. When they went to bed, the monks took off their outer habits and shoes, but kept on the tunics they wore during the day.

At midnight a bell rang. The monks rose, dressed and went silently to the church where they sang psalms and said prayers. This service was called **matins**. After about half an hour, they returned to bed, but they were up again at 6 a.m. for the service of **prime**.

Cormac's Chapel on the Rock of Cashel, Co. Tipperary

THE CHAPTER HOUSE

After prime, the monks went to the **chapter house**, one of the most important buildings in the monastery. All stood silently in their places until the abbot was seated. They then bowed to him and sat down. In the chapter house, the monks dealt with the business of the monastery. They might have talked about a new roof for the church or whether they should build a new barn. Discipline was also enforced at the chapter meetings. A monk who had done something wrong confessed and was punished. Punishments ranged from a week on bread and water to complete expulsion for breaking the solemn vows. Finally, a chapter of the Rule was read so that everyone would remember that they must live by it. This is how the "chapter house" got its name.

MASS

The next service was **terce** which was held at 9 a.m. It was followed by **High Mass**, the most magnificent service of the day. On Sundays and holy days, peasants came from the nearby villages to join in. During Mass, the church was filled with the voices of the monks singing **plain chant**, a kind of music which is sometimes sung today.

ONE MEAL A DAY

When Mass was over, the monks broke their fast in the **refectory**. They ate in silence while one monk read from a holy book. They usually ate vegetables, beans, eggs, cheese, and bread. They washed it down with ale or wine. On Fridays they had fish, and meat on special feast days.

The Rule said that from September to Easter this was to be their only meal each day. In summer, however, they had a light supper before going to bed.

THE DUTIES OF THE DAY

At midday there was a service called **sext** after which the monks went to work. Different monks had different duties. The **cellarer** met local merchants at the gate and bought food and wine from them. The **infirmarian** went to the infirmary to nurse any monks who were sick. Other monks copied manuscripts in the scriptorium or studied books in the library.

The **master of novices** taught Latin to his charges. They had to learn it because the Rule, as well as all their prayers and books, were in Latin. Classes were held in the **cloister**, a square garden in the centre of the monastery. Around it there was a covered walk which gave shelter in bad weather.

A medieval manuscript showing monks at work

A REFUGE FOR TRAVELLERS

The Rule said the monks must welcome every traveller "as if he were Christ himself". Therefore every monastery had a **guest house** where a weary traveller could be sure of a night's shelter and a warm meal. The **guest master** looked after them.

They were not charged for their lodgings but were expected to give whatever they could afford to the monastery. The abbot himself entertained important guests, such as bishops, lords or even the king, in his own house.

The poor were not neglected by the monks. Beggars, sick people, and even lepers whom no one else would help, were taken into the **almonry** where the **almoner** gave them food, shelter and nursing care, if they needed it.

🏛 THE LAST PRAYERS OF THE DAY

The monks had three more services to attend. These were **none** at about 3.00 p.m., **vespers** at about 6.00 p.m., and **compline** at sunset. After that they went to bed and slept until the first bell of a new day called them to prayer once again.

CHAPTER 21

Life in a Medieval Town

🏛 Towns in the Middle Ages

There had been towns in Europe since ancient times. The Greeks and Romans lived in towns and cities. But after the fall of the Roman Empire, towns became less important until the Middle Ages.

In the eleventh century, medieval kings and lords discovered that towns could be useful. They needed skilled craftspeople like masons, smiths and carpenters to build their castles and churches – and these people lived in towns. Peasants also paid **tolls** to sell their produce in the towns, which also increased the kings' or lords' wealth.

🏛 TOWN CHARTERS

Kings and lords gave people **charters** to build towns near their castles. A charter was a document which guaranteed the townspeople certain rights in return for paying a tax to the king or the lord.

The usual rights in a charter were:
- ◪ the right to elect a town council (or corporation) which could make decisions about the government of the town.
- ◪ the right to collect their own taxes and use them for the good of the town.

🏛 IRISH TOWNS AND CITIES

The first towns in Ireland developed during the Middle Ages. The Vikings established some like Dublin, Waterford and Limerick. The Normans encouraged more. Their leader, King Henry II, gave charters to Dublin and Waterford. Norman lords helped to found Carlow, Kilmallock, Drogheda, Carrickfergus, Nenagh and many others.

THE SIZE OF TOWNS

By our standards, medieval towns were small. Around the year 1300 AD, Dublin probably had a population of about 15,000. Towns in other parts of Europe were much larger, with London and Paris each having about 30,000 inhabitants.

TOWN WALLS

Most medieval towns were surrounded by walls. Wars were common in the Middle Ages. Towns were always in danger of being attacked, so the walls gave the townspeople some security. Towns walls were rather like the castle walls you saw on page 51, only bigger. There was sometimes a moat outside the walls for extra protection.

The medieval gate at Drogheda, Co. Louth

HERE IS PART OF A POEM CALLED *THE WALLING OF NEW ROSS*. IT WAS WRITTEN IN 1265 WHEN NEW ROSS WAS THE BUSIEST PORT IN IRELAND. READ IT AND ANSWER THE QUESTIONS.

THEY WERE FEARFUL OF A WAR
THAT WAS GOING ON BETWEEN TWO BARONS.
HERE IS WRITTEN THEIR TWO NAMES –
LORD MAURICE AND LORD WALTER.

WHAT THEY FEARED WAS THAT THEIR TOWN
   HAD NO WALLS.
TO THEIR COUNCIL THEY WENT ONE DAY,
THEY MADE THIS RESOLUTION:
THAT WALLS OF STONE AND MORTAR
THEY WOULD BUILD AROUND THE TOWN.

WHAT REASON DOES THE POEM GIVE FOR WANTING A WALL? WHAT WOULD THE WALLS BE MADE OF? WHO WOULD BUILD THEM?

Looking at the evidence ▽ ▽ ▽ ▽ ▽ ▽ ▽

TOWN GATES

There were usually several gates in the wall which led to the different roads in and out of the town. Some town gates had a portcullis and a drawbridge. The gates were very narrow and, with their towers, were easy to defend.

Gates were guarded day and night by soldiers or armed townsmen. They questioned any stranger about his business before they let him inside the walls. Anyone wanting to sell goods in the town had to pay a toll.

At sunset, the gates were closed and they were not opened again until dawn.

STREETS AND HOUSES WITHIN THE WALLS

Inside their walls, medieval towns were very crowded. There was one wide High Street running between two of the gates. Near the centre, the street widened into a square where there was a **market cross**. A market was held there once a week.

The High Street was paved with wooden planks or stones. There was often an open, stone-lined drain running down the centre. People threw their sewage and other rubbish into it. Most other streets were narrow and unpaved.

Life in a medieval town

THE EVIDENCE FROM WINETAVERN STREET

In the 1960s and 1970s, archaeologists excavated a medieval street in Dublin called Winetavern Street. They unearthed the foundations of many houses and discovered a great deal about life there in the Middle Ages. Here is some of what they found.

TOWN HOUSES

Most of the houses in Winetavern Street were one storey high and made of wood with thatched roofs. The windows were holes in the wall, sometimes covered by shutters. Inside there were two or three rooms where the whole family lived. Behind the houses there were long gardens, some with fruit trees and even grass where cows, pigs and hens were kept.

The people who lived in these houses made goods which they sold to the public. Their shops and workshops opened straight onto the street, with their family's living room behind.

In the living room there was a fire in the middle of the floor, with the smoke seeping out through the windows or the thatch. There was very little furniture, only stone benches along the walls which acted as seats during the day and beds at night.

A few richer men could afford to build two-storey houses with four or five rooms. They furnished their houses with beds, chests and tables, hung carpets on the walls for warmth and colour, ate from pewter dishes and even put glass in some of the windows.

Later in the Middle Ages, some rich merchants even built stone houses. Stone houses were safer than wooden ones as they were less likely to go on fire. Today, the wooden houses have all disappeared, but some stone ones still exist in many of our towns.

This medieval house in Kilkenny was built by the wealthy Rothe family.

CHURCH BUILDINGS

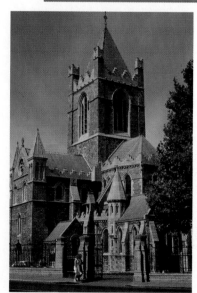

Christchurch Cathedral in Dublin

Towns also had a parish church and often a monastery or a friary. These were built of stone by the local craftsmen. The townspeople were proud of their churches and spent time and money making them beautiful. They usually built them in the latest Romanesque or Gothic styles (page 59).

Today, these stone churches are the main medieval buildings that still remain in our towns.

CRAFTSMEN

Medieval towns were always crowded with people. Some lived and worked there, while others came to buy and sell goods at the regular markets or fairs.

The most important people were the **craftsmen** who made the things that people needed.

HERE IS A LIST OF CRAFTSMEN WHO WORKED IN DUBLIN IN 1200 AD. READ IT AND MAKE A LIST OF THE THINGS THAT WERE MADE IN THE CITY. USE A DICTIONARY TO LOOK UP ANY WORDS YOU DO NOT UNDERSTAND.

GOLDSMITHS	TANNERS	MASONS
TAILORS	SADDLERS	MILLERS
SHOEMAKERS	LORIMERS	BAKERS
WEAVERS	SMITHS	VINTNERS
CORDWAINERS	CARPENTERS	BUTCHERS
MERCERS	COOPERS	FISHERMEN

Activity

Medieval trades - a shoemaker's shop, a goldsmith at work with his apprentices, and a butcher

IN MEDIEVAL TOWNS, PEOPLE WITH THE SAME TRADE OFTEN LIVED TOGETHER IN THE SAME STREET. WHICH OF THE CRAFTSMEN WOULD YOU EXPECT TO FIND IN THESE DUBLIN STREETS: WINETAVERN STREET, FISHAMBLES STREET, COOK STREET AND SKINNERS' ROW?

Finding out

ARE THERE ANY STREETS IN YOUR AREA WHICH SEEM TO HAVE MEDIEVAL NAMES? FIND OUT ABOUT THEM AND ABOUT THE TRADES WHICH MAY HAVE BEEN CARRIED ON IN THESE STREETS.

Activity

Guilds

All the people who practised a particular craft had to belong to a **guild**. There was a bakers' guild, a masons' guild and so on. A guild had a lot of power.

- It set examinations for people who wanted to enter that craft.
- It saw that the goods produced by its members were of a high standard.
- It fixed wages and prices.
- It helped members who were old or ill.

If a person wanted to work in a town, he had to belong to the local guild. There were three ways to do this: being born the son of a member, marrying the daughter of a member, or going through a long and difficult training. This training had three stages.

APPRENTICE

At the age of twelve, a boy went to work for a **master** as an **apprentice**. He lived in his master's house and learned his trade. He started with simple tasks and when he could do them, he moved on to more difficult ones.

An apprentice had to stay with his master for seven years. He was not paid, but was given his food and clothes. A good master treated a boy well, but a cruel master could make life miserable for his apprentices.

JOURNEYMAN

After seven years, the apprentice became a **journeyman**. (The word "journeyman" comes from the French word *journée*, meaning "a day".) Now he was paid for each day's work he did. He could leave his old master to work for someone else, or go to another town to get better wages. Journeymen in some trades travelled all over Europe looking for work. We know that skilled masons from the west of England helped to build Christchurch Cathedral in Dublin.

MASTER CRAFTSMAN

If a man wanted to have his own shop, he had to become a **master**. First, he had to pass a test set by the guild. They asked him to make a **masterpiece** which would show his skill. For example, a tailor might be asked to make a fine gown, or a carpenter a piece of furniture. If he passed, he became a member of the guild and could open his own workshop, employ apprentices and journeymen and sell his work to the public.

A master craftsman's shop, workshop and home were all in the same small building. The front room, which opened onto the street, was the shop. In the room behind it, the master and his men worked side by side. And alongside them, the master's family lived, ate and slept.

WOMEN IN THE GUILDS

As the word "craftsmen" shows, medieval guilds were for men only. Girls could not be apprentices or journeymen. We have records of a few women who were guild members, but we do not know how this happened. They may have learned the craft at home alongside their brothers. It is more likely, however, that they were widows who continued the family business after their husbands had died. There were probably far more women involved in the crafts than the records show.

Fairs and markets

Towns were centres where people went to buy and sell goods. Every town had a weekly **market** and the bigger towns had an annual **fair**.

MARKETS

Once a week, peasants from nearby manors went to the town. They paid a small **toll** (fee) for permission to set up a stall around the market cross in the town centre. They sold corn, chickens, eggs, vegetables or cheese to the townsfolk. They also sold hay to feed animals, straw to cover floors, and moss which was used as toilet paper. With the money they earned, the peasants then bought shoes, knives, pots or other things they needed in the craftsmen's shops.

FAIRS

Every October, thousands of people gather at the fair in Ballinasloe, Co. Galway, just as they did during medieval times.

Fairs were much bigger and more important than markets. They were usually held once a year on the fair green outside the city or town walls. Some of these medieval fairs survive to the present day, including Puck Fair in Killorglin, Co. Kerry or the annual horse fair in Ballinasloe, Co. Galway.

Merchants

People came from far and wide to visit the fair. The most important of these were the **merchants**. They were traders, either Irish or foreign, who brought foreign goods to sell to the local people. They also bought local produce and exported it from Ireland. Merchants paid the townspeople for permission to set up their stalls on the fair green.

On the fair day, the lords from the local manors came with their carts laden with wheat, wool and hides. They also brought herds of cattle and horses which they sold to the merchants. The lords then bought salt, wine, spices, rich cloth, furs or other things that were not made locally.

Craftsmen also bought things they needed at the fair. Smiths bought iron, tanners bought hides (animal skins), weavers bought dyes, and chandlers bought wax to make candles.

Fair day was a holiday for the peasants and townsfolk. On the fair green there were dozens of stalls selling food, ale, honey, ribbons or knives. There was plenty to see: musicians, jugglers, wrestlers and men showing off strange animals such as camels.

The fair day was the high point of everyone's year. On that day they met strangers from England, France or Italy who passed on gossip of distant wars and the deaths of kings and popes. In the days before newspapers or television, this was the only way for people to hear about what was happening outside their own area.

IRISH MERCHANTS AND THEIR TRADE

Many Irish merchants took part in these fairs. They exported hides, wool and other things produced in Ireland and imported things which the people needed. Merchants often made long journeys in small boats and were in constant danger from storms and pirates. But if a merchant was lucky and successful, he could become very rich.

Two of Ireland's main medieval imports came from Bordeaux in France. These were salt and wine. Salt was important because the only way to preserve food for the long winter months was to salt it. Wine was drunk by Norman and Irish lords.

Merchants also imported spices (pepper, cloves, nutmeg, ginger) and dried fruit and nuts like almonds, raisons and figs. (Archaeologists found fig seeds when they were excavating in Dublin.) Other imports such as silks and fine woollen cloth came from Italy. Rich furs from the Baltic adorned the clothes of wealthy lords and ladies.

Irish merchants belonged to the merchant guild, the richest and most important guild in each city. In many cities, the council was controlled by these merchants.

How medieval towns were governed

THE TOWN COUNCIL

Most towns had a charter which set out the rights of the townsmen, or the **burgesses** as they were called. The burgesses' most important right was to elect a **town council** which governed the town. The head of the town council was called the **provost.** In bigger cities like Dublin, Galway, Limerick or Waterford, the head of the council was the **mayor.**

A town council had many duties.

- It collected taxes from the citizens and tolls from traders.
- It paid some of this income to the king and used the rest to keep the walls in good repair.

- It held courts and punished wrongdoers.
- It made laws to regulate the lives of the townspeople.

FIRE

Fire was a big problem for town councils. If one wooden house went on fire, the blaze spread quickly to the whole street. To reduce the risk, councils ordered that all household fires had to be put out at night.

At sunset, a bell rang to tell the people that it was **curfew** – time to put out the fire. It also signalled that the gates were closing and that everyone was expected to go to bed. Only thieves or murderers went out after curfew. Councils hired watchmen to patrol the streets at night, keeping guard against wrongdoers and watching out for fires.

DIRT AND DISEASE

Medieval towns were filthy. Butchers and fishmongers threw their waste into the street where it rotted away. Tanning hides for leather, which was carried on in most towns, caused a terrible smell. There were no underground pipes, so people threw sewage out of the houses, straight into the drains that ran down the centre of the streets.

Rubbish was piled up in odd corners or thrown over the town walls. (Archaeologists have found this a very useful habit, as they can learn a lot from piles of old rubbish!) People kept pigs and cattle in their back gardens, and pigs often escaped and rooted in the rubbish – alongside thousands of rats.

Town councils tried to improve conditions. They fined people who let their pigs loose or who threw rubbish straight into the street. They also tried to get supplies of clean water.

In 1224, the Dublin Council diverted the River Dodder so that it flowed into a special tank. This gave a supply of fresh water to the citizens. Most people carried it away in buckets, but the council allowed rich people to pipe the water directly into their homes. The pipes were made of wood and the council ordered that they must be "no wider than a goose quill". This greatly reduced the amount of water the pipes could carry.

Not long after the council provided this fresh water, it had to order people not to wash their clothes in it. This shows how difficult it was for councils to keep their cities clean.

THE BLACK DEATH

The dirty conditions of medieval towns caused many diseases. The worst example was the **Black Death** which started in 1345. It was a plague caused by fleas on the rats which had come from Asia on merchants' ships.

A friar in Kilkenny, John Clyn, kept a diary which said the plague reached his city in 1348. When the Black Death struck, men, women and children died. About a third of the population of Europe died from the plague, which was especially bad in crowded cities. As a result, cities declined in both population and importance.

Finding out

1. ARCHAEOLOGISTS CAN LEARN ABOUT MEDIEVAL LIFE BY LOOKING THROUGH THEIR RUBBISH DUMPS. SUGGEST FIVE PIECES OF EVIDENCE THEY MIGHT DISCOVER IN THESE DUMPS.
2. FIND OUT WHAT THE FRIAR, JOHN CLYN, HAD TO SAY ABOUT THE BLACK DEATH IN IRELAND.

QUESTIONS

1. List six of the craftsmen who worked in a medieval city. Pick out one from the list and write an account of his life. You should include: (a) how he learned his craft; (b) how he joined the guild; (c) his shop and house; (d) his business at a market and a fair.
2. Write a sentence explaining the following words: craftsman, charter, guild, town council, apprentice, masterpiece, curfew.
3. Would you like to have lived in a medieval city? Give reasons for your answer.

Activity

IMAGINE YOU WERE WALKING THROUGH A MEDIEVAL TOWN ON THE FAIR DAY. DESCRIBE THIS EXPERIENCE BY WRITING ABOUT WHAT YOU SAW AND HEARD.

SECTION 5

THE RENAISSANCE

CHAPTER 23

How we know about the Renaissance

The end of the Middle Ages

After the Black Death, life in medieval Europe began to change. These changes first started in Italy. Italian people turned away from medieval ideas. Instead, they began to revive the ideas of the ancient Romans and Greeks.

Historians say that these ancient ideas were **reborn** in Italy. This rebirth began in the fourteenth century and continued on into the fifteenth and sixteenth centuries. Historians call this period in European history the **Renaissance** which means "rebirth".

The Renaissance in Italy

There are a number of important sources which we can study to find out about the Renaissance in Italy.

MANUSCRIPTS AND PRINTED BOOKS

During the Renaissance, many people wrote books which give information about life at that time. At first, these books were in manuscript form – they were written by hand. In the middle of the Renaissance, printing was invented. Books could now be copied quickly and sent all over Europe.

70

Printed books were also much cheaper to produce than manuscripts. As a result, many more people could afford to buy and read them.

ARCHIVES

An **archive** is a collection of documents such as reports, letters, diaries, accounts and notebooks dealing with everyday matters.

During the Renaissance, many rulers, government officials and private citizens saved their personal papers. These have been collected and stored safely in libraries throughout Europe. Historians have studied many of these documents. From them they have learned a great deal about the private lives of people who lived during the Renaissance.

Michelangelo wrote this poem and drew the little sketch of himself while he was painting the ceiling of the Sistine Chapel.

BUILDINGS, PAINTINGS AND SCULPTURES

During the Renaissance, architects designed new buildings, painters produced great works of art, and sculptors made statues out of marble and bronze. Today, we can study these buildings and see Renaissance paintings and sculptures in art galleries and museums.

GIORGIO VASARI (1511-1574)

In 1550, a famous book called *The Lives of the Most Excellent Painters, Architects and Sculptors* was published. It was written by an Italian called **Giorgio Vasari** who was also a successful painter and architect. Vasari knew that many changes had taken place in painting, architecture and sculpture. So he decided to write down all he knew about them.

Vasari travelled around Italy and gathered as much information as he could about painters, architects and sculptors. His book contains details about the lives and works of 150 Renaissance artists. It is one of our most important sources of information about the Renaissance. Many of the quotations in this section come from Vasari's work.

Three examples of Renaissance art - the Medici palace in Florence, Michelangelo's statue of Bacchus, the Roman god of wine and Botticelli's La Primavera (Spring)

QUESTIONS

1. Whose ideas did the Italians begin to revive during the fourteenth century?
2. List three sources of information about the Renaissance.
3. Choose one of these sources and write a paragraph about it.
4. Which kind of source do you think could tell us most about the Italian Renaissance? Give reasons for your answer.

CHAPTER 24

Italy in the Fifteenth Century

The Renaissance began in Italy because:
- ☑ Italy was richer than other countries.
- ☑ Italy was not a united country, so each area ran its own affairs.
- ☑ More Italians lived in cities than elsewhere in Europe.

🏛 Italian merchants

On page 68, you read about foreign merchants who went to medieval fairs. Many of these people were Italians. At fairs all over Europe, Italian merchants sold fine woollen cloth, glass, armour and weapons.

Each Italian city had its own speciality. Venice was famous for shipbuilding and glass. Milan made the best armour, weapons and cutlery. Crafts-people in Florence made beautiful woollen and silk cloth.

Italian merchants also travelled to Asia to buy spices, jewels, perfumes and silk which they brought back to Europe and sold at a large profit.

🏛 Italian bankers

All this trading made Italian merchants very rich. To protect their wealth, some of them became bankers. Italian bankers lent money to other merchants as well as to kings and popes. They charged high rates of interest, which made them even richer than before.

🏛 Italian cities

At the end fourteenth century, more people in Italy lived in cities than anywhere else in Europe. For example, in both Milan and Venice there were more than 100,000 inhabitants, and more than 50,000 people lived in Florence. There were other large cities like Genoa, Rome and Naples.

Many Italian cities were **city-states**. They were made up of the city itself and the surrounding towns and countryside. Like ancient Athens, each city had its own rulers and ran its own affairs.

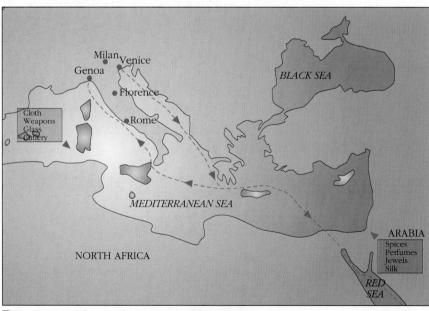

▲ *Trade to and from Italy during the fifteenth century*

▲ *The most important city-states in Italy during the fifteenth century*

FLORENCE

The most famous Italian city was Florence. It stood on the River Arno and was surrounded by high walls. In the centre was a large square with a palace where the city's government met. Nearby were the palaces of the rich Florentine merchants and bankers.

▲ *Florence on the River Arno*

Other streets were narrow and lined with the workshops of craftsmen. The most important were the wool and silk weavers who made the cloth on which the wealth of Florence depended. There were also hundreds of other workshops for stonemasons, cabinet makers, goldsmiths, marble workers and so on.

The people of Florence were very proud of their city. They thought it was the richest and most beautiful in Italy. Other Italians did not agree. The rivalry between cities can be seen in this letter which a Florentine merchant, **Benedetto Dei**, wrote to a friend of his in Venice in 1472.

"Florence is more beautiful than your Venice. We have 30,000 homes owned by noblemen, merchants, craftsmen and citizens. Our city has 270 shops belonging to the Wool Merchants' Guild and 83 splendid warehouses of the Silk Merchants' Guild. We also have 84 cabinet makers' shops: 54 workshops for stonecutters and marble workers: 44 goldsmiths and jewellers and 33 banks. If you travel to all the cities in the world, nowhere will you ever be able to find artists equal to those we have in Florence."

Pride in their own cities led to rivalry among Italians. Everyone wanted to make their own city the best and most beautiful in Italy. So the rulers and wealthy merchants hired the best architects to design new buildings. They also employed sculptors to carve statues and artists to paint pictures.

PATRONAGE

People who are rich enough to pay architects, sculptors and painters to work for them are called **patrons.** During the Renaissance, wealthy Italian merchants, nobles and bishops became patrons, encouraging young artists and giving them work. **Patronage** was very important during the Renaissance because it gave work to artists who wanted to try out new ideas.

Looking at the evidence ▶

READ BENEDETTO DEI'S LETTER CAREFULLY. WHICH OF ALL THE THINGS HE LISTS IN FLORENCE IS HE MOST PROUD OF? GIVE REASONS FOR YOUR ANSWER.

▲ *Wealthy bankers and merchants like these were patrons of Renaissance artists.*

◢ QUESTIONS ◣

1. Write a paragraph explaining why Italy was the richest country in Europe at the beginning of the fifteenth century.
2. What is a city-state? Draw a map of Italy and mark in the most important city-states.
3. What does patronage mean? List three different kinds of people who became patrons during the Renaissance.

CHAPTER
25

Renaissance Architecture

Florence looks at the past

At the end of the thirteenth century, the citizens of Florence decided to build a huge new cathedral in the centre of the city. When work began, the **Gothic** style of architecture was still popular in Europe. (Turn back to pages 59-60 and look again at the pointed doors and windows, the flying buttresses, the towers and stained glass in a Gothic church.)

Work on Florence's new cathedral was slow and difficult, and the architect who designed it died before it was finished. By 1400, there was still a huge hole nearly forty-five metres wide over the main altar. By then, the Florentines had become bored with Gothic style churches. They wanted to do something different with their new cathedral.

The Italians had always been proud of the fact that one thousand years earlier, their country had been the centre of the old Roman Empire. Everywhere around them they saw the ruins of ancient buildings and they realised what great architects their Roman ancestors had been.

▲ *Buildings like the Colosseum made Italians proud of the skills of their ancestors.*

Filippo Brunelleschi (1377-1446)

A young Florentine architect called Filippo Brunelleschi was fascinated by old Roman buildings. He wanted to learn the secrets of the ancient Roman builders. He found a book written by a Roman architect named **Vitruvius** and studied it carefully.

Brunelleschi also spent twelve years in Rome examining the ancient buildings for himself. He studied the Colosseum, the Roman Forum and especially the Pantheon, measuring them carefully and making accurate drawings of everything he saw.

When Brunelleschi returned to Florence, he heard that the Wool Guild had called a meeting to discuss how to finish the cathedral. He had already made a model for a giant dome, similar to that on the Pantheon. When the Wool Guild saw it, they were so impressed that they decided to give him the job.

▲ *Brunelleschi's cathedral towers over Florence. The tower on the right is not part of the cathedral. It was built nearby by the artist, Giotto (page 81).*

BRUNELLESCHI'S DOME

Brunelleschi began work on the dome in 1420. It took sixteen years to build and people came from far and wide to see it. It was the largest dome in the world at that time. Brunelleschi became a hero and rich merchants hired him to work for them. He built several other churches and a hospital in Florence, all in the style of ancient Roman buildings.

A close-up view of Brunnelleschi's magnificent dome

The Renaissance style of architecture

After Brunelleschi died, this new Renaissance style of architecture became very fashionable in Italy. It was based on the Roman style of building with columns, domes and rounded arches.

Renaissance buildings were square, rectangular or round. Roofs and ceilings were usually flat, and there were sometimes tall, narrow columns outside. Large windows with plain glass made the buildings brighter inside. New churches always had a dome rather than a tower or a spire.

Soon the rulers of Italian cities, wealthy merchants, bishops and even the pope in Rome

hired architects to design palaces and churches in this new style. During the next two centuries, hundreds of new buildings appeared all over Italy. This is what **Antonio Filarete**, a fifteenth-century Florentine architect, wrote.

"Italian cities should not hold back from building great and beautiful buildings because of the expense. No country ever became poor, nor did anyone ever die, because of the construction of buildings."

The Pitti Palace in Florence is still a popular tourist attraction.

QUESTIONS

1. Why was the building of the cathedral in Florence left unfinished for so long? What problem had to be solved before it could be finished?
2. The Florentines wanted a new style of architecture. What was this style based on? Name two buildings which gave them their ideas.
3. Write a short essay on Brunelleschi and his work.
4. List three ways in which Renaissance architecture was different from Gothic architecture.

The de Medicis of Florence: Renaissance Patrons

Cosimo de Medici (1389-1464)

Cosimo de Medici was a great patron of the arts.

During the fifteenth century, Florence was a **republic**, which means that its citizens elected the city council. While Brunelleschi was building the dome of the cathedral, a wealthy banker named **Cosimo de Medici** gained control of the council by bribing the politicians and the voters. Cosimo used his control over the council to avoid war with other city-states, which helped Florence to prosper.

Cosimo was a great patron of the arts. He admired Brunelleschi's work and paid him to design the church of San Lorenzo near where he lived. Cosimo had special tombs built in the church where all the members of his family were buried. He also encouraged the sculptor **Donatello** (page 78) to work for him.

Like many other Florentines, Cosimo de Medici greatly admired the ideas of the ancient Greeks and Romans. He paid people to travel around Europe, looking for lost copies of their writings. When these manuscripts were brought back to Florence, he built a special library to house them.

When the Greek city of Constantinople was captured by the Turks in 1453, Cosimo encouraged Greek refugees to settle in Florence. Many of them brought important Greek manuscripts with them. These scholars taught Greek to the citizens of Florence. Cosimo set up a special school called the **Platonic Academy** where people could discuss the works of Plato, a famous Greek philosopher.

Lorenzo de Medici (1444-1492)

When Cosimo died in 1464, his eldest son, Piero took over. He was in bad health and died after five years. Piero's own son, Lorenzo, described what happened next.

"Two days after my father died, the most important men of the city came to my house. They asked me to take care of the city as my father and grandfather had done. As I was only twenty, I feared danger and did not agree at first. In the end, I did so, in order to protect our friends and our property, for it is unwise for anyone in Florence who has great wealth not to have control of the government."

Lorenzo the Magnificent helped artists such as Michelangelo.

The spread of Renaissance ideas

People all over Italy soon learned that something new and exciting was taking place in Florence. They wanted to do the same in their own cities. Wealthy merchants in Milan, Venice and other cities encouraged artists to work for them. The pope and cardinals in Rome did so too.

Soon, the rulers of France, England and Germany joined in. They all copied the new styles of building, the new ways of carving statues, and the new ways of painting pictures. In this way, the ideas of the Renaissance began to spread throughout Europe.

QUESTIONS

1. Two of the greatest patrons of the Renaissance were Cosimo and Lorenzo de Medici. Pick one of them and write a paragraph about his life and work.
2. Why did the ideas of the Renaissance spread outside Florence?

Lorenzo ruled Florence until his death in 1492. He was the most famous member of the de Medici family and was known as **Lorenzo the Magnificent**.

Lorenzo was also a great patron of the Arts. He set up a special school for young artists where they could improve their skills. **Michelangelo** (page 84) was one artist who went there. Lorenzo also held pageants in Florence and encouraged music and dance. This is what a friend said about him.

"Lorenzo loved music, painting, architecture and sculpture. As a result, all the artists competed with each other in order to please him all the more. He was very generous because he gave pensions to talented artists and supplied them with the tools they needed."

LOOK AGAIN AT THESE THREE PIECES OF EVIDENCE ABOUT LORENZO DE MEDICI:
- WHAT LORENZO SAID AFTER HIS FATHER DIED
- THE PORTRAIT OF LORENZO
- THE DESCRIPTION OF LORENZO BY HIS FRIEND

WHICH PIECE OF EVIDENCE TELLS THE MOST ABOUT LORENZO DE MEDICI? GIVE REASONS FOR YOUR ANSWER.

Looking at the evidence

Donatello and Renaissance Sculpture

🏛 Ancient statues

The ancient Greeks had been famous for their statues (Section 3). Many Greek statues showed the nude human body. They were free-standing and very life-like. The ancient Romans admired Greek statues and copied them.

Renaissance sculptors admired statues like this one of Greek wrestlers which was made in the second century BC.

During the Middle Ages, however, people stopped making these kinds of statues. Instead, medieval sculptors carved statues which were part of the decoration in churches.

During the Renaissance, Italians found statues buried in the ruins of old Roman buildings. Renaissance sculptors admired them. They rejected medieval forms of sculpture and instead tried to copy what the Romans and Greeks had done.

🏛 Donatello (1386-1466)

One of the artists who worked for Cosimo de Medici was a Florentine sculptor called **Donatello.** He was a friend of Brunelleschi and travelled to Rome with him. While Brunelleschi studied old Roman buildings, Donatello studied Greek and Roman statues.

Donatello was one of the first men in Italy to carve statues in the Roman manner. People were amazed at how life-like he made them. Donatello thought so himself! When Donatello was working on one statue, Vasari says that he would look at it and mutter, "Speak, damn you, speak!"

Donatello and other sculptors made their statues so realistic by carefully studying human anatomy. Sometimes they dissected dead bodies to study the muscles, bones, sinews and tendons. Then they tried to show these in their statues.

🏛 DONATELLO'S *DAVID*

Donatello carved many statues during his long lifetime. One of the most famous shows the boy David just after he had killed Goliath. A number of things show that Donatello's *David* is a Renaissance statue, not a medieval one.

David *by Donatello*

◪ The statue is realistic with the arms, legs and head all in proportion.

◪ David is almost nude, so that you can see the bones and muscles on his arms and legs.

It is free-standing and not part of the decoration in a church.

Vasari says that Donatello's work was

". . .considered nearer to what was done by the ancient Greeks and Romans than that of any other artist".

LOOK CLOSELY AT THE PICTURES OF GREEK SCULPTURE AND RENAISSANCE SCULPTURE. WHAT SIMILARITIES OR DIFFERENCES DO YOU SEE IN THE WAYS IN WHICH THEY ARE CARVED?

Looking at the evidence ▼ ▼

Donatello's friend Lorenzo Ghiberti (1378-1455) sculpted these ten bronze panels for the door of Baptistery in Florence. Michelangelo thought they were so magnificent that he called them "The Gates of Paradise".

■ QUESTIONS ■

1. How did Renaissance sculptors learn about Roman and Greek statues?
2. Write a short paragraph on the life of Donatello.

CHAPTER

28

Renaissance Painting

Changing styles of painting

Medieval artists painted many fine pictures. Most of them, however, were only concerned with the Christian religion. Medieval artists painted religious pictures to inspire holy thoughts. They were not interested in painting real people.

During the Renaissance, medieval styles of painting went out of fashion. Although many paintings were still based on religious themes, Renaissance artists were freer to express their own ideas and to use their imagination. They wanted to show that Christ and the saints were real people, living in a real world. They concentrated on painting real faces, real bodies and real scenery behind the figures.

Like the sculptors, Renaissance painters studied the human body to see how it worked. They dissected corpses and made drawings of bones, joints and muscles. They then used this knowledge to make the people in their pictures more life-like.

Here are four important differences between medieval and Renaissance paintings.

PERSPECTIVE

During the Renaissance, artists wanted to make their pictures look real, so they worked out ways to make a painting look three-dimensional. This is called **perspective**. Perspective gives depth to a painting. It makes people and objects appear in their proper proportions.

An artist's demonstration of the use of perspective. Comment on what this drawing shows.

COLOUR, LIGHT AND SHADE

Medieval artists used dark colours and lots of gold paint. Renaissance artists discovered that there are three basic colours – red, yellow and blue – which they called **primary colours**. They mixed these colours to produce many different shades and hardly ever used gold.

Renaissance artists also studied light and shade. They noticed where shadows fell and what shapes they made. They saw that faces had shadows around the nose, mouth and eyes. By putting these areas in shadow and putting light on other parts, they could paint a more realistic portrait of a person.

Lavinia Fontana (1552-1614) was a Renaissance woman who became famous for her realistic portraits and paintings of historical scenes.

TEMPERA AND OIL PAINT

During the Middle Ages, painters used a paint called **tempera** which is like modern water-colour paint. It was made from the juices of berries added to water, gum and egg yolks. During the Renaissance, artists still used tempera, but they also began to paint in oil. Oil painting was probably invented by a Belgian artist called **Jan van Eyck** (1390-1441) (page 87). This is what an artist at the time had to say about oil paint.

"It dries more slowly than tempera so you can make changes more easily. You can apply many more coats of paint and work in a lot more detail using a brush, or a knife or even your finger. You can make paintings shiny or rough or smooth and as a result, they are more true to life."

CANVAS

Medieval artists painted mainly on wooden panels. Many Renaissance artists painted on canvas, which is a type of cloth made from cotton or linen. Canvas had many advantages over wooden panels since it was lighter and did not warp and crack as wood did.

Look at these two paintings.

The one on the top is a medieval painting called The Intercession of the Virgin. *It was painted on a wooden panel. The one below it is a Renaissance painting,* The Taking of Christ. *This famous painting by Caravaggio was recently discovered in Ireland and presented to the National Gallery. Compare these two paintings using these headings: perspective; colour, light and shade; type of paint.*

◣ QUESTIONS ◢

1. Look at the painting on page 89. Was it painted during the Middle Ages or during the Renaissance? Give three reasons for your choice.
2. Explain in your own words what perspective means. Find examples of perspective in the pictures in this chapter.
3. Besides perspective, list three ways in which Renaissance painting differed from medieval painting. Pick one Renaissance painting and write a short paragraph about it.

Great Artists of the Renaissance

🏛 Giotto (1267-1337)

🏛 THE FIRST RENAISSANCE PAINTER

Much of our information about the lives and works of Italian Renaissance artists comes from Vasari's book (page 71). He tells us that the first painter to bring new ideas to painting was **Giotto**. This is what he says about him.

*"As a young boy, Giotto was always sketching what he saw around him. One day while he was scratching the picture of a sheep on a rock, using a pointed stone, an artist called **Cimabue** was passing by. He stopped in amazement to watch him. Cimabue asked Giotto to go and live with him in his studio and Giotto's father agreed. Soon Giotto brought to life the great art of painting as we know it today. Once when Cimabue was not looking, Giotto painted a fly on the nose of the face Cimabue was working on. It looked so real that Cimabue tried to brush it away."*

▲ *Part of Giotto's fresco showing scenes from the life of St Francis of Assisi. His work is almost as vivid today as it was over six hundred years ago.*

Giotto soon became the most famous painter in Italy. When the Franciscans wanted to decorate a church in Assisi in memory of St Francis, they employed Giotto. He covered the walls with **frescoes** depicting the life of St Francis. Giotto showed emotions and feelings in the faces of the people. He also succeeded in creating the illusion of depth on a flat surface.

🏛 FRESCOES

Giotto painted many of his pictures on the walls of churches and monasteries. These paintings are called **frescoes.** The word **fresco** comes from the Italian word meaning "fresh", because the painting had to be done on wet plaster, a little at a time.

🏛 THE EFFECTS OF THE BLACK DEATH

Giotto died in 1337 and ten years later, the Black Death broke out (page 69). Millions of people died and the population of Europe was halved. Many artists became pessimistic about life and they returned to the old styles of painting. It was many years before artists copied and improved upon Giotto's new styles.

🏛 Leonardo da Vinci (1452-1519)

🏛 PAINTER AND INVENTOR

Leonardo da Vinci was one of the greatest artists of the Renaissance. Vasari says that he was born in a small village called Vinci near Florence. As a boy, he was always drawing – bats, snakes, lizards and even dragons. Most of all, he loved to draw horses and birds.

His father realised that Leonardo had a lot of talent. One day he showed some of his son's drawings to a famous artist called **Verrocchio** who had a studio in Florence. At once Verrocchio took Leonardo on as his apprentice. Leonardo soon learned everything his master had to teach him.

One day, while Verrocchio was working on a picture of Christ, he asked Leonardo to paint one of the angels. Leonardo set to work and when he was finished Verrocchio was amazed. He knew the angel was much better than the one he had done himself, and much better than anything he could ever do. Verrocchio decided to give up painting and spent the rest of his life working as a sculptor and goldsmith.

When Leonardo was twenty, he became a master in the Artists' Guild in Florence. His fame spread and many people commissioned paintings from him.

One of Leonardo's most famous paintings is *The Last Supper* which he painted on the wall of a monastery in Milan. He took so long to finish it that the abbot complained. But Leonardo replied that "men of genius achieve most when they work least".

While he was working on *The Last Supper*, Leonardo experimented with a new way of mixing paints. But it was not a success. Even before Leonardo died, the paint had already started to peel.

The Last Supper *by Leonardo da Vinci. No one had ever painted the scene like this, with Jesus and the apostles on one side of the table. Jesus has just told the apostles of his betrayal and they are all surprised, except Judas (the third man to Jesus' left). Judas' face is in shadow and he his lower than the other apostles. Why do you think Leonardo did this?*

Another famous painting by Leonardo is the *Mona Lisa*, a portrait of the wife of a wealthy Florentine merchant. While he worked, Leonardo hired musicians and singers to keep her amused. Is this how he captured the mysterious smile on her face?

Leonardo used a technique called **sfumato** (an Italian word meaning "smoky") to paint the hands and face. Sfumato blends one colour into another to produce the appearance of real skin. When people saw the *Mona Lisa*, they were amazed to find it so

Leonardo used a technique called sfumato *when he painted the* Mona Lisa *in 1501.*

life-like and many artists later copied this technique. The king of France was so impressed by this picture that he bought it and took it to Paris where it now hangs in the Louvre Museum.

LEONARDO'S STUDY OF THE HUMAN BODY

One reason Leonardo's paintings are so good was his study of anatomy. He often went to the place in Florence where bodies were kept before burial and examined them carefully. He wrote:

"I have cut up more than ten human bodies. I have destroyed all the different limbs and removed even the smallest part of the flesh surrounding the veins without even spilling the smallest drop of blood. One body was not enough. It was necessary to cut up as many as ten so that my knowledge was complete. For an artist will paint nothing that is any good if he just copies the work of others. I have studied the veins, the

muscles, the tendons and sinews. In fact, I have studied all parts of the human body in order to paint better."

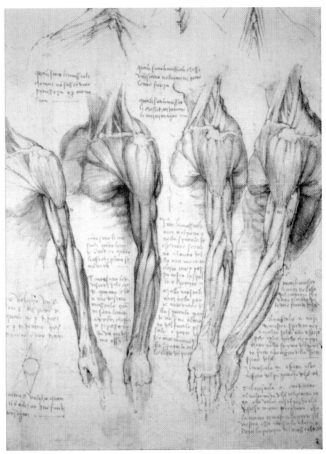

Two more drawings from Leonardo's notebooks - a woman's face, and his notes and designs for a flying machine

Leonardo's sketches of muscles in the arm and shoulders and the notes he made about them

🔲 LEONARDO'S NOTEBOOKS

Leonardo always had a notebook with him in which he sketched flowers and animals and the faces of people he saw in the streets. Leonardo was always full of new ideas which he recorded in his notebooks. Some of his designs resemble submarines, parachutes, bicycle chains, catapults and even aeroplanes. When he died he left more than 5000 pages of notes behind him.

Leonardo also wrote comments in his notebooks using mirror writing. We do not know why he wrote like that. He was left-handed so maybe it was easier for him to write that way. Or he may have wanted to keep his ideas secret. What do you think?

When Leonardo applied to the Duke of Milan for a job, he told the duke:

"I can design portable bridges and cannon-proof ships. I can also make gun carriages and

catapults. In times of peace I can paint anything you want. I can work as an architect or an engineer and I can make statues in marble, bronze and clay. I am also good at philosophy, poetry, mathematics, physics, chemistry, botany and mechanics."

It is not surprising that Leonardo's many talents got him the job. While in Milan he drew up plans for the city walls and designed sets and costumes for plays which were put on at the duke's court. However, he was easily bored and often did not finish the work he began. Vasari says:

"Clearly it was because of his profound knowledge that Leonardo started many things without finishing them; for he was convinced that his hands, for all their skill, could never perfectly express the subtle and wonderful ideas of his imagination."

In 1517, Leonardo went to work for Francis I, the king of France. The two men became good friends. Leonardo told the king that he had offended God by not working at his art as he should have done. He died in France in 1519, aged sixty-seven years.

A self-portrait of Leonardo. It was drawn in red chalk when he was sixty years old.

▲ *A self-portrait of Michelangelo. From this painting, what kind of person do you think he was?*

Michelangelo (1475-1564)

SCULPTOR AND PAINTER

Michelangelo was born near Florence into a wealthy family. His mother died when he was a small boy.

At that time, Lorenzo de Medici ruled Florence. He set up a school for sculptors and Michelangelo became a pupil there. Vasari tells us:

> *"One day, Michelangelo decided to copy a faun's head which had been found in the garden. It had been carved more than a thousand years earlier by a sculptor in ancient Rome. Although this was the first time that he had ever touched a chisel or worked marble, Michelangelo copied it so well that Lorenzo was amazed. He gave Michelangelo his own room and looked after him as if he was one of the family."*

MICHELANGELO THE SCULPTOR

Like Leonardo da Vinci, Michelangelo was good at many things, including architecture, engineering, music, poetry and painting. But more than anything else he loved sculpture. He believed that he could bring marble to life. He said that as he chiselled away at the marble, he could see the statue trying to escape. He once wrote:

> *"The best of artists has no idea that is not contained within a piece of marble itself with its unnecessary shell, and this the hand discovers only by obeying the intellect."*

One of Michelangelo's most famous statues is called the **Pietá**, a word which means "sorrow" in Italian. The statue now stands in St Peter's in Rome. It shows Mary mourning over the body of her son, Jesus Christ. People say Michelangelo cheated because he made the Virgin Mary too young looking to be the mother of a man of thirty-three. What do you think?

Vasari tells us this story about the Pietá.

"One day, Michelangelo went to where the statue was and found a crowd of people looking at it and praising it. Then one of them asked another who had sculpted it. Someone replied, 'Old Gobbo from Milan'. Michelangelo stood there not saying a word, but later that night taking a chisel with him, he crept into the church where the statue stood and carved his name on it."

It is the only one of his statues that he ever signed.

The Pietá *- one of the only statues which Michelangelo ever signed*

CARVING *DAVID*

In 1501, Michelangelo went back to Florence where he was offered a 6-metre high block of marble which another sculptor had damaged. No one thought it was any use, but Michelangelo decided to carve a huge statue of David.

Vasari says:

"Because there were flaws in the marble, Michelangelo could not always carve it the way he wanted to. But he created a miracle by restoring to life something that had been left for dead. Without doubt, this figure has put in the shade every other statue, ancient or modern, Greek or Roman."

When Michelangelo's *David* was finished in 1504, it was the largest free-standing statue made since classical times. It was put up in the main square in

Michelangelo's David. *Do you think this figure is in perfect proportion or not?*

Florence where it stood for over three centuries. The city council then decided to replace it with a copy and to put the real *David* in a museum for safety.

> COMPARE MICHELANGELO'S *David* WITH DONATELLO'S *David* ON PAGE 78. NOTE THE DIFFERENCES AND SIMILARITIES BETWEEN THE TWO. WHICH DO YOU PREFER? GIVE REASONS FOR YOUR ANSWER.
>
> *Activity*

MICHELANGELO THE PAINTER

Julius II was elected pope in 1503. He became a great patron of the arts and paid many famous artists to decorate his palace in the Vatican. He asked Michelangelo to go to Rome to design his tomb. Michelangelo spent eight months in the marble quarries at **Carrara** where he picked out forty giant blocks which he sent by sea to Rome. Michelangelo planned a giant tomb with forty statues, some as high as three metres.

However, the pope decided that it was bad luck to build his tomb before he died so he told Michelangelo to stop. By then, Michelangelo had only carved a single statue, one of Moses.

PAINTING THE CEILING OF THE SISTINE CHAPEL

The pope then asked Michelangelo to paint frescoes on the ceiling of the Sistine Chapel in the Vatican. Although Michelangelo had very little experience of frescoes, he began work on the ceiling in 1508 and it took four years to complete. He erected scaffolding twenty metres high and spent most of the time lying on his back. He wrote this poem to a friend describing his experience.

"My stomach is pushed up towards my chin
My beard curls up towards the sky
My head leans over onto my back
And my chest is like that of an old witch.
The brush drips endlessly onto my face
And coats it with many different colours.
I move blindly without being able to see my feet
And I am as curved as a Syrian bow."

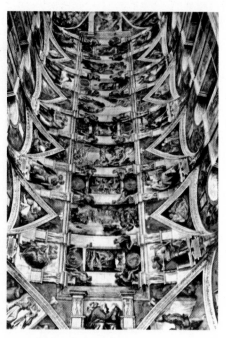

The ceiling of the Sistine Chapel was 12m wide and 40m long. On it, Michelangelo painted more than 300 figures showing scenes from the Bible.

THE LAST JUDGMENT

Twenty-five years after he had finished the ceiling of the Sistine Chapel, another pope asked Michelangelo to work there again. On the wall behind the high altar, he painted a huge fresco called *The Last Judgment*. This tells the story of Christ sitting in judgment on the Last Day, deciding who should go to heaven or to hell.

Michelangelo used many bright colours like blue, pink and mauve. Although some people said it was a masterpiece, others thought that it was not very religious looking. In 1564, Pope Pius IV ordered that some of the naked figures be painted over.

The Last Judgment. Do many of the figures look like pieces of sculpture?

THE DOME OF ST PETERS

When Michelangelo was seventy-two years old, the architect who was building St Peter's Basilica died and Michelangelo was asked to finish it. He changed the design and worked on it till his own death at the age of ninety in 1564.

The dome of St Peter's in Rome. Compare it with the dome of the cathedral in Florence (page 75). How are they similar?

⬛ THE DEATH OF MICHELANGELO

Although Michelangelo became very wealthy, he always lived a simple life and never married. He said, "The works I leave behind will be my sons. Even if they are nothing they will live after me for a while." More than five centuries later, his magnificent paintings and sculptures still amaze everyone who sees them.

◼ QUESTIONS ◼

1. List three pieces of sculpture by Michelangelo and describe one of them.
2. Where did Michelangelo paint his frescoes? Tell the story of one of these paintings.

Activities

◼ WRITE AN ACCOUNT OF THE LIFE OF MICHELANGELO. YOU SHOULD INCLUDE: (A) HIS EARLY LIFE AND TRAINING; (B) HIS WORK AS A SCULPTOR AND SOME OF THE STATUES HE CARVED; (C) HIS WORK FOR POPE JULIUS II; (D) HIS LATER LIFE.

◼ IF THERE IS A SCULPTOR OR A STONEMASON LIVING NEAR YOU, ASK PERMISSION TO VISIT HIS/HER STUDIO OR WORKSHOP TO SEE THE KIND OF WORK HE/SHE DOES AND THE DIFFERENT TOOLS HE/SHE USES.

Finding out

POPE JULIUS II WAS A GREAT RENAISSANCE PATRON WHO EMPLOYED MANY ARTISTS. ONE OF THEM WAS THE PAINTER RAPHAEL. FIND OUT ABOUT RAPHAEL IN YOUR LIBRARY AND LOOK AT SOME OF THE PICTURES HE PAINTED FOR THE POPE.

CHAPTER 30
Painting outside Italy

⬛ Jan van Eyck (1390-1441)

While many changes in painting were taking place in Italy, painters in other parts of Europe were also trying out new ideas. One of the most famous was Jan van Eyck. He was born in Flanders (modern Belgium) in 1390 and was one of the first painters to show ordinary people in their own homes. He was also one of the first artists to use oil paint. Vasari said:

"Jan's discovery of oil colouring is a very beautiful invention and a great help to the art of painting."

Jan van Eyck's most famous picture is *The Arnolfini Wedding*. Arnolfini was an Italian merchant who got married in Flanders. Van Eyck painted a record of the marriage ceremony that took place. In it, the man is raising his right hand and promising to love and honour his wife. She puts her hand in his and promises to do the same.

There are many symbols in this picture which people at the time could read better than we can. For example, the lighted candle represents Christ, the light of the world. The couple have taken off their sandals because they believe they are standing on holy ground. The little dog is the symbol of faithfulness between husband and wife.

The Arnolfini Wedding *by Jan van Eyck*

In the mirror in the background, the artist has painted the backs of the bride and groom. Two other figures are also visible – the witness to the wedding and the artist himself. Above the mirror is a sentence in Latin which reads, *Johannes van Eyck fuit hic -1434.* What do you think that means?

The spread of the Renaissance

As the Renaissance developed in Italy, many artists from northern Europe travelled there to work in the studios of the Italian masters. They also learned about anatomy, perspective and all the other skills that the Italians had developed. Of course, the information was not all one way. Artists from Flanders brought the technique of oil painting with them and taught it to the Italians.

Albrecht Dürer (1471-1528)

One of the artists who went to study in Italy was a German called Albrecht Dürer. He was born in Nuremberg where his father and grandfather had been goldsmiths. He learned their trade but then gave it up to become a painter. He visited Italy several times.

When he returned to Nuremberg, Dürer set up his own studio where he painted many pictures in both oil and tempera. Many of his paintings were self-portraits. Some people have suggested that this shows he was vain about his appearance.

Albrecht Dürer painted this self-portrait in 1493, when he was twenty-two years old. No one is certain what the plant he is holding represents. What do you think?

WOODCUTS AND ENGRAVINGS

Dürer also became interested in different art forms. He made **woodcuts** and **engravings**, some of which were used to illustrate books. Woodcuts were the first kind of pictures that ordinary people could afford to buy.

To make a woodcut, Dürer took a block of wood, polished it smooth and traced a picture on it. He then carved out all the wood that was not part of the picture. Next he coated the picture with ink and pressed it down on a sheet of paper. He could then make as many copies of it as he wished.

Engravings are similar to woodcuts, but the picture is carved onto a copper plate. During his lifetime, Dürer made hundreds of woodcuts and engravings.

In Ireland, we are lucky to have a great collection of Dürer engravings in the Chester Beatty Library in Dublin. Chester Betty was a wealthy man who collected works of art. When he died, he left them to the Irish nation.

▲ *This hare is one of Dürer's most famous pictures.*

Activity

IT MAY BE POSSIBLE FOR YOUR CLASS TO ARRANGE A VISIT TO THE CHESTER BEATTY LIBRARY TO SEE SOME OF DÜRER'S ENGRAVINGS AND OTHER GREAT ART TREASURES.
▼

◪ QUESTION ◪

Name two artists who worked outside Italy during the Renaissance. Pick one of them and write a short account of his life and work. You should mention: (a) where he came from; (b) what was special about his art; (c) and describe and name one of his pictures.

Looking at the evidence

LOOK AGAIN AT THE PAINTING OF *The Arnolfini Wedding.*

1. DESCRIBE ONE EXAMPLE OF EACH OF THE FOLLOWING IN THE PAINTING: PERSPECTIVE, LIGHT AND SHADE, AND THE USE OF COLOUR.
2. ARE THERE OTHER SYMBOLS OR SIGNS IN THE PAINTING BESIDES THE ONES DESCRIBED? WRITE DOWN WHAT YOU THINK THEY ARE AND WHAT YOU THINK THEY MIGHT REPRESENT.

◄ *Peter Breughel was another painter of the Northern Renaissance. He was famous for his lively paintings of village life like this one,* The Peasants' Dance. *Comment on this picture using the headings: perspective, colour, and light and shade. How is Breughel's work different from other Renaissance paintings you have studied? What do you think of* The Peasants' Dance?

CHAPTER 31

Learning during the Renaissance

Humanism

During the Renaissance, many wealthy and educated people became interested in the thoughts and ideas of the ancient Greeks and Romans. From the fourteenth century onwards, they began to collect the works of ancient writers and to study their lives and ideas.

This interest in the literature of Greece and Rome is called **humanism**. Those who studied the writings of the ancient authors are called **humanists.** Renaissance scholars were greatly influenced by these writings.

FRANCESCO PETRARCH (1304-1374)

One of the first humanists was the Florentine, Francesco Petrarch. He was a lawyer and a poet. He wrote poetry in Italian and dedicated it to a young girl called Laura whom he fell in love with, but who died during the Black Death. His poems are called **sonnets** and they contained fourteen lines which rhymed in a special way.

▲ *A Renaissance portrait of Petrarch. He is wearing a crown of laurel leaves which he was given when he was made Poet Laureate in Rome – the poet's highest honour.*

Petrarch's main interest was in the works of the ancient Greek and Roman writers. During his lifetime, he discovered many of their writings which were hidden away in monastic libraries. Like most humanists, Petrarch thought that Latin was the greatest language in the world, but he also studied Greek.

> LOOK IN YOUR ENGLISH BOOKS TO FIND OUT MORE ABOUT SONNETS.
>
> *Finding out*

POPE NICHOLAS V (1447-1455)

Renaissance popes were also interested in ancient literature. For example, Pope Nicholas V sent out hundreds of men to search for ancient manuscripts. When the Turks captured Constantinople in 1453, he sent his secretaries to rescue as many Greek manuscripts as possible.

Nicholas V encouraged Greek scholars to travel to Italy and paid them to translate Greek works into Latin. He also built the magnificent Vatican Library to house his collection of manuscripts. After he died, his librarian wrote:

> *"Pope Nicholas V must be praised for his kindness to scholars. He supported them with money, encouraged them to give lectures and to write new works. He also encouraged the translation of Greek authors into Latin so that Greek and Latin writings which had been hidden away in darkness for six hundred years, could again be re-born and re-read."*

CHAPTER 32

The Invention of Printing

Manuscripts

One reason why Renaissance ideas spread all over Europe was the invention of printing. Today, we are so used to the idea of printing that we do not often think about its importance.

This book and all your other school books are printed, as are the newspapers and magazines you read. Until 1456, however, all books were manuscripts which means they were written by hand. Just imagine how long it would take to write this book by hand.

During the Middle Ages, booksellers often had workshops where scribes worked long hours copying manuscripts. One person usually sat at the front of the room and read slowly from a book while the scribes wrote down what was dictated on parchment. In this way, several copies of a popular book could be made at the same time. However, it still took a long time, which made books very expensive. As a result, only rich people could afford to own books.

In the thirteenth century, Europeans copied the Chinese idea of making paper by grinding up wood shavings and old rags. Paper was much cheaper to produce than parchment, so it reduced the price of books.

Johann Gutenberg (1398-1468)

The man who invented printing was a German called Johann Gutenberg. We know very little about his early life except that he trained as a goldsmith and knew a great deal about various metals.

Johann Gutenberg's printing press

THE INVENTION OF MOVEABLE TYPE

One day, Gutenberg began to make tiny metal letters, like those on a typewriter. He made dozens of copies of each letter. Then, he made a wooden frame with lines drawn on it. He picked the letters he needed for his first word and fitted them on to the first line. He continued in this way until the whole page was put together.

Using a piece of wool, he spread ink on the letters and pressed a sheet of paper down hard on them, using an old wine press. When he lifted the sheet

A paper-maker and his apprentice at work. Describe what they are doing.

off, the page was printed upon it. He could now make as many copies as he wanted.

When he had finished one page, Gutenberg lifted out the letters from the frame and used them again to make up the next page. He had invented **moveable type** – letters which could be used over and over again.

🏛 GUTENBERG'S BIBLE

Gutenberg decided to print the Bible, which is a very big book. He borrowed money from a merchant named Johann Fust to pay for it. After four years, however, he was still not finished and Fust demanded his money back. He took Gutenberg to court and won. Fust took over Gutenberg's printing press as well as his partly-finished Bible, which Fust published himself in 1456.

▲ The Gutenberg Bible. It was written in Latin and contains 1300 pages. The colour decorations were added later by hand.

🏛 William Caxton (1422-1491)

After Gutenberg's Bible appeared, other people copied his idea and the skill of printing spread to other countries. Paper which was by then widely available in Europe made books cheap to print and to buy. The first man to print books in English was **William Caxton**, a cloth merchant.

🏛 CAXTON IN ENGLAND

Caxton worked in Belgium where he learned about printing. He returned home in 1476 and set up a printing press near Westminster Abbey in London. He called his shop **The Red Pale**.

Over the next fifteen years, Caxton printed more than one hundred different books. These included popular works like *The Canterbury Tales, King*

🔼 *The beautiful printer's mark used by William Caxton*

Arthur and the Knights of the Round Table and *Aesop's Fables*. Three kings of England bought books from him.

Caxton hardly ever put a date on his books, but he used this emblem with his initials on it and the words "Printed by me, William Caxton, at Westminster."

🏛 The spread of printing

By 1500, there were more than one thousand printing presses in cities all over Europe and more than ten million printed books had already appeared. Many of these books were the works of ancient Greek and Roman writers.

But printers also wanted to make money, so they began printing popular books in the local language – French, German or English. Some were tales and legends; others were about medicine, architecture, nature and the travels of famous explorers like Christopher Columbus.

The invention of printing is one of the most important events in the history of Europe. Here are some of the main results.

🏛 THE SPREAD OF LITERACY

Before printing, few people could read and write. The invention of printing made books cheaper and more common. As a result, more and more people learned to read until, by the twentieth century, we assume that everybody should be literate.

THE GROWTH OF VERNACULAR LANGUAGES

As more people learned to read, they read books printed in their own languages – English, French, Italian or German. These are called the **vernacular languages**, those which people speak every day. By the sixteenth century, famous writers began to use their own language rather than Latin. For example, William Shakespeare (page 95) wrote his plays and poems in English. The first book in Irish was printed in Dublin in 1550.

STANDARDISING VERNACULAR LANGUAGES

Printing books in the languages people spoke every day caused a few problems. In any country, there might be a dozen different ways of pronouncing or spelling a word. Which of these should a printer use?

In most countries, printers began to use the form of word which the people used in the capital city. In England, for example, it was the form of English used in London. In this way a standard form of writing and spelling emerged in each language and the old local forms gradually disappeared.

THE SPREAD OF NEW IDEAS

Before printing, new ideas were written in manuscript form, of which only a few copies were made. These manuscripts could easily be lost or destroyed. Popes or kings could suppress ideas they disliked by ordering all copies to be burned.

When new ideas were printed in books, hundreds of copies were made, so that it was unlikely that all of them would be lost or destroyed. It became much more difficult for popes or kings to suppress ideas they disliked. The best example of this occurred during the Reformation (Section 7). Martin Luther, who started the Reformation, was successful because his ideas were printed in books and spread throughout Germany.

QUESTIONS

1. How were books produced before 1450? Give two disadvantages of this way of producing books.
2. Tell the story of Gutenberg's invention of printing in your own words. You should: (a) describe his background; (b) say where he got money for his invention; (c) explain how he printed a page; and (d) describe his famous book.
3. Name one other famous printer and give a brief account of his life.
4. List four of the main results of printing. Select the one you think is the most important and explain your choice.

Activity

HOLD A DISCUSSION IN CLASS ON THE TOPIC: "PRINTING WAS ONE OF THE MOST IMPORTANT INVENTIONS IN THE LAST FIVE HUNDRED YEARS." ▼

Finding out

HAVE YOU EVER READ ANY OF THE STORIES PRINTED BY WILLIAM CAXTON? YOU CAN FIND SOME OF THEM IN YOUR LOCAL LIBRARY. (IT IS IMPORTANT TO REMEMBER THAT CAXTON PRINTED THESE STORIES, BUT HE DID NOT WRITE THEM.) ▼ ▼

The Theatre and William Shakespeare

🏛 Putting on plays

During the sixteenth century, the invention of printing encouraged new writers to use their native languages to write novels, poetry and plays. Unlike novels and poems, however, plays were written to be performed on the stage.

Going to the theatre had been a popular pastime in ancient Greece and Rome. But during the Middle Ages, many people disapproved of the theatre. Sometimes a medieval guild put on a short play based on stories from the Bible, but there were no proper theatres like the Greeks and Romans had. This began to change during the Renaissance.

🏛 THE THEATRE IN ENGLAND

In England, small groups of actors went around from town to town, putting on plays in the courtyards of inns. During the reign of Queen Elizabeth I (1558-

1603), the theatre began to flourish. The queen loved plays and many were put on in her court.

In 1576, the first theatre was built in London. It was so successful that others followed. These **Elizabethan** theatres were based on the Greek models. They were round or oval in shape and had no roofs. Plays were always put on in daylight because it was dangerous to light a theatre at night using candles.

🏛 AN ACTOR'S LIFE

All the actors were men. Women's parts were played by young boys whose voices had not yet broken. An actor had a tough life. He had to learn his lines and be able to sing, dance and fence. A young actor usually joined a band of travelling players. If he had talent, he might get a job with one of the London theatres.

◄

Drawings of Elizabethan Theatres. The one on the left shows the Swan Theatre which could hold more than 3000 spectators. The poorer people always stood on the ground in front of the stage and were known as "groundlings". The stage was made of wooden planks. The doors at the back of the stage led to the dressing rooms where the actors changed their costumes. They were known as the "tiring rooms". Can you think why? The hut at the top is where the scene shifters worked. From there, they made special effects for thunder and rain. The man blowing the trumpet is announcing that a play is about to begin.

Shakespeare's last play, *Henry VIII* was being performed. After that, he retired to Stratford-on-Avon where he died in 1616. A few years later, Shakespeare's plays were printed and became popular all over the world. Today, they are still performed in theatres and can be seen on television and heard on the radio.

William Shakespeare, one of the world's most famous writers

SHAKESPEARE WAS NOT THE ONLY FAMOUS RENAISSANCE WRITER. TWO OTHERS WERE **Cervantes**, WHO WAS SPANISH, AND **Rabelais,** WHO WAS FRENCH. LOOK THESE WRITERS UP IN AN ENCYCLOPAEDIA AND WRITE A SHORT ACCOUNT OF THEIR LIVES.

Finding out

Elizabeth I was very fond of the theatre. Shakespeare wrote a number of plays in her honour.

William Shakespeare (1564-1616)

We know about one such actor, William Shakespeare. However, he is famous, not for his acting, but because he wrote plays which are still performed today.

Shakespeare was born in Stratford-on-Avon where his father was a glove-maker. When William was eighteen, he married a girl called Anne Hathaway who was eight years older than he. The couple had three children.

We do not know what Shakespeare worked at before he got married. However, when he was twenty-eight, we know he was living in London, working as an actor and writing poems and plays in his spare time. In 1599, Shakespeare bought shares in the Globe Theatre where most of his plays were performed.

William Shakespeare wrote thirty-five plays. Some are comedies like *A Midsummer Night's Dream* and *As You Like It*. Others are tragedies like *Hamlet* or *King Lear*. He also wrote plays about ancient Rome such as *Julius Caesar* and *Antony and Cleopatra*.

In 1613, the Globe Theatre burned down while

QUESTIONS

1. Write a short account of the life of William Shakespeare. You should include: (a) his early life; (b) his time as an actor; (c) the names of some of his plays; (d) his later life.
2. Have you ever read a play by Shakespeare? You may have seen one in a theatre or on television. If you have, give the title of the play and write a brief account of it.

Medicine during the Renaissance

Medieval doctors

During the Middle Ages, doctors relied on the medical knowledge of the ancient Greeks and Romans. The most famous book on medicine was by a Greek doctor named **Galen** who had lived in the second century AD. Medieval doctors believed everything Galen and other ancient doctors had written and followed them without question.

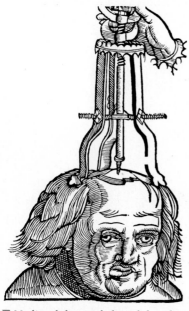

In the 16th century, however, some doctors became convinced that the ancient doctors did not have all the answers. They began to carry out experiments of their own. They also learned a great deal from the detailed drawings of the human body by Leonardo da Vinci and other artists. These doctors soon discovered that the ancient doctors were often wrong.

▲ *Medieval doctors believed that this screw-like device would cause demons to leave the brain.*

Andreas Vesalius (1514-1564)

One of the most famous Renaissance doctors was Andreas Vesalius. He was born in Brussels and studied medicine at Louvain and at Paris. Later, he became professor of anatomy at Padua university in Italy.

Although the Church said it was wrong to dissect dead bodies, Vesalius believed that it was the only way to improve medical knowledge. He sometimes stole bodies from graveyards or sent out his students to cut down the bodies of criminals hanging from the gallows. He dissected them carefully to find out

▲ *One of the drawings from Vesalius' book*

how the human body worked.

In 1543, Vesalius published a book called *The Structure of the Human Body*. He got an artist to make 270 drawings for it, illustrating every part of the body including the bones, muscles, veins, heart and even the brain. Vesalius now believed that Galen was wrong in certain matters. For example, Galen had claimed that:

"The jaw of an ape is formed of two bones, like the jaw of man. There are also the same number of bones in the spine of a monkey as in a man's spine."

From his research, Vesalius proved that apes had fewer bones in their spines and that the human jaw has only one bone, not two like the apes. He now encouraged other doctors to test their own ideas. Vesalius went on to invent many of the medical terms for parts of the human body which doctors still use today. He was also he first to use a special knife called a **scalpel** for performing operations. By the time he died, he had become known as the **Father of Modern Anatomy**.

Ambroise Paré (1510-1590)

Ambroise Paré was another Renaissance doctor. When he was twenty-five, he joined the French army where he treated soldiers with terrible wounds. The usual practice at the time was to put boiling oil on a wound to stop the bleeding, but this obviously caused great pain. One day after a battle, Paré was treating some wounded soldiers, but there was no oil available. Here is his description of what he did:

"Instead of using oil, I made a substance from eggs, oil of roses and turpentine and I applied it cold to the wounds of the soldiers. That night I could not sleep because I was afraid that in the morning I would find the wounded either dead or poisoned. But beyond my greatest hopes, I found those soldiers on whom I had put the new substance, feeling only a little pain and their wounds were not swollen. After that I decided never to use boiling oil again on poor men wounded by gunshot."

Paré devoted the rest of his life to improving methods of surgery. He found a way to stop soldiers bleeding to death from a torn artery. He devised a new way of mending broken arms by binding them tightly. He even made artificial limbs for soldiers who had lost a leg or an arm in battle.

In 1575, Paré published a book called *The Collected Works of Surgery* which was used as a medical text-book by students for many years. Paré is now regarded by many as the **Father of Modern Surgery.**

◤ QUESTIONS ◣

1. Select one of the doctors mentioned here and write a short account of his life and the medical discoveries he made.
2. Do you think there are similarities between the ways Vesalius and Paré changed our knowledge of medicine? Explain your answer.

CHAPTER
35

Renaissance Science

🏛 Astronomy

Astronomy, or the study of the universe, is the oldest of all the sciences. The ancient Greeks were great astronomers. They studied the planets and tried to work out the movements of the sun, the moon and the stars. So did the ancient Egyptians. In Ireland, the Stone Age people who built Newgrange knew where the sun would be in mid-winter (page 17).

Some of the questions that ancient astronomers wondered about were:

*Was the earth round or flat?

*Did the sun go around the earth, or did the earth go around the sun?

Different astronomers had different answers to these questions. For example, in the fourth century BC, a Greek astronomer and mathematician called **Aristotle** said that the earth revolved around the sun. Several hundred years later in the third century AD, an Egyptian astronomer called **Ptolemy** wrote a book called *Geography* in which he said that the sun, stars and the planets revolved around the earth.

During the Middle Ages, most people accepted Ptolemy's view that the earth was the centre of the universe and that the sun and all the other planets moved around it. This theory seemed to fit in with what the Bible said and with their own observations of the sun's movements across the sky.

During the Renaissance, however, the writings of the Greek astronomers were rediscovered and astronomers began to ask these questions again.

🏛 Nicholas Copernicus (1473-1543)

One of these astronomers was Nicholas Copernicus. He was from Poland and had studied mathematics, law and medicine. He learned Greek and became interested in the writings of ancient astronomers.

Copernicus set up a small observatory in his house along the Baltic Sea. Every day, he watched

A portrait of Copernicus which stands above an astronomical clock.

Galileo Galilei (1564-1642)

Other astronomers read Copernicus' ideas and tried to prove him right. The most famous of them was an Italian called Galileo Galilei.

Galileo studied mathematics and carried out experiments on gravity. In 1608, an event took place in Holland which was to change Galileo's life and turn his attention to the study of astronomy. This was the invention of the telescope.

Galileo - his ideas about the universe were proved to be right.

THE TELESCOPE

A telescope is really a very simple idea. Lenses for reading glasses had been in use for hundreds of years. In 1608, a Dutchman called **Jan Lippershey** put two of these lenses at either end of a tube and discovered that he could see distant objects more clearly. In 1609 Galileo wrote:

"About ten months ago, I heard that a Dutchman had built a telescope and I decided to make a similar instrument myself. I prepared a tube of lead and at each end of it, I fitted two glass lenses. Both were flat on one side and on the other, one concave and the other convex. When I put it to my eye, I saw objects nearer and larger. Later I made another telescope which magnified objects more than sixty times. Finally, I succeeded in building a telescope so much better that objects seen through it appear magnified nearly one thousand times."

the movements of the sun, the moon and the stars and kept detailed notes on everything he saw. Telescopes had not yet been invented, so he could only see what was visible to the human eye.

From his observations, Copernicus decided that the medieval idea that the earth stood still and that the sun and the planets revolved around it was wrong. He put forward two ideas – the earth revolved around the sun; and the earth also revolved on its own axis. However, he could not prove these theories.

For thirty years, Copernicus worked on a book setting out his ideas. It was called *The Revolution of the Heavenly Spheres*, but he was afraid to publish it. He feared that the Catholic Church would disapprove of his ideas because they seemed to go against the Bible. At last, when he was an old man, a friend persuaded him to get it printed. He was given a copy of it as he lay dying in 1543.

Galileo now spent much of his time looking at the sky through his telescope. Because it was so powerful, he saw things no one had ever seen before. He observed mountains and craters on the moon, dark spots on the sun and moons circling Jupiter. Everything he saw convinced him that Copernicus was right – that the sun was the centre of the universe and the earth revolved around it.

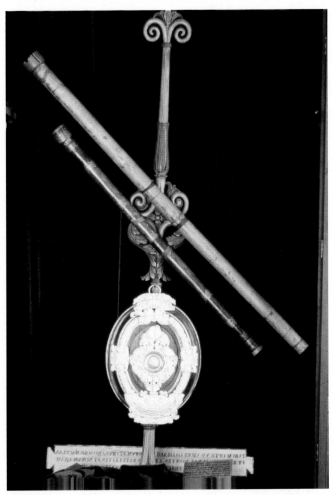

During his lifetime, Galileo made more than one hundred telescopes. This is one of the few which has survived.

THE CHURCH REJECTS GALILEO'S IDEAS

When the Church learned of Galileo's theories, it rejected them completely because it believed that God must have made the earth the centre of the universe. In 1611, Pope Paul V ordered Galileo to Rome where he told him to stop spreading his ideas. All of Galileo's books were banned, as were those of Copernicus.

Galileo was a good Catholic, but he was sure he was right and the pope was wrong. However, he still could not prove his theories. He returned home and worked quietly on a book which was published in 1632. Once again, he was ordered to go to Rome. This time, he was put on trial.

By then Galileo was an old man and his trial lasted for several months. At last, worn out by questioning and afraid that he might be burned as a heretic, he agreed to say he was wrong. He wrote a document in which he took back everything he had written in his books. This is part of what he wrote.

"I, Galileo Galilei, aged seventy, do swear that I have always believed and do now believe all that is taught by the Holy Catholic Church. I will never defend or teach false doctrines and I curse and detest my errors and heresies which are contrary to the teachings of the Church. I have signed this document in my own hand on 22 June 1633."

As a punishment, Galileo was sent back to Florence where he was not allowed to receive any visitors. He was also forbidden to study or write about astronomy. When he died in 1642, the pope refused to allow Galileo to be honoured in any way.

But Galileo's ideas lived on after him. All over Europe people continued to study astronomy until they had enough proof to show that Galileo had been right all along.

 QUESTIONS

1. Why did people become interested in astronomy during the Renaissance?
2. Who was Nicholas Copernicus? What two important theories did he have?
3. Write a short paragraph on the invention of the telescope.
4. Tell the story of Galileo's life in your own words. You will find other books about him in your library.
5. Copernicus was the first to say that the earth was not the centre of the universe. Galileo only repeated what he said. Why, then, do you think Galileo is more famous? Give reasons for your answer.

CHAPTER 36

The World in 1400

As far back as we can go in history, people have always been interested in discovering new lands. The Egyptians, the Greeks, the Celts, the Romans and the Vikings all travelled over land and sea. They went to conquer or to trade, to look for adventure – or just to see what was there.

At the beginning of the fifteenth century, a new age of exploration began in Europe. It was the greatest age of exploration the world had ever seen and within one hundred years, Europeans had learned more about the world than they had ever known before.

Map A: Europe's view of the world in 1400

Map B: Europe's view of the world today

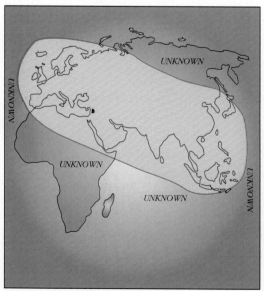

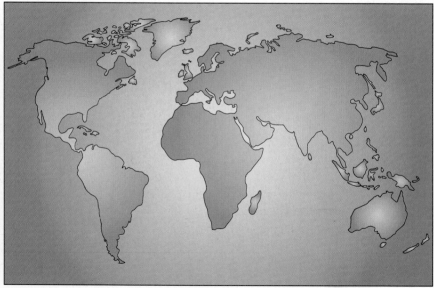

LOOK AT THE TWO MAPS OF THE WORLD ON
PAGE 100. MAP A SHOWS THE WORLD AS IT WAS
KNOWN BY PEOPLE IN EUROPE IN 1400 AD.
MAP B SHOWS THE WORLD WE KNOW TODAY.

COMPARE THE TWO MAPS CAREFULLY. NAME
(A) THREE CONTINENTS, (B) TWO OCEANS AND
(C) FIVE RIVERS THAT EUROPEANS DID NOT
KNOW ABOUT IN 1400.

Activity ▼ ▼ ▼ ▼ ▼ ▼

The world: some medieval ideas

Today, we know exactly what our world looks like –
its size, shape, the continents and oceans. We can
even see photographs of the earth taken from space.

During the Middle Ages, people had none of our
modern ways of finding out about the world. They
got most of their knowledge from the ancient
Greeks and their ideas made sense to medieval
people.

▲ *Marco Polo (1254-1324) and his
family brought back goods from
the East. Their stories fascinated
Europeans of the time. Find out
more about the voyages of Marco
Polo.*

Every day, they
saw the sun rise in
the east and set in
the west. So they
believed the sun
moved around the
earth. Since the sun
seemed to move,
they believed that
the earth stood still.
People could see no
sign that the earth
curved, so they
presumed that it was
flat. However, by
1400, a few people
were beginning to
believe that the
world was round.

Trade in the Mediterranean

Trade helped medieval people to find out more
about the world. During the Middle Ages, merchants
sailed across the Mediterranean to Egypt where they
traded with the Arabs. They bought silk, cotton,
precious stones and perfumes. Arab traders bought
these goods in Asia. The map at the top of the page
shows the trade routes and where the goods came
from.

▲ *Italian and Arab trade routes around 1400*

SPICES

Of all the things which merchants brought back to
Europe, spices were the most popular and the most
expensive. Europeans discovered that spices could
be used to preserve food and improve its flavour.
Some spices were also used as medicines. The most
popular and expensive spices were pepper, nutmeg,
cloves, ginger and cinnamon.

▲ *Arab traders sold their goods to European merchants.*

Spices only grow on tropical islands, and the most
important of these were the Spice Islands, or the
Moluccas, in the Indian Ocean. Locate them on the
map above.

Italian merchants became very wealthy from this spice trade. The rulers of other European countries were jealous of Italy's wealth. They wondered if there might be another way of getting to the Spice Islands. The first country to discover such a route was Portugal.

◢ QUESTIONS ◣

1. (a) List three things that people in 1400 believed about the world and explain how they go these ideas. (b) Do you think they were right to believe these things? Explain your answer.
2. For what reasons did some Europeans travel to other countries during the Middle Ages?

Looking at the evidence

LOOK AGAIN AT THE MAPS ON PAGE 100. SAY WHETHER THE FOLLOWING STATEMENTS ARE TRUE OR FALSE. EXPLAIN YOUR REASONS FOR SAYING SO.

IN 1400, EUROPEANS KNEW THAT:
1. NORTH AND SOUTH AMERICA EXISTED.
2. AFRICA IS THREE TIMES LARGER THAN EUROPE.
3. A CONTINENT CALLED AUSTRALIA EXISTED.
4. THE NORTH AND SOUTH POLES ARE FROZEN OVER.

CHAPTER

37

Prince Henry the Navigator

🏛 Portugal and Africa

The map shows that Portugal faces the Atlantic Ocean and that Africa lies to the south of it.

▣ *Portugal and North Africa*

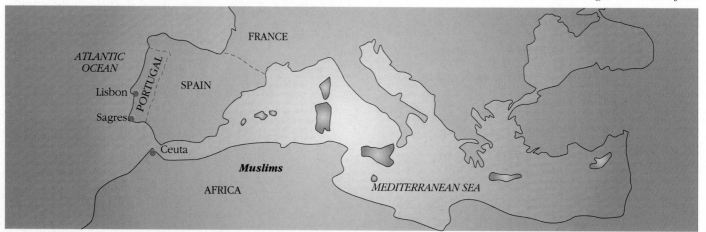

In 1415, Prince Henry of Portugal (1394-1460) fought against the Arabs in North Africa and captured a fortress called **Ceuta**. These Arabs were Muslims, and the Portuguese believed it was their duty to conquer them and convert them to Christianity.

Prince Henry was very curious about Africa, even though Portuguese sailors were terrified to travel farther south than **Cape Bojador**. Many of them had heard the ancient Arab legend which said:

"Beyond Cape Bojador the sun grows hotter, the sea boils and becomes coated with a scum of green weeds and hideous monsters. Near the equator there are huge sea serpents which would crunch ships like a biscuit."

Portuguese sailors were terrified that sea serpents would attack their ships.

Prince Henry wanted to discover the truth of this legend for himself and encouraged his sailors to explore the west coast of Africa. Although he never went on any voyages himself, he is still remembered as **Prince Henry the Navigator**.

WRITTEN SOURCES

A friend of Prince Henry's, **Gomez de Azurara**, wrote a book called *The Chronicle of the Discovery and Conquest of Guinea* which tells us a great deal about Henry the Navigator. This is an extract from the chronicle.

"Henry wanted to know what lay beyond Cape Bojador. Nothing existed in writing, nor in anyone's memory, of what the land there looked like. Some said that Saint Brendan had passed it, while others said that two ships had gone there and had never returned. Henry believed he could trade there, perhaps even find allies against the Muslims, and spread the Christian faith."

The school at Sagres

Prince Henry wondered how he could overcome his sailors' fears. He realised that they needed better ships, better maps and charts, and better navigational instruments. So he set up a school at Sagres on the southern tip of Portugal. There, he invited the best shipbuilders to design new ships and the best map makers to make new maps and charts. Astronomers and mathematicians were asked to invent new navigational

Prince Henry the Navigator

instruments. Work at the school led to many improvements in ships and sailors' skills over the following century.

CARAVELS

Henry's workmen designed a new type of ship called a **caravel**. The planks of the ship were fitted edge-to-edge over a strong frame, making the sides totally smooth. This made a caravel faster than the old ships because it cut through the water much more efficiently.

Lisbon harbour in the fifteenth century. A caravel with triangular lateen sails is at the right.

Ships at that time had one large square sail. The caravel had several smaller triangular sails called **lateen** sails. The idea was copied from Arab ships. Lateen sails could be turned round more easily. They also helped the ship to sail against the wind or to catch the wind when it was blowing sideways.

PORTOLANS AND MAPS

The Portuguese made special kinds of maps called **portolans** to help sailors plot a safe course. A portolan was not just a map of the coastline. It gave details about winds, currents and the depth of the ocean. As most sailors liked to sail close to land, a portolan also showed where dangers lay, such as rocks and shallow harbours. Most portolans were drawn on sheepskin and many of them were decorated in colour.

case. Underneath the needle was a card with the thirty-two points of the compass marked on it. The captain could now immediately see in which direction his ship was sailing even when it was out of sight of land.

MEASURING SPEED AND DISTANCE AT SEA

Sailors also discovered a way to measure speed at sea. They threw a long rope with knots four or five metres apart into the sea. A small piece of wood was attached to the end of the rope. As the ship sailed on, the wood remained floating where it fell. A sailor slowly unwound the rope. After one minute, he pulled it in and counted the number of knots that had gone over the side. He could then work out the ship's speed and how far it had travelled. The term "knots" is still used to measure distances at sea.

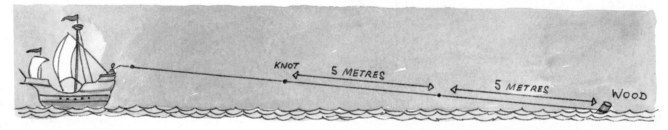

A BETTER COMPASS

Ships in Europe had used compasses since the twelfth century. The old compass was made by putting a magnetic needle on a block of wood and floating it in a bowl of water. The Portuguese improved on this by placing the needle on a tiny pivot so that it could move freely.

To keep it safe, the compass was put in a glass

Measuring distance at sea using knots

THE QUADRANT

Portuguese sailors learned to work out their **latitude** (how far they were from the equator) by calculating the height of the North Star above the horizon. To do this, they used an instrument called a **quadrant**. It was similar to the **astrolabe** used by Greek and Arab sailors.

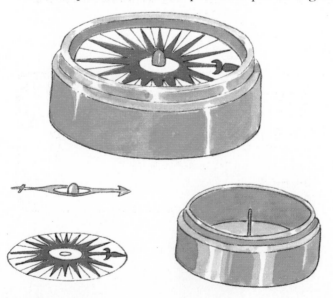

Although no examples have survived, this is the type of compass that was probably used around 1400.

An astrolabe

The drawing shows a sailor holding a quadrant. At the base of the quadrant, all the lines of latitude are marked. The sailor first looks along the top of the quadrant towards the North Star. When he does so, a thin piece of cord with a weight attached (called a **plumb line**) hangs down from the top of the instrument and positions itself at the correct line of latitude. Another sailor then reads the measurement.

⬕ *Sailors using a quadrant*

South of the equator, sailors had to work out their latitude by measuring the height of the sun above the horizon at noon. But the height of the sun changes with the seasons, so a special book was written which gave the height of the sun above the horizon at noon for every day of the year.

Sailors were not able to work out their **longitude** (distance from east to west) until accurate clocks were made in the seventeenth century.

PRACTICAL EXPERIENCE

By using a compass and measuring the distance travelled, the navigator then marked out the ship's course on a chart. This was called **dead reckoning**. This needed great skill because the navigator had to remember that changes in winds and currents could take his ship off course.

Of course, practical experience was just as important as good instruments. Most navigators could judge the depth of the water by its colour. They would watch the sky for birds and the sea for floating twigs. Both might be signs of land. They also had to be familiar with the trade winds and the directions in which they blew.

◪ QUESTIONS ◪

1. Which continent lies directly south of Portugal? Trace a map of this continent, showing only those parts that Europeans knew about in 1400.
2. (a) Give four reasons why Portuguese sailors were afraid to travel south of Cape Bojador. (b) Do you think they were right to be afraid?
3. (a) Write down four things which Prince Henry thought would help sailors to overcome their fears of sailing too far from home. (b) If you were a sailor living in the fifteenth century, which of these things do you think would have helped you the most? Give reasons for your answer.

1. DRAW A PICTURE OF THE KIND OF SHIP BUILT AT SAGRES.
2. USING LABELLED DIAGRAMS, ILLUSTRATE THE FOLLOWING: THE COMPASS, MEASURING LATITUDE, MEASURING THE SPEED OF A SHIP.

Activities ▼ ▼

The Portuguese Voyages

🏛 New discoveries

With better ships, better maps and better instruments, Portuguese sailors became more brave and confident. They soon began to travel farther and farther down the coast of Africa. Portuguese explorers discovered **Madeira** (1418), the **Azores** (1432) and the **Cape Verde Islands** (1444). Other discoveries quickly followed. The map shows the most important places and the year in which each was discovered.

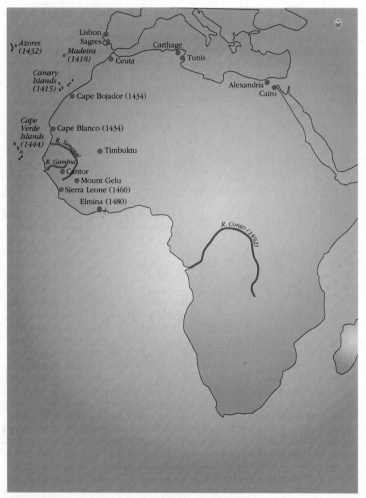

▲ *Early Portuguese discoveries: 1415 -1486*

🏛 Descriptions of north-west Africa

In 1455 and 1458, two Portuguese sailors – **Luigi Cadamosto** and **Diego Gomez** – explored the west coast of Africa for Prince Henry. Both wrote accounts of what they saw.

🏛 LUIGI CADAMOSTO'S ACCOUNT

"From Cape Blanco, I travelled on for another six hundred kilometres until I reached the mouth of a large river (the Senegal) which I sailed up. The king who lives here rules over very poor people. There is no city in this country, but only villages with huts made of straw."

🏛 DIEGO GOMEZ'S ACCOUNT

"I went up the River Gambia as far as Cantor. People came from Timbuktu in the north and Mount Gelu in the south to see us. I was told that there was plenty of gold to be found there and that Arabs came to trade from as far away as Carthage, Tunis, Alexandria and Cairo."

🏛 Trade with Africa

The Portuguese found it profitable to trade with people along the west coast of Africa. Every month, caravels left Lisbon carrying wool, linen, iron and other goods which were exchanged for gold, ivory and exotic animals and birds.

The horrors of the slave trade also began during these times. This is Azurara's account of taking African slaves back to Portugal.

"Mothers clasped their infants in their arms and threw themselves on the ground, so that they could prevent their children from being separated from them. But these slaves were treated with kindness and no difference was made between them and the free-born citizens of Portugal."

Bartholomew Diaz rounds the Cape of Good Hope: 1488

When Henry the Navigator died in 1460, King John II of Portugal continued to encourage explorers. During his reign, Bartholomew Diaz was the first man to sail as far as the southern tip of Africa.

Diaz set sail from Lisbon in 1487 with three ships. He travelled more than 5500 kilometres southwards, farther than any Portuguese sailor had ever sailed before. You can trace his journey on the map.

Early in January 1488, Diaz and his ships were blown off course by a great storm. The ships drifted onwards and soon lost sight of land. When the storm ended, Diaz discovered that his ships were no longer sailing southwards as he had expected. Instead, they were sailing eastwards. He ordered his ships to turn northwards again and to sail back the way they had come.

On 3 February 1488, Diaz sighted land again and his ships anchored at a place called **Mossel Bay**. Diaz named the tip of Africa the **Cape of Storms**. When he returned to Portugal with the news, King John II renamed it the **Cape of Good Hope**.

HAVE A CLASS DISCUSSION ABOUT WHY KING JOHN II DECIDED TO CALL THE TIP OF AFRICA THE CAPE OF GOOD HOPE. MAKE A LIST OF AS MANY REASONS AS YOU CAN THINK OF.

How do we know about Diaz's voyage?

The Portuguese were very secretive about their voyages. Maps, charts, portolans and log books were immediately handed over to the government in Lisbon when the explorers returned home. Many of these documents survive to this day and can be seen in the state archives in Portugal.

Unfortunately, Bartholomew Diaz did not leave a written account of his voyage. Instead, we must rely on other evidence.

PADRAOS

Many Portuguese explorers carried crosses called **padraos** on their voyages. They erected them on headlands of newly-discovered lands. Bartholomew Diaz erected a padrao at the Cape of Good Hope in 1488.

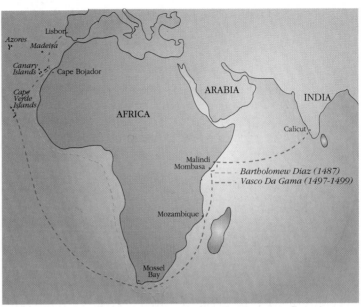
The voyages of Bartholomew Diaz and Vasco da Gama

Vasco da Gama sails to India: 1497-1499

In July 1497, nine years after Diaz sailed to the Cape of Good Hope, another Portuguese sailor called Vasco da Gama set out from Lisbon with four caravels. He believed he could sail around the Cape of Good Hope, cross the Indian Ocean and reach the Spice Islands.

We know a great deal more about da Gama's voyage because a member of his crew kept a journal of what happened. By March 1498, da Gama's ships had sailed around the Cape of Good Hope. The journal says:

15 March 1498
"We entered the bay at Mozambique where we discovered the people are Muslims and their language is the same as the Moors in North Africa. Many of them are merchants who trade with the Arabs. There were four Arab ships in the port at the time, full of gold, silver, cloves, pepper, ginger, pearls and rubies, all of which the people here use."

7 April 1498
"When we arrived at Mombassa, we saw a dhow (an Arab boat) which was full of Arabs, so we did not enter the harbour. At midnight, a dhow with about one hundred men, all armed with cutlasses and shields, approached our ships. The captain, however, allowed only four or five of the

most important looking men to board his ship. They said that orders had been given to capture us as soon as we entered the harbour. We then immediately sailed on to Malindi."

The Portuguese hired an Arab pilot to guide them across the Indian Ocean to **Calicut** in India.

28 May 1498

"When the King of Calicut's advisers saw the presents the Portuguese had brought with them, they laughed, saying that if they wanted to give a present to the king, it should be in gold. Later, when da Gama visited the king, he greeted him by putting his hands together and then raising them towards Heaven. He said that he was the ambassador of the King of Portugal."

Da Gama and his crew stayed in Calicut for three months. Then, with a load of spices and precious stones, they set sail for home and reached Lisbon in July 1499.

Three years later, in 1502, da Gama made a second voyage to India with a fleet of twenty ships. As a reward for discovering a new route to the Spice Islands, da Gama was appointed viceroy (ruler) of India.

The Portuguese built this church in India in 1550.

🏛 The Portuguese take control of the Spice Islands

The Portuguese had better guns and ships than the Arabs or the Indians. They took control of a number of ports in India and Ceylon. In 1511, they finally conquered the Spice Islands.

By the middle of the sixteenth century, Portugal had become a great empire. With a population of only one million people, she now controlled trade around the entire coast of Africa, as well as much of India and south-east Asia.

The Tower of Belem stands on the River Tagus not far from Lisbon. It was built in 1520 in honour of Vasco da Gama.

◤ QUESTIONS ◥

1. Read the accounts written by Cadamosto and Gomez. Which one do you think Prince Henry would have been happier to hear? Give reasons for your answer.
2. Write an account of the voyages of Vasco da Gama. You should include in your answer: (a) how we know about him; (b) the route of his first voyage; (c) the places he visited; (d) the difficulties he experienced; (e) why he succeeded.

Activities

1. COPY A MAP OF AFRICA INTO YOUR WORKBOOK. MARK IN THE ROUTE THAT DIAZ TOOK FROM PORTUGAL TO THE CAPE OF GOOD HOPE. MARK IN AND NAME FIVE MODERN COUNTRIES ALONG THE ROUTE.
2. IMAGINE YOU WERE A PORTUGUESE EXPLORER IN THE FIFTEENTH CENTURY. IN YOUR WORKBOOK, DESIGN A MONUMENT WITH A SUITABLE INSCRIPTION WHICH YOU MIGHT HAVE USED TO REMEMBER YOUR VOYAGE.

Life on board a Ship

The crew

Ships in the fifteenth and sixteenth centuries were very small. Most were about the size of a modern fishing boat.

Most sailors who travelled on the great voyages of discovery had some seafaring experience. They were often hand-picked by the captain himself.

Every ship had a **captain**, as well as a **master** and **navigator**. The **master** was next in rank to the captain and was responsible for the daily running of the ship. The **navigator** or **pilot** steered the ship using his own charts and instruments. Usually, several ships sailed together as a fleet. The ship on which the captain sailed was called the **flagship.**

Each sailor on board had special duties to perform. The **boatswain** looked after the sails and anchors. The **helmsman** was in charge of the rudder. Some sailors were skilled carpenters, sail makers and painters. Others worked as cooks or were in charge of the cannon and ammunition on board. A ship often had some young boys on board who ran errands or acted as pages to the captains.

▲ *Time was kept using an hour glass .*

Keeping time

Each day was divided into six watches of four hours. As there were no clocks on board, sailors used a **half-hour glass** or an **hour glass**. These were filled with sand and turned over each time the sand ran through. Each turn was marked with chalk on a slate, or a peg was placed in a hole on a special piece of wood called a **traverse board**.

Food

On a long voyage, ships had to carry enough food to last for one or two years. The food was stored in barrels and often went bad. Some was eaten by rats or infested with insects. Water was particularly difficult to keep fresh and had to be rationed.

There are many records which tell us the kind of food put on board a ship. Most ships took supplies of:

dried biscuits
sugar
salted meat and fish
dried fruit
lentils, beans and peas
anchovies
cheese
wine
garlic
mustard

A FIREBOX

Food was cooked on the main deck over a large three-sided iron box called a **firebox**. The base of the box was covered with sand and firewood was then placed on top. When the food was ready, the crew lined up at the firebox, each man carrying a wooden plate on which the food was served.

As there was always the danger of a fire, buckets of sea water were kept close by.

◣ *Cooking in a fire box*

Careening a ship

When a ship travelled a great distance, it had to be docked where it could be cleaned and repaired. This was called **careening.**

The masts and the sails were taken down and all the cargo on board was placed on the beach. At high tide, the ship was floated up onto the beach, anchored securely, then turned on its side.

When the tide flowed out, seaweed and barnacles were scraped off the sides of the ship. Rotten planks were replaced with new ones and the keel was retarred. With the next high tide, the ship was turned on its other side and the work was repeated.

Dangers at sea

Life on board ship was both dangerous and difficult. Only the captain had his own cabin. Other members of the crew usually slept on the open deck.

Sailors were often injured when loading heavy goods, or when pulling on ropes and weighing anchor. Others hit their heads on low beams or were crushed to death by cargo which had come loose in heavy storms.

Many sailors became bored on long voyages and they argued and fought with one another. Some got drunk, fell overboard and drowned.

DISEASES

Sailors on long sea voyages also faced death from storms and ship wrecks. Many also died from diseases such as **scurvy** which was caused by the lack of fresh fruit and vegetables. On Vasco da Gama's voyage around the Cape of Good Hope, scurvy is said to have killed one hundred of his 170 men.

◣ *Careening a ship. Explain what the sailors are doing and why.*

This is how one sailor described scurvy.

"My gums rotted and gave out black blood. My thighs and lower legs were black and had gangrene and I was forced to use my knife each day to cut into the flesh in order to release this black and foul blood."

Sailors also died from **typhoid** which they got from drinking infected water. Many more suffered from sun stroke and frostbite. The rats and lice which swarmed all over the ships carried other diseases. So it is no wonder that many sailors did not survive to tell their tales.

◢ QUESTIONS ◣

1. Who were the three most important people on board a ship?
2. List four skills which were needed on a ship. Explain why these skills were so important.
3. Make a list of some of the difficulties and dangers which crews faced on long journeys.
4. Make your own labelled drawings of: an hourglass; a firebox.
5. Write a short paragraph explaining how sailors careened a ship on a long voyage.
6. Imagine you are a sailor living in 1500. Write an account of your life on board ship under these headings: (a) what job you have; (b) living conditions; (c) accidents and diseases; (d) the places you have seen.

CHAPTER

Christopher Columbus Sails Westward

🏛 Toscanelli's chart

Paolo Toscanelli was a famous map maker from Florence who was certain the world was round. He got his idea from an Egyptian geographer called **Ptolemy** who had lived in the second century AD.

In the middle of the fifteenth century, a map of the world which Ptolemy had made was rediscovered. Although it was inaccurate, it clearly showed the earth was a sphere.

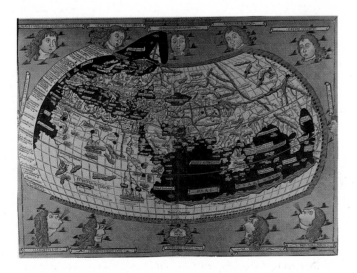

Ptolemy's map clearly shows the earth as a sphere. The ten faces represent the winds of the world.

Toscanelli was fascinated by this map. In 1474, he wrote to a young sailor from Genoa in Italy. This is part of Toscanelli's letter.

"Greetings, Christopher Columbus:
I know of a shorter way to the Spice Islands than that which takes you along the coast of Africa. I have worked this out from the shape of the earth. I enclose a chart which I have made myself. Do not be surprised if I say that the places where the spices grow lie towards the west, when others usually say to the east."

☑ Japan was four times farther away than he thought.
☑ A great undiscovered continent lay between Europe and Japan.

Columbus was a poor sailor who wanted to make his fortune, so he was very excited by this letter. If what Toscanelli said was true, Columbus realised that he could get to the Spice Islands more quickly than the Portuguese. He spent many years looking for support to make such a voyage westwards across the Atlantic.

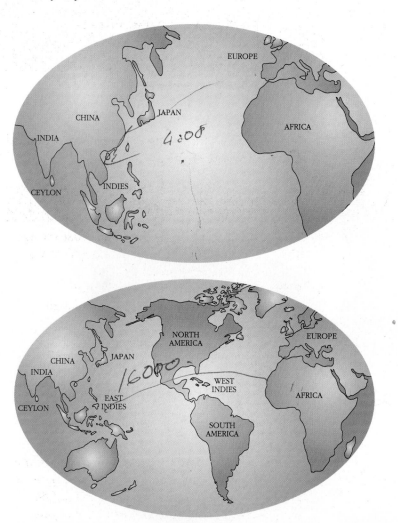

▲ *Although no one knows what Christopher Columbus really looked like, this picture shows him as a big, dark-haired man. What does he seem to be holding? Why do you think he is shown pointing to the stars?*

▲ *The top map shows Toscanelli's and Columbus' idea of the world. The world as we know it today is shown below. Compare the two maps. Comment on the ways in which Columbus and Toscanelli were wrong.*

Toscanelli told Columbus that if he sailed westwards for about 4000 kilometres, he would reach Japan which he said was close to India. However, like Ptolemy, there were two important facts which Toscanelli did not know.

🏛 Columbus looks for support

Columbus first asked the King of Portugal to finance his trip, but the king turned him down, saying:

"Columbus is a big talker and boastful and is full of fancy and imagination about Japan."

Finally, **King Ferdinand** and **Queen Isabella** of Spain agreed to give him money to equip three ships. This is part of the agreement which they made with Columbus in 1492.

"We are sending you on a voyage to the regions of India to discover certain islands and mainlands in the ocean. You shall be admiral, viceroy and governor of all the lands that you find. You shall also have ten per cent of all the gold, gems, spices or other goods got by trading in those lands."

An exact replica of Columbus' flagship, *the* Santa Maria

Ferdinand and Isabella of Spain hoped that Columbus would bring back many riches for them.

was more suitable for sailing in rough weather and could carry more men and provisions.

How do we know about the voyages of Columbus?

- Columbus kept a journal during his first voyage. This journal has been lost, but a copy of it was made by a Spanish historian called **Bartholomew Las Casas** shortly after Columbus died. This is our most important source.
- Columbus also wrote 36 letters to different people, many of which refer to his voyages across the Atlantic.
- Columbus' son Hernando travelled with his father on his fourth voyage. He wrote a biography of Columbus called *A Life of the Admiral.*
- **Fernandez de Oviedo** (1478-1557) lived in the New World for many years. He wrote *A General History of the Indies* in which he gives a first-hand account of the discoveries of Columbus.

The ships

Columbus hired and equipped three ships for his voyage.

Ship	Size	Crew	Captain
Santa Maria	100 tonnes	40	Admiral Columbus
Niña	50 tonnes	21	Captain Vincent Pinzon
Pinta	60 tonnes	27	Captain Martin Pinzon

The *Niña* and the *Pinta* were caravels. The *Santa Maria* was a **nao** which was larger and broader. It

On the wide Atlantic

Columbus' three ships left **Palos** in Spain on 3 August 1492. When they reached the Canary Islands, they set sail in a westerly direction across the Atlantic Ocean. Columbus knew that winds blew steadily westwards from the Canaries, so he could rely on them to gain speed.

This artist's impression shows Columbus setting out from Palos on his great voyage of discovery on 3 August 1492.

Here are three entries from Columbus' *Journal* towards the end of the westward crossing of the Atlantic.

10 October 1492

"The sailors began to complain about the length of the journey. The Admiral cheered them up as best he could by telling them of the advantages they would gain."

11 October 1492

"One sailor spotted petrels (small seabirds) and green reeds near the ship. Another picked up a small stick shaped with an iron tool. At these signs, all on board breathed again and were happy. Later that night another sailor saw a moving light. With these signs of land, the crew were filled with hope. The ships anchored and waited for daylight."

12 October 1492

"At dawn they saw a stretch of land which was large, flat and very green. The Admiral went ashore in a small armed boat with Martin and

Vincent Pinzon. He took the Royal Spanish standard and a large wooden cross with him. When he reached the shore, Columbus fell on his knees and wept tears of joy. He said, 'Praise to the Lord! We take this land for the King and Queen.'"

An artist's impression of Columbus landing in the New World on 12 October 1492. How accurate and realistic do you think these two paintings are?

In the West Indies

Columbus named the island **San Salvador** (see map, page 116), which means "Holy Saviour". (Today it is known as Watling Island in the Bahamas.) Columbus thought he had reached India, so he called the people Indians. The lands he discovered were called the West Indies. He did not know that he had discovered a new continent. Here is Columbus' description of the people he met.

"The natives go as naked as when their mothers bore them. I believe they will easily become Christians because they seem to have no religion of their own. They know nothing about arms because when I showed them our swords, they took them by the blade and cut themselves."

Columbus gave the natives red caps and glass beads which they hung around their necks. In return, the natives gave the Spaniards some parrots and balls of cotton thread.

Columbus continues his search

From the natives on San Salvador, Columbus learned that there was a larger island nearby which they called **Cuba**. He believed this had to be Japan. On reaching Cuba, Columbus sent some of his men into

Natives of the New World harvesting fruit, cooking fish and smoking tobacco. Describe other interesting things you notice in these drawings.

the interior, but they found no large cities or evidence of great wealth. All they saw were men "eating smoke".

Columbus then sailed on to another island which he called **Hispaniola** (Haiti and Dominican Republic, see map, page 116). He still hoped to find great cities and wealthy rulers, but the people he found there were poor. There were no spices and only tiny amounts of gold which the people used to make rings.

⌂ THE LOSS OF THE *SANTA MARIA*

On Christmas Day 1492, disaster struck when strong currents carried the *Santa Maria* onto a sand bank. This is a description of what happened.

"The Admiral rushed up on deck and ordered masts to be cut down and the ship to be lightened as much as possible to see if she would come off

the sand bank. But as the water continued to rise, nothing more could be done. The Santa Maria fell on her side, then the timbers opened and the ship was lost."

Using the timber from the wrecked ship, Columbus and his men built a wooden fort on Hispaniola. Forty men agreed to remain behind to search for gold. They were given a year's supply of bread and wine and were left some crossbows and muskets.

⌂ Columbus returns to Spain

The rest of the sailors crowded onto the *Niña* and the *Pinta* and on 16 January 1493, they set sail for Spain. Half-way across the Atlantic, a great storm separated the two ships and they did not meet again until they reached home on the 15 March 1493.

Columbus was certain that he had found the Indies. So were King Ferdinand and Queen Isabella, who granted him all the titles and privileges which they had promised.

Columbus brought back pineapples, sweet potatoes, maize, exotic birds, six natives and some gold ornaments. But he exaggerated his discoveries because he needed the king's and queen's support to undertake another voyage. He lied when he told them there was as much gold and as many slaves as they could ever want.

⌂ THE LATER VOYAGES

Columbus made three more voyages across the Atlantic: 1493-96, 1498-1500 and 1502-1504. On the second voyage, which was the largest, he sailed with seventeen ships and a crew of 1200 men.

On each voyage, more islands in the West Indies were discovered, including **Trinidad**, **Puerto Rico** and **Jamaica**. Columbus also explored the **Gulf of Mexico** and parts of **Central America** including **Panama**. But he never reached Japan, the land he had always dreamed of finding.

after another Italian explorer, **Amerigo Vespucci**.

In 1501, Vespucci explored thousands of kilometres of the South American coastline. He decided that Columbus' calculations were wrong and that the West Indies was not part of Asia, but a new continent, a New World. This new land became known as **America**, after Amerigo Vespucci.

The Treaty of Tordesillas: 1494

After Columbus' voyages, the Spanish and the Portuguese became rivals in the discovery of new lands. In 1494, with the help of Pope Alexander VI, both countries signed the Treaty of Tordesillas in which they agreed to divide all newly-discovered lands between them. The treaty said:

"We agree to draw a boundary line on the map, running from north to south, 370 leagues west of the Cape Verde Islands. All lands, islands and mainlands west of this line belong to Spain. All lands, islands and mainlands east of this line belong to Portugal."

The Treaty of Tordesillas seemed like a good idea at first. But the world was round, and no Europeans had travelled to the other side. So no one could decide where the line should be drawn on the far side of the world.

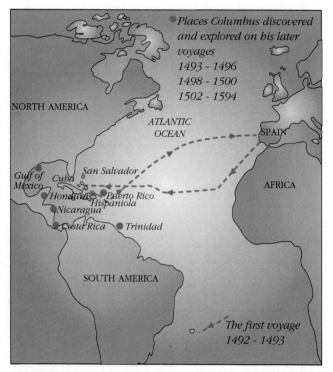

The voyages of Columbus

The death of Columbus

Columbus died in 1506, believing that his life had been a failure. He did not discover a new route to the Spice Islands. But he had discovered a "New World" – the continents of North and South America. It was this land mass which had blocked his way to the East and the spices and gold he had hoped to find.

AMERIGO VESPUCCI (1451-1512)

Some people say that the New World should have been called **Columbia** after Christopher Columbus. Instead it was named

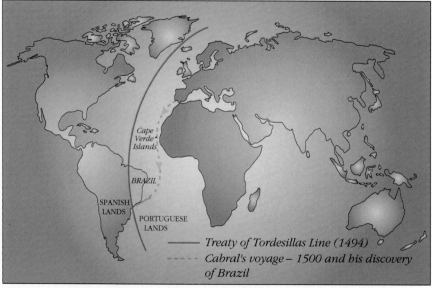

The Treaty of Tordesillas divided land in the New World between Spain and Portugal.

Cabral and the discovery of Brazil: 1500

In 1500, a Portuguese captain named **Pedro Cabral (1467-1519)** was sailing down the west coast of Africa on his way to India. His ship was blown off course and he landed instead in South America.

The Portuguese realised that this land was less than "370 leagues west of the Cape Verde Islands". Under the Treaty of Tordesillas, it belonged to them. They named the country Brazil because of the large amounts of Brazil wood which grew there.

Portuguese traders soon settled in Brazil and exported the wood to Europe where it was used for dying cloth. Today, the people of Brazil still speak Portuguese and not Spanish, like most other South Americans.

1. DIVIDE THE CLASS INTO TWO TEAMS. HOLD A DEBATE ON THE MOTION THAT "THE NEW WORLD SHOULD HAVE BEEN CALLED COLUMBIA, NOT AMERICA".
2. HOLD ANOTHER DISCUSSION ON WHAT THE NATIVE PEOPLE OF THE NEW WORLD MIGHT HAVE THOUGHT ABOUT THE TREATY OF TORDESILLAS.

Activities

QUESTIONS

1. Write a short paragraph on Toscanelli's map (page 112). Was it a help or a hindrance to Columbus? Give reasons for your answer.
2. What were the terms of the agreement which Ferdinand and Isabella made with Columbus (page 113)? Do you think they were generous terms? Give reasons for your answer.
3. Calculate how many days Columbus' first voyage took, from the time his ships left Spain until they reached Watling Island. Compare this time with the length of Vasco da Gama's voyage to Calicut.
4. Read the descriptions about Columbus' voyage on page 114. Which one do you find the most interesting? Give reasons for your answer.
5. Write an account of Columbus' life. You should include: (a) his early life; (b) his agreement with Ferdinand and Isabella; (c) his first voyage; (d) his later life.
6. Columbus died without realising two important facts about the discoveries he had made. What were they?
7. Write a paragraph about the Treaty of Tordesillas and say whether it was a good idea or not.
8. How is Brazil different from the rest of South America? Write a paragraph explaining how that came about.

CHAPTER 41

The Destruction of Two Great Civilisations: the Aztecs and the Incas

The Aztecs

When European explorers first arrived in America, many different tribes were living in the area we now call Mexico. The most powerful of these were the **Aztecs**. Their city was called **Tenochtitlán**. It was built on several small islands in the middle of a large lake. Nearly 200,000 people lived there.

In order to please their gods, the Aztecs carried out human sacrifices. These two artefacts from Aztec times – the mask of the Serpent God, and the head-dress worn by the Aztec leader, Montezuma – were used in their ceremonies.

HERNÁN CORTÉS (1485-1547)

Hernán Cortés went to live in the New World when he was only nineteen years old. He spent his life savings on preparing for his expedition to Mexico.

In 1519, a Spanish adventurer, Hernán Cortés, decided to conquer the Aztec empire. In 1520, he gathered together an army of 100,000 men. Most of them were from other Mexican tribes who hated the war-like Aztecs. The siege of Tenochtitlán lasted three months. This is how a Spaniard, Bernal Diaz, describes the city after the defeat of the Aztecs and their leader, Montezuma.

"The lake was full of heads and corpses. In the city itself, we could not walk except among the corpses and the heads of dead Indians. They stank so much that none of us could bear it. Even Cortés was ill from the smell which filled his nostrils."

The Spanish conquerors rebuilt Tenochtitlán and renamed it Mexico City. A cathedral was built on the site of the great Aztec temple and many Aztecs who survived the slaughter were converted to Christianity. All the conquered lands of the Aztecs were called New Spain. In 1522, Hernán Cortés was appointed governor of these lands by King Charles V of Spain.

The Incas

The Incas were another ancient civilisation in South America. They lived high in the Andes mountains in Peru. As architects and engineers, the Incas were even more advanced than the Aztecs.

Francisco Pizarro (1475-1541), a Spanish adventurer, had heard rumours about the Inca empire and its great riches. In 1530, he set out to find the Inca empire with a small number of men. They travelled through swamps and rain forests and were often attacked by native Indians.

Francisco Pizarro seized enough Inca gold to fill a room 7m long and 5m wide, but killed thousands of Incas in the process.

With sixty horses, Pizarro and his troops marched across the Andes. It was three years before they reached **Cuzco**, the Inca capital. The Inca armies were no match for the Spaniards' guns and cavalry and they were quickly defeated.

The Spaniards seized enough gold and silver to fill a room seven metres long and five metres wide. Later, Pizarro founded a new city called Lima, the modern capital of Peru.

Artefacts like this gold knife convinced the conquistadores of the wealth which could be found in the New World.

QUESTIONS

1. In which modern country did the Aztecs live? Write down three interesting facts about their civilisation.
2. Write a short account of Cortés' conquest of the Aztecs. You will find more information about it in your local library.
3. In which modern country did the Incas live? Who conquered them and why?

THE FULL STORY OF THE CONQUEST OF THE INCAS IS BOTH SAD AND FASCINATING. SEE IF YOU CAN FIND OUT MORE ABOUT IT.

Finding out

The Inca settlement at Machu Pichu was built high in the Andes.

All the gold from the New World was stored in the Tower of Gold in Seville, Spain. The king always kept one-fifth of the treasure for himself.

The New World becomes Spanish

🏛 Conquistadores

Cortés, Pizarro and the other Spanish explorers who conquered land in America were called **conquistadores**, the Spanish word for "conquerors". The king of Spain appointed governors to rule over the lands they conquered. He also ordered that one-fifth of all the gold and silver found in the New World should be given to him. By the end of sixteenth century, Spain had become the wealthiest and most powerful country in the world.

🏛 Colonies

Many Spaniards were eager to go to the New World where they believed they could make their fortunes. They heard stories about gold and silver mines and rich farming land. During the sixteenth century, about 200,000 Spaniards settled in the New World. They were farmers, craftsmen, traders, priests and government officials. Very few women went, so most Spaniards married Indian women.

The people who settled in the New World were called **colonists**, and the lands in which they settled were called **colonies**.

Spain was the first European country to have colonies in the New World. All the Spanish colonies belonged to the king of Spain. The colonists were his subjects and obeyed his laws. They brought about many changes to daily life in South and Central America. Let us look at some of them.

🏛 EUROPEAN CROPS AND ANIMALS

Spaniards who went to the New World brought along with them many things which were not found there. They took seeds of wheat, barley and rye and cultivated these crops. They also took animals such as horses, cows, pigs and sheep which bred and multiplied quickly. Forests were cut down and Spanish horses grazed on the land. Today, great herds of cattle still roam the plains of South America.

🏛 Treatment of the native people

The colonists needed help to farm the land, so they forced the native people to work for them as slaves. In the silver and gold mines of Mexico and Peru, all the work was done by natives who were treated badly by the European colonists. Many were tortured and killed because the Spaniards thought they were lazy. They were also forced to become Christians against their will. The colonists behaved as if the native people had no rights at all.

▲ *Native people in the New World were treated like slaves. They were forced to work in the mines and to pan for gold in the rivers.*

The Spanish government grew concerned about this harsh treatment of the native people. In 1542, it issued rules telling the colonists to treat the natives better. These were called the **New Laws** which stated three important things:

- ☑ The native people were free subjects of the King of Spain.
- ☑ Slavery was forbidden.
- ☑ Natives must be properly paid.

Were these laws successful? The information in the graph will help you to decide. It shows the number of native people living in New Spain when Cortés conquered it in 1519 and how their numbers changed over the next hundred years.

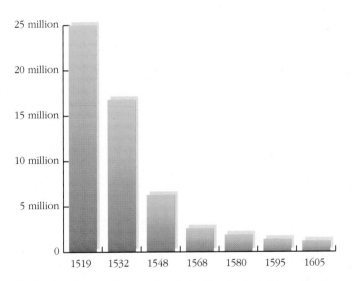

The population of native people in New Spain between the arrival of Cortés (1519) and 1605. Comment on what this graph shows.

Why did the population fall so rapidly? Historians think there were two main reasons. One was the harsh way in which the Spaniards treated the Indians. Many of them were overworked and ill-treated in the silver and mercury mines and died from exhaustion.

The other reason is that Europeans brought diseases like smallpox and measles with them when they went to the New World. The Indians had never suffered from these illnesses before. Their resistance to new diseases was low, so millions of them died. The native population in the New World declined, while the Spanish population grew.

THE SPANISH LANGUAGE

As more and more Spaniards arrived in the New World, Spanish soon became the common language for everyone. The native people spoke many different languages, so it was easier for the colonists to make them learn Spanish. Books were printed in Spanish and the natives were taught to read and write.

> **Activity**
>
> FIND A MAP OF CENTRAL AND SOUTH AMERICA IN YOUR ATLAS. YOU WILL SEE THAT MANY OF THE CITIES, RIVERS AND MOUNTAINS HAVE SPANISH NAMES.
>
> HERE IS A LIST OF THE MOST COMMON SPANISH WORDS WITH THEIR ENGLISH MEANINGS. SEE HOW MANY PLACES YOU CAN FIND CONTAINING THESE WORDS.
>
> SAN/SANTA (SAINT)   CRUZ (CROSS)
> RIO (RIVER)   COSTA (COAST)
> MONTE (HILL)   PUERTO (PORT)
> SIERRA (MOUNTAIN RANGE)   LAS/EL (THE...)
>
> SPANIARDS ALSO SETTLED IN NORTH AMERICA. USING THESE PLACENAMES, WORK OUT THE STATES IN WHICH THEY SETTLED.

THE SPREAD OF CHRISTIANITY

Spaniards who colonised the New World believed it was their duty to convert the native people to Christianity. Hundreds of missionaries left Spain to preach the word of God. By 1600, there were thirty Spanish bishops and more than 12,000 churches in the New World. Today, most people in Central and South America are Catholics.

A SPANISH WAY OF LIFE

The Spaniards believed that their culture was superior to that of the Indians. New buildings, particularly churches, were built in a style similar to those in Spain. All over America today, the influence of Spanish architecture can be seen. The Spaniards also destroyed a great deal of native craftsmanship and taught the Indians Spanish crafts instead.

GOODS FROM THE NEW WORLD

The discovery of America also changed the way in which Europeans lived. Many new kinds of food arrived in Europe from the New World. Sugar, chocolate, potatoes, turkeys, peanuts, pineapples and tomatoes all came from America. So did the practice of smoking tobacco.

Because Spain was the first country to discover America, she became the richest country in Europe during the sixteenth century. Other European countries soon grew jealous of her wealth. The English, Dutch and French conquered different parts of America and set up colonies too.

◤ QUESTIONS ◢

1. Give three reasons why so many Spaniards settled in the New World. What were these settlers called?
2. Write down five changes which the Spaniards brought to the New World. Comment on whether these changes were positive (good) or negative (bad).
3. What did the Spaniards learn from the Indians? How did the conquest of America affect life in Europe?
4. How did the Spanish colonists treat the Indians? Suggest three reasons for their behaviour. Were they right or wrong to behave in this way? Explain your answer.

CHAPTER 43

Special Study: A Voyage Round the World: 1519-1522

 ## Proving the world is round

After Columbus discovered America, many explorers wanted to prove once and for all that the world was round. They dreamed of being the first to make such a voyage. One of them was a Portuguese sailor named Ferdinand Magellan.

Ferdinand Magellan (1480?-1521)

Ferdinand Magellan was born about 1480 in northern Portugal. As a boy, he was fascinated by the stories of Bartholomew Diaz, Vasco da Gama and Christopher Columbus. When he was twenty-five, Magellan sailed with a Portuguese fleet around the Cape of Good Hope. He was on the first ship to reach the Spice Islands by sailing eastwards.

Magellan was certain that it should also be possible to reach the Spice Islands by sailing westwards. After the voyages of Columbus, Magellan knew that North and South America blocked the way. He wondered just how large these continents were and whether it would be possible to sail around them.

Magellan began to study the maps drawn by explorers who had sailed along the coast of South America. He also knew that in 1513, a Spaniard called **Balboa** had seen another great ocean on the west coast of Central America. Balboa had named it the Great South Sea, but we know it as the Pacific Ocean.

Magellan became convinced that there must be a **strait** (a narrow channel of water) somewhere along the American coast that would let him sail through to the Pacific Ocean. From there, he could sail across the Great South Sea to the Spice Islands. He put his idea to the King of Portugal, but the king was not interested.

CHARLES V OF SPAIN

Magellan then decided to seek the assistance of Charles V, the new the King of Spain. Charles V was very interested in exploration. After all, his grandparents, King Ferdinand and Queen Isabella, had helped Christopher Columbus. The king listened to Magellan and he agreed to pay for the voyage.

How do we know?

Magellan kept a log (diary) in which he recorded the events of the voyage, but it has been lost. None of the letters which he wrote during the voyage has survived.

Fortunately, one of Magellan's crew members, an Italian called **Antonio Pigafetta**, kept a journal. Pigafetta was an observant man who was interested in everything that went on. He kept a detailed diary of all that happened and it is now the only surviving account of the voyage. This makes it a very important piece of evidence for historians.

> ✏ Throughout the story of Magellan's voyage, you will read Pigafetta's descriptions of what happened.
> ✏ You should also look at the map on page 127 and check each stage of the journey.

MAGELLAN'S SHIPS

Magellan's fleet consisted of five old merchant ships called **naos**. They were large enough to carry provisions for long ocean voyages. However, they needed many repairs before they could set sail.

The charts below show Magellan's ships and the goods they carried.

Name	Size	Crew	Captain
Santiago	75 tonnes	32	Juan Serrano
Victoria	85 tonnes	42	Luis de Mendoza
Concepcion	90 tonnes	45	Gaspar de Queseda
Trinidad	110 tonnes	55	Ferdinand Magellan
San Antonio	120 tonnes	60	Juan de Cartagena

Weapons & Armour	Instruments	Trading goods
62 large cannon	23 maps	230kg of glass beads
10 small cannon	6 compasses	10,000 fish hooks
2200kg of gunpowder	21 quadrants	4800 knives
100 suits of armour	18 hour glasses	20,000 small bells
100 helmets	35 needles	1000 small mirrors

There were also hundreds of swords, crossbows, lances and enough food to last for two years.

MAGELLAN'S CREW

Most of the crew were Spaniards, including three of the captains. They were jealous of Magellan because he was a Portuguese admiral leading a Spanish fleet. The only captain that Magellan could trust completely was Juan Serrano, who was also Portuguese.

The crew included Greeks, Germans and Flemings as well as Spaniards and Portuguese. The youngest member of the crew was only fourteen and the oldest was forty-four. Magellan also brought with him a slave named **Enrique**. Years earlier, Magellan had brought him back from the Spice Islands.

> *Looking at the evidence*
>
> LOOK AT THE LIST OF WEAPONS AND ARMOUR. WHAT DO THESE LISTS TELL YOU ABOUT MAGELLAN'S VOYAGE?

The fleet departs

Magellan's fleet set sail on 20 September 1519. He ordered his five ships to sail as closely together as possible. Since he was admiral of the fleet, his flagship, the *Trinidad* sailed in front.

To give orders on the voyage, Magellan used flags during the day and lights at night. The lights were either wooden torches or small lanterns with lighted candles in them. The other ships flashed a single light to show that they understood the orders.

In October 1519, when the fleet reached Guinea on the African coast, Magellan commanded the ships to sail westwards across the Atlantic. Late in November 1519, the ships reached the coast of Brazil. Sailing farther southwards, they anchored at **Rio de Janeiro** where Magellan and his crew spent their first Christmas away from home. Pigafetta wrote:

*"We tasted pineapples and sweet potatoes for the first time and saw natives sleeping in cotton nets which they call **hammocks**."*

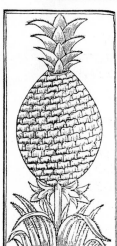

These engravings were made around the time of Magellan's voyage. They show some things which he and his crew saw – a native hammock, a pineapple, and a strange creature called a manatee. In his journal, Columbus wrote that it was a mermaid!

Searching for the strait

Magellan was anxious to find the strait which led to the Pacific. On 12 January 1520, the fleet reached the mouth of the River Plate (Rio de la Plata). Magellan explored the estuary, but all he found was fresh water, so he knew that this was not the strait he was looking for.

The fleet then continued its journey southwards. Magellan stopped to examine every bay and inlet, no matter how narrow.

The sailors saw strange animals and birds for the first time, including sea lions, penguins and llamas. This is how Pigafetta describes what they saw.

"These places are full of sea wolves as big as calves, with large teeth and small round ears. They have no legs, but limbs like hands and so they cannot run. There are also geese without wings. They are black and fat with beaks like crows and they cannot fly. There are also animals with a head and ears as big as a mule, the neck and body of a camel, the legs of a deer and the tail of a horse. We loaded a large number of these onto the five ships."

PATAGONIA

As the ships sailed deep into the southern hemisphere, snow fell and ice formed on the masts. On 30 March 1520, Magellan decided to anchor his fleet at a place he named St Julian's Bay. There the sailors spent the winter and careened the ships (page 110). Pigafetta tells us this interesting story.

"For two months we saw nobody. Then one day, we saw a naked giant standing on the shore. He was so tall that the tallest of us only came up to his waist. His face was painted red and his eyes were painted yellow. He had only a little hair on his head which was painted white."

During the next few months, many more of these "giants" were seen. Magellan named them **Patagóns**, which means "big feet". Today, that part of Argentina is still known as Patagonia. Later explorers said that the Patagonians were simply "taller than average Europeans", and not giants.

MUTINY

While in St Julian's Bay, many of the sailors grew impatient. Magellan discovered that the three

Spanish captains were plotting a mutiny. In the struggle which followed, two of the captains were killed and the third was left behind in Patagonia. Forty others were also found guilty of mutiny, but were later pardoned.

THE LOSS OF THE *SANTIAGO*

When the weather improved, Magellan sent the *Santiago* to explore the coastline to the south. However, the ship was driven onto rocks and sank. Although the sinking of the *Santiago* was a great loss, all but one of the crew was saved. The remaining four ships set sail once more.

MAGELLAN'S VESSELS IN A STORM.

An artist's impression of the storms and rough seas which faced Magellan's fleet in the South Atlantic

Finding the strait

Three months later, in August 1520, Magellan noticed a wide estuary. He ordered the *Antonio* and the *Concepcion* to sail ahead and explore it. The *Victoria* and the *Trinidad* remained at the mouth of the estuary.

On either side of the estuary there were huge snow-capped mountains. The sailors saw fires burning on the mountains and named the place **Tierra del Fuego**, which means "the land of fire". (We now know that these fires were lit by the natives in their hollowed-out canoes. Since these primitive people did not know how to make a new fire, they always had to keep a fire burning.)

Sailing for three days, the captains of the *Antonio* and the *Concepcion* were about to turn back when they noticed a channel leading into a large bay. There was a tide flowing into this bay from the other side. They sailed back to Magellan to report what they had found. This is how Pigafetta describes their return.

"They came into view with their flags flying and their mortars firing round after round. Then the whole fleet joined in the cheering, all of us thanking God and the Virgin Mary that the strait had been found."

The Straits of Magellan, with its many channels and bays, surrounded by high mountains

The four ships now made their way slowly up the strait. As the map shows, the strait divides in two half way across, and Magellan was not sure which direction to take. So he ordered the *Victoria* and his own ship, the *Trinidad*, to go in one direction and the other two ships in the opposite direction.

It was the *Victoria*, closely followed by the *Trinidad*, which first reached the end of the strait. According to Pigafetta:

"When the Captain General heard the news, he wept for joy. He named the end of the strait Cape Desire, because he had desired it for so long."

THE *SAN ANTONIO* DESERTS

A few days later, Magellan learned that the *San Antonio* had deserted and had returned to Spain. This was a terrible blow to everyone. Not only was the *San Antonio* the largest ship; it also carried most of the food supplies. But Magellan was not prepared to give up. He told the crew:

"We will continue the voyage as we have promised the king, even if we have to eat the cowhides from the masts."

Crossing the Pacific Ocean

On 28 November 1520, Magellan's three remaining ships – the *Trinidad*, the *Concepcion* and the *Victoria* – sailed into the Great South Sea. Magellan spoke to his crew.

"Gentlemen, we are now entering waters where no ship has sailed before. May we always find this sea as peaceful as it is this morning. With this hope, I shall name it the Pacific Ocean."

But Magellan had no idea of just how big the Pacific Ocean was. The Spice Islands were actually 10,000km to the west. Pigafetta describes what happened next.

"We were three months and twenty days without any kind of fresh food. We ate what were supposed to be biscuits, but they were really powdered crumbs, swarming with worms and stinking of rats' urine. The water we drank had turned yellow. Nineteen men died from scurvy. I really think the likes of this voyage will never be seen again."

At last, on 6 March 1521, a sailor saw a small island. When they went ashore, the islanders attacked the crew and stole their boats. Pigafetta called the place the **Island of Thieves**. Today it is known as Guam.

THE PHILIPPINES

A week later, the three ships reached a group of small islands. Magellan called them the Philippines, after Philip, the son of King Charles V. There they found fresh water and plenty of fish and coconuts.

Magellan spent most of his time in the Philippines trying to convert the natives to Christianity. Everywhere he went, his slave Enrique acted as an interpreter.

When Magellan learned that the king on the island of **Mactan** did not want to become a Christian, he decided to attack him. The Battle of Mactan was perhaps the saddest event of the whole voyage. Pigafetta has left us a marvellous description of it.

26 April 1521

"1500 natives of Mactan had formed three divisions on the shore. When they saw us coming,

they charged at us with loud cries, one division in front and one on either side of us. They fired arrows and bamboo spears, as well as pointed stakes and stones so that we could hardly defend ourselves. . .

When our Admiral was shot through the right arm with a poisoned arrow, he ordered our men to retreat slowly. But the natives continued to attack us in the water, picking up the same spear five or six times and hurling it at us again and again. . .

The Admiral then tried to take out his sword, and when the enemy saw this, they charged at him and wounded him in the left leg. This caused our leader to fall face downwards into the water. Then they charged at him again with bamboo spears and cutlasses until they had killed our mirror, our light, our comfort and our true guide."

THE LOSS OF THE *CONCEPCION*

After the death of Magellan, the crew decided to leave the Philippines. But there were no longer enough men to sail three ships. So they decided to destroy the *Concepcion* which was leaking badly. All her cargo was transferred to the *Trinidad* and the *Victoria*. It took the two remaining ships another four months to find the Spice Islands. This is what Pigafetta wrote.

6 November 1521

"We came in sight of four islands which we knew were the Spice Islands. We thanked God for this moment, after spending twenty-seven months in search of them. We bartered for cloves with all that we had. For one hundred pounds of cloves, we gave a brass chain worth a few pence.
So much was packed into the ships' holds that the Trinidad *burst her seams and began to leak."*

It was decided that the *Victoria* should return to Spain alone. In the end, only forty-seven men set sail and a few Moluccans decided to sail with them. The remaining fifty-four crew members stayed on the Spice Islands.

"Those who stayed behind wrote letters which they gave us for their families and friends. It was with tears and embraces that we departed."

Crossing the Atlantic

The captain of the *Victoria* was **Sebastian del Caño.** He decided not to go back across the Pacific, the way they had come, but to cross the Indian Ocean and find the Cape of Good Hope. The crew now suffered from intense heat and terrible storms. Many more sailors died from starvation and disease.

On 6 September 1552, almost four years after she had set out, the *Victoria* sailed into Seville harbour. The ship was a floating wreck, with torn sails and broken masts. There were only eighteen men on board and all of them were sick. These are the last words of Pigafetta.

"We anchored close to the quayside at Seville and fired a salute with all our guns. Then altogether, coatless and barefooted and with lighted candles, we went to the Shrine of Our Lady of Victory to give thanks. We had sailed 14,460 leagues (69,408km)) and completed the circuit of the world."

The greatest voyage ever undertaken was over.

QUESTIONS

1. Write a paragraph on the early life of Magellan.
2. Answer the following questions about Magellan's ships.
   (a) How many ships were there in Magellan's fleet? (b) What were these ships called? (c) What kind of ships were they? (d) Which ship was the largest? (e) Which ship was the smallest? (f) Which ship did Magellan captain? (g) How many crewmen were there altogether? (h) Why were some captains jealous of Magellan? (i) Which captain did Magellan trust and why?
3. Who was Antonio Pigafetta? Why is he so important to the story of the voyage?
4. Throughout the voyage, Pigafetta describes many interesting things. Read all the extracts from his journal again. Write down which you think is (a) the most interesting and (b) the least interesting entry. Give reasons for your answer.
5. Imagine you had travelled with Magellan's fleet and decided to stay on the Spice Islands. Write a letter home to your family in Spain. In it, tell the story of your voyage with Magellan and explain why you are remaining behind.

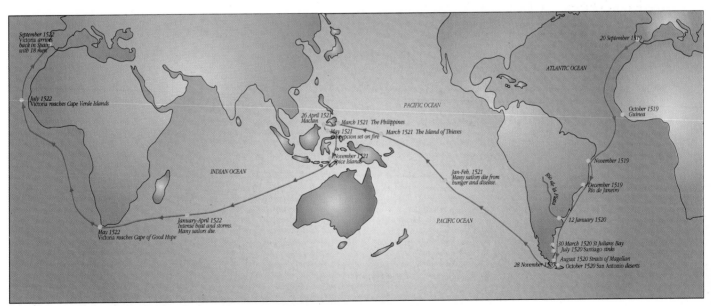

The voyage of Magellan. Look back at the story of his journey around the world and find the places mentioned in the text on this map. Tell what event took place for each date and place on the map.

CHAPTER

44

The Origins of the Reformation

🏛 Dissatisfaction with the Catholic Church

In the year 1500, nearly everyone in western Europe was a Christian. They were all united in one Catholic Church whose head was the pope in Rome.

Many Christians were dissatisfied with the Church, however. Complaints were made about Church leaders - the popes, the bishops and the priests who were supposed to set a good example to the people.

🏛 THE POPES

The trouble with the Catholic Church began at the top. In the fifteenth and early sixteenth centuries, several bad popes had been elected. An account written in the 1490s tells how a Spanish cardinal, Rodrigo Borgia, became Pope Alexander VI.

"Borgia openly bribed many of the cardinals, some with money, others with promises of profitable jobs..."

Another pope, Julius II, even led his armies into battle against rival Italian princes. A report from 1511 says the pope was "employed in person in managing a war started by himself."

◄ *Pope Julius II. He led his armies in battle against rival princes.*

THE BISHOPS

All across Europe, bishops ruled over the Christians who lived in their dioceses. It was a bishop's job to see that the people were being trained in their faith and that priests were doing their jobs properly. However, popes like Alexander VI and Julius II were not likely to encourage good behaviour in their bishops. As a result, abuses grew within the Catholic Church.

THE MOST COMMON ABUSES

▶ **Simony**: Buying or selling positions of power in the Church.

▶ **Absenteeism**: A bishop, abbot or priest living away from the area he was supposed to serve.

▶ **Pluralism**: A bishop, abbot or priest holding more than one Church office at the same time.

▶ **Nepotism**: A person using his position in the Church to promote relatives to jobs, even when they were not suitable.

Looking at the evidence

HERE ARE SOME PEOPLE WHO ABUSED THEIR POWER OR POSITIONS. LOOK AT THE BOX SHOWING THE MOST COMMON ABUSES. TELL WHICH ABUSE EACH OF THESE PEOPLE WAS GUILTY OF.

▶ JEAN DE LORRAINE, A FRENCH NOBLEMAN, WAS APPOINTED A BISHOP AT THE AGE OF THREE.

▶ ALBRECHT OF BRANDENBURG, A GERMAN NOBLE, PAID TO BECOME ARCHBISHOP OF MAINZ. HE WAS ALREADY BISHOP OF TWO OTHER DIOCESES.

▶ KING FERDINAND OF ARAGON GOT APPOINTMENTS IN THE CHURCH FOR HIS ILLEGITIMATE CHILDREN.

▶ IN ENGLAND, CARDINAL WOLSEY WAS BISHOP OF SEVERAL DIOCESES AND THE ABBOT OF MANY MONASTERIES, AS WELL AS THE CHIEF MINISTER OF KING HENRY VIII.

▶ POPE SIXTUS IV MADE HIS NEPHEWS CARDINALS.

▲ *This woodcut illustration from a book published in 1497 is critical of the Church. Cartoons like this were a very powerful way of getting messages across to people who could not read or write. Explain how you think this woodcut gets its message across.*

THE CLERGY

Many monks lived in luxury rather than praying and fasting as the rules of the monastery required. People complained that priests were poorly educated. All Church services were in Latin. But in 1493, a German monk had this to say about his fellow monks.

> *"They lack all education. They understand nothing of what they sing and the Bible is never seen in their hands."*

THE RELIGION OF THE ORDINARY PEOPLE

There were many complaints that ordinary people were ignorant of their religion. It was said that they did not even know simple things like the Lord's Prayer or the Ten Commandments. Instead, they were superstitious, believing in witches and magic spells.

▰ QUESTIONS ▰

1. In your own words, write the meaning of the following: nepotism, absenteeism, simony, pluralism, diocese.
2. Write a paragraph describing three things that were wrong with the Church in 1500.

CHAPTER 45

The Early Life of Martin Luther

🏛 How do we know about Luther ?

Some people decided that it was time to reform the Catholic Church. One of them was **Martin Luther (1483-1546)** Because he became one of the most important men of the sixteenth century, we know a great deal about him. This knowledge comes from many sources.

- ✏ Luther himself wrote hundreds of **books and pamphlets**. He also wrote many **letters** which were collected after his death.
- ✏ Luther's students wrote down many of his conversations and stories about his early life. These writings are known as the ***Table Talk***. Some of these stories were told by Luther himself thirty or forty years after the events.
- ✏ **Other people** wrote about Luther, both during his life and after his death.
- ✏ We have **portraits of Luther** painted by Lucas Cranach and other artists.

🏛 LUTHER'S BOYHOOD

Martin Luther was a German. He was born in Eisleben in Saxony in 1483. Martin's family was very strict, as Luther himself said.

"My mother caned me for stealing a nut... My father once whipped me so that I ran away.... At school I was caned in a single morning fifteen times..."

When he was seventeen, Luther entered the University of Erfurt. There he played the lute and loved music. He discussed things with other students so much that they nicknamed him "the philosopher". His father hoped he would become a lawyer, but Luther had other ideas.

🏛 LUTHER BECOMES A MONK

Martin Luther as a young man studying at the University of Erfurt

In 1505, Luther entered the monastery of the Augustinian friars at Erfurt. Later he explained why he did this.

"When travelling not far from Erfurt, I was so shaken by lightning that I cried out in terror: 'Help me, St Anne, and I will become a monk'. Afterwards I regretted the vow, but I stuck to it. My father was angry..."

After further studies, Luther began to teach at the University of Wittenberg in 1507.

Luther as a monk. What differences do you notice between these two portraits of Luther?

Luther has doubts about the Catholic Church

As a monk, Luther led a simple and holy life. He did all the things that were expected of a monk but he was not happy. Luther was convinced that God was good but that he himself was wicked. He wondered how a fair God could let such a wicked person into heaven.

According to the Catholic Church, people could earn **salvation** (go to heaven) if they believed in Jesus Christ, avoided sin and did good works like praying, fasting and helping the poor. But Luther was not convinced. He wrote:

"I used to confess my sins... yet I doubted and said: 'You did not do that correctly. You were not sorry enough. You left this or that out of your confession.'"

After much prayer and study, Luther found the answer he had been looking for in the Bible. In one of St Paul's letters to the Romans, Luther found the words: "The just man shall live by his faith". He took this to mean that people could only be saved if they put their absolute trust in God's power. Nothing anyone did mattered in the least, only their faith in God. Luther called this idea **salvation through faith alone** (without good works).

This idea comforted Luther. And it would not have mattered much to anyone else but for an event that took place in Europe in 1517.

 ### ☑ QUESTIONS ☑

1. What sources do we have about Luther's life? Which of these sources do you think are the most reliable? Give reasons for your answer.
2. Write a paragraph on Luther's life from his birth in 1483 until 1517.

SOME OF THE QUOTATIONS USED IN THIS CHAPTER COME FROM LUTHER'S *TABLE TALK*. REMEMBER WHEN THEY WERE WRITTEN. SHOULD WE TRUST THE *TABLE TALK* AS A SOURCE FOR LUTHER'S EARLY LIFE? GIVE REASONS FOR YOUR ANSWER.

Activity

CHAPTER
46

The Row over Indulgences in Germany

 ## Indulgences

Early in the sixteenth century, Pope Leo X decided that St Peter's Church in Rome should be replaced by a magnificent new cathedral built in the latest Renaissance style. He issued a special **indulgence** to anyone who performed certain religious duties and contributed money towards the building costs.

WHAT IS AN INDULGENCE?
The Church taught that if people were truly sorry for their sins and did certain good works, they could gain an indulgence. This meant that they themselves or someone they cared about would spend less time in Purgatory suffering for their sins. The pope declared that making a contribution for the rebuilding of St Peter's was one such good work.

A woodcut showing the sale of indulgences. Describe what you see in this picture. Was it made by someone who was for or against the sale? Give reasons for your opinion.

🏛 THE INDULGENCE IN GERMANY

Luther's archbishop, Albrecht of Mainz, also needed money so he made a deal with the pope – Albrecht could keep half the money raised in his diocese for himself and send the other half to Rome.

Albrecht sent a Dominican friar, **John Tetzel**, around his diocese to persuade people to buy the indulgence. Tetzel gave people the impression that giving money was far more important than performing good works. One witness said that Tetzel preached that:

"....so soon as the coin rang in the chest, the soul for whom the money was paid would go straightaway to heaven".

🏛 Luther complains

Tetzel's behaviour worried Luther. He wrote a very humble letter to Archbishop Albrecht.

"With your highness's consent, the papal indulgence for the rebuilding of St Peter's is being carried through the land... I regret the false meaning that the simple folk attach to it... It has gone about, doubtless without your knowledge, that those who purchase the indulgence do not need to repent their sins..."

Luther also drew up *95 Theses* (arguments) against the indulgence. Legend says that he pinned a copy of these theses to the door of All Saints Church in Wittenberg. He hoped that other professors and students would read what he had written and be willing to debate these points.

Luther had no idea of the huge row he was about to start.

John Tetzel selling indulgences. The last lines of the poem say: "As soon as gold in the basin rings/Right then the soul to heaven springs." What does this rhyme say about the sale of indulgences?

⚔ QUESTIONS ⚔

1. What was meant by an indulgence?
2. Have you heard about Albrecht of Mainz before? Does the information in this chapter fit in with what you already know about him?
3. Why did Luther write a letter to Albrecht? What attitude to Albrecht is shown in the way in which Luther writes?

Luther's Career: 1519 – 1546

The spread of Luther's ideas

Luther wrote to Albrecht in Latin. His *95 Theses* were also written in Latin. At the time, Latin was used by educated people all over Europe to write to each other. If Luther's protest had stayed in Latin, only a small number of people would have heard of it. But someone translated his ideas into German, the language of the ordinary people. Printers made copies of them and they began to sell all over Germany.

Ego ſum Papa.

▲ *This woodcut is called "Ego Sum Papa" (I am the pope). Why do you think it was made? Suggest who might have made it. What is it trying to say about the pope?*

Soon, people all over Germany were talking about Luther. Germans who were worried about the abuses in the Catholic Church began to side with Luther.

THE POPE GETS INVOLVED

Albrecht of Mainz complained to Pope Leo X about Luther. Leo agreed with Albrecht and arranged a debate to discuss some of Luther's ideas. This was held at Leipzig during the summer of 1519. On one side was Luther. On the other, representing the pope, was **John Eck**. This is how an eye-witness at the debate described Luther.

> *"He is wonderfully learned in the Bible and he has almost all the texts from memory... In daily life he is cultivated and friendly... He is a joker in company... You would hardly believe he is the man to do such great things unless he is inspired by God."*

Eck was a clever debater and forced Luther to go further than he had before. In the end, Luther openly attacked the power of the pope. The debate ended without anything being settled. It was clear, though, that Luther was moving away from the main beliefs of the Catholic Church. He was becoming what the Church called a **heretic** (a person who teaches false ideas).

POPE LEO X CONDEMNS LUTHER

In 1520, Pope Leo decided to take stronger action against Luther. He issued a papal letter (called a **bull** in Latin). It condemned Luther's teachings and gave him sixty days to withdraw his words. If Luther disobeyed, he knew he would be called a heretic and **excommunicated** (cut off from the Church). This was a terrible decision because heretics were burned alive at the stake. But Luther had made up his mind. He said: "I am not afraid. God's will be done. I am happy to suffer for so noble a cause."

In this woodcut made in 1557, Luther burns a copy of the pope's bull.

In December 1520, a young student watched Luther as he burned a copy of the pope's letter in Wittenberg.

"The next day, Dr Luther warned us it was easy to burn copies of the pope's letter and books... Dr Luther said it would be better to live lonely in a desert than under the laws of the pope."

◤ QUESTIONS ◤

1. How did printing help to spread the message of Luther? (You may want to refer to pages 91-93 for further information.)
2. Why do you think Albrecht and the pope were so anxious to condemn Luther?
3. Why do you think Luther chose to publicly burn a copy of the papal bull in 1520?

Emperor Charles V

In 1519, Charles Hapsburg was crowned Charles V and became the new emperor of Germany. Charles was already king of Spain and ruler of many other parts of Europe. The emperor was a very powerful man who saw himself as the leader of the Christian world. Just after he was elected, Charles wrote:

"The first thing at which I must aim, and the best that God could send me, is peace. I must therefore make great efforts."

Charles V became emperor of Germany in 1519.

To protect the Christian world, Charles thought he had to lead it against the enemies of Christ. One of these enemies, Charles soon came to believe, was Martin Luther.

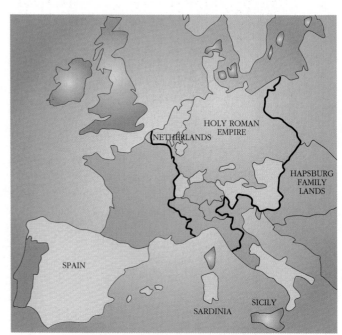

This map shows the lands in Europe ruled over by Charles V. Because he was king of Spain, Charles also ruled over the vast new lands taken over by Spaniards in America and elsewhere.

Luther and Frederick the Wise

After his debate with John Eck at Leipzig, Luther had been very busy writing many pamphlets to explain his ideas. By 1520, almost 30,000 copies of these had been printed. Luther's message was also spread through the woodcuts which were used to illustrate the pamphlets.

One of Luther's supporters was Frederick the Wise, the ruler of Saxony. Frederick was very proud of his new university at Wittenberg. He liked the idea that one of his professors was becoming famous throughout Europe. The pope expected Charles V to arrest and punish Luther, but Charles did not wish to annoy Frederick. The emperor decided to allow Luther to explain his ideas at a **Diet** (assembly) which he was planning to hold at Worms.

▲ *Luther on his way to the Diet of Worms. Some people are trying to block his way. Who do these figures represent?*

🏛 The Diet of Worms: 1521

The **Diet of Worms** met in 1521. All the German rulers were present because they wanted to meet their new emperor. Charles himself promised Luther a safe passage so he could come to defend his ideas.

Cardinal Aleander, the pope's representative, wrote to the pope about the mood in the city during the Diet.

"Now the whole of Germany is in full revolt. Nine-tenths raise the war cry 'Luther!'. Others say 'Death to the cardinals in Rome!'. A while ago at Augsburg, they were selling Luther's picture with a halo..."

Luther appeared before the Diet on 17 April 1521. A large stack of books was placed on the table in front of him. Cardinal Aleander described what happened.

"An official spoke to Luther as follows: 'Martin Luther, the emperor has summoned you hither that you may say whether you have composed these books and to let us know whether you intend to stand by these books...'"

Luther said that the books were indeed his. The next day, he made this courageous statement.

"I stand convinced by the scriptures I have studied. I cannot and I will not take back anything. To act against my conscience is neither safe nor honest. God help me."

The emperor's decision came in a letter the next day.

"According to Luther, the whole of the Christian world has been wrong for a thousand years... I regret having delayed so long against his false beliefs... He is not to preach or tempt the people with his evil teaching. I have decided to move against him as a heretic..."

As a heretic, Luther was declared an outlaw of the empire. The citizens of the empire were not to provide him and his supporters with food or shelter. Rulers were told to seize and burn all of Luther's writings. If Luther was caught, he should be burned as a heretic.

🏛 LUTHER DISAPPEARS (1521-22)

Many Germans did not agree with the emperor's decision to outlaw Luther. This is what the ambassador of Venice wrote.

"He (Luther) has many powerful followers who encourage him and against whom nobody would dare act. His books are sold publicly in Worms, although the pope and the emperor have banned them."

Luther left Worms before Charles declared him a heretic and vanished. Some of his supporters thought he had been killed. The artist Albrecht Dürer wrote in his diary: "...if Luther be dead, who will explain the holy gospel with such clearness?"

▲ *Luther gives communion to Frederick the Wise.*

1. What did Charles V see as his main job as emperor? Do you think he had much time to attend to problems in Germany? Give reasons for your answer.
2. Write a paragraph describing what happened at the Diet of Worms.
3. Why did Frederick the Wise kidnap Luther?
4. How did Luther spend his time at Wartburg?

Lutheranism spreads throughout Germany

At the Diet of Worms, the emperor Charles V had condemned Luther. But many Germans ignored this decision. Lutheran ideas spread quickly, especially in the cities. An English sailor visiting the German city of Bremen in 1520 noted: "The people did follow Luther's works and no Masses were said."

In 1524, a representative of the pope described the city of Nuremberg like this.

> *"The citizens make fun of the pope's rights. In Lent they eat meat openly... They take bread and wine at communion... They consider Martin Luther their light and that, until now, they have been in darkness."*

A DIVIDED GERMANY

By 1526, Germany was divided into Catholic and Lutheran states. For this reason, the punishment of Luther that Charles had ordered at Worms was never carried out. When the pope's order against Luther was issued once again in 1529, the Lutheran rulers **protested**. It is from this we get the word **Protestant**. From then on, the followers of Luther were often called Protestants.

During the next twenty years, Lutherans and Catholics fought each other in a series of civil wars in Germany. In the end, neither side won and a peace was eventually signed at Augsburg in 1555.

The Peace of Augsburg: 1555

The peace of Augsburg accepted that Germany was permanently divided by religion. The following decisions were made.

◢ Two religions were recognised in Germany – Roman Catholicism and Lutheranism.

But Luther was quite safe. Frederick the Wise of Saxony had sent soldiers to kidnap him on his way home from Worms. It was many months before Germans learned that Luther was safe in Frederick's castle at Wartburg.

Luther's translation of the Bible

While he was in hiding at Wartburg, Luther began to translate the New Testament into German. Because he could write in a lively way that ordinary people could understand and remember, his translation became famous. He also wrote hymns with memorable tunes and stirring words. An example is the well-known hymn which is still sung today – "A mighty fortress is our God".

During the year in which Luther lived at the Wartburg, more and more people began to believe as he did. People spoke about a new religion called **Lutheranism** with believers known as **Lutherans**.

■ Each ruler would decide which religion he and his people would follow.

Luther's later years

Luther believed that priests should be allowed to marry. In 1525, he himself married Catherine von Bora, who had been a nun. For the rest of his life, Luther was a family man as well as a religious leader. He was devoted to his wife and children. When one of his daughters died in 1542, he was very upset: "He fell down before the bed on his knees and wept bitterly."

Luther's house was always crowded with his followers and other visitors.

"The house of Luther is occupied by a varied crowd of boys, students, girls, old women and youngsters…".

Surrounded by all this company, Luther was both hospitable and generous. He liked to sing and dance and was popular with everyone who met him.

LUTHER'S DEATH

Martin Luther died of a heart attack on 18 February 1546. The religious wars which raged in Germany in his final years had saddened him greatly. Two days before he died, Luther wrote a short passage from St John's gospel in a friend's book, then added a few words of his own.

" 'If anyone obeys my teaching, he shall never know what it is to die' (St John). How incredible is such a text and yet it is the truth. If a man takes God's Word in full sincerity and believes in it and then dies, he slips away without noticing death and is safe on the other side."

■ QUESTION ■

How do you think Luther felt about the division of Germany into Lutheran and Catholic states and the fighting between them? Give reasons for your answer.

Activity

MAKE OUT A LABELLED TIME CHART WITH ALL THE IMPORTANT DATES IN LUTHER'S LIFE, 1483-1546.

Finding out

FIND A COPY OF LUTHER'S HYMN "A MIGHTY FORTRESS IS OUR GOD". WHAT CAN YOU SAY ABOUT THE WORDS? LISTEN TO A RECORDING OF THE HYMN, IF YOU CAN. WHAT DO YOU THINK OF LUTHER'S TUNE?

Luther's Teachings

Luther's main ideas

When Luther protested about the sale of indulgences in 1517, he was still a Catholic who wanted to reform the Church. However, after much study and reading, he decided that the Church was completely wrong. He developed new ideas which were different from those of the Catholic Church.

These are the main teachings:

1. Luther taught that people could only be saved by having **faith in God**. No amount of good works could help them get into heaven.
2. Everything God wanted of us is in **the Bible**. The Bible alone has the truth. Popes and bishops are not needed to explain it.
3. Because all people could get God's teachings from the Bible, they belonged to the **priesthood of all believers**. Specially consecrated men were not needed to help people get to heaven.

SUBJECT	CATHOLIC BELIEFS	LUTHERAN BELIEFS
Salvation	Both faith *and* good works are needed to get to heaven.	Faith alone is enough.
Finding out about God	People need the advice and guidance of the pope and bishops to understand what God says in the Bible.	People must read and understand the Bible for themselves.
Priests	Priests are specially consecrated men with powers to say Mass, forgive sins and lead people to God.	People can read the Bible and pray to God themselves. The people themselves are priests and only need ministers to preach.
Language	Latin, the language of the priests, is to be used in the Bible and in all Church services.	Since people must read the Bible, it and all Church services must be in the people's own language.
Sacraments	There are 7 sacraments – Baptism, Penance, Eucharist, Confirmation, Marriage, Holy Orders, Blessing of the Dying	Only 2 sacraments are clearly stated in the Bible – Baptism and Eucharist.
Eucharist	Bread and wine are changed into the body and blood of Christ. This is known as **transubstantiation**.	Bread and wine *and* the body and blood of Christ are all present in the Eucharist. This is known as **consubstantiation**.
Saints	Praying to the saints can help Christians reach God.	Since only faith is needed, praying to saints is useless.
Clergy	Priests must not marry.	Priests are allowed to marry, since some of the apostles were married.

🏛 Catholic beliefs and Lutheran beliefs

This table sets out some of Luther's teachings and how they differed from those of the Catholic Church.

◢ QUESTIONS ◣

1. What did Luther say people had to do to get to heaven? How was this different from the Catholic teaching?
2. In your own words, tell how Luther's teaching differed from the Catholic idea on each of the following: (a) the use of Latin; (b) marriage for the clergy.

1. WRITE AN ESSAY ON THE LIFE OF MARTIN LUTHER. YOU SHOULD INCLUDE THESE POINTS: (A) HIS YOUTH; (B) HIS LIFE AS A MONK; (C) LUTHER AND INDULGENCES; (D) THE DIET OF WORMS; (E) LUTHER'S IDEAS; (F) HIS LATER LIFE.
2. LOOK CLOSELY AT THE DRAWINGS OF THE CATHOLIC AND LUTHERAN CHURCHES. MAKE TWO COLUMNS IN YOUR NOTEBOOK. ON ONE SIDE, WRITE DOWN THE FEATURES OF THE CATHOLIC CHURCH. ON THE OTHER, NOTE THE FEATURES OF THE LUTHERAN CHURCH.

CHURCH SERVICES

These illustrations show the main differences between a traditional Catholic service and one organised by the Lutherans.

CHAPTER 49

The Reformation outside Germany

🏛 The spread of Protestantism

In the years after Luther started the Reformation, Protestant ideas spread outside Germany. But not all those who became Protestant followed Luther's ideas. Other reformers preferred to go to the Bible to discover the truth for themselves.

🏛 John Calvin (1509-1564)

One important reformer was the Frenchman, John Calvin. When he was young he studied law in the University of Paris. At first he was a Catholic, but in 1533 he became a Protestant.

John Calvin was a reformer who believed in predestination.

🏛 CALVIN'S TEACHINGS

Calvin set out his ideas in a book, *The Institutes of the Christian Religion*. He accepted many of Luther's ideas but added some of his own.

- Calvin believed that God had chosen some people (**the elect**) to go to heaven. Everyone else would go to hell. It did not matter what a person did in this life; even good works could never change God's decision. This idea is called **predestination**.
- Calvin thought the Church should not be run by bishops. Instead, the people in every parish should elect their own leaders, called **presbyters**, and their own minister. Because of this idea, Calvinism is sometimes called **Presbyterianism**.

🏛 CALVIN IN GENEVA

In 1536, the king of France began to persecute Protestants. Calvin was forced to flee to Geneva in Switzerland. The people there asked him for help in starting their own reformation. Reluctantly, Calvin agreed to stay and by 1541 he was in complete control of the city.

Calvinists attacking a Catholic church in the Netherlands in the late 1570s. Explain what they are doing and why.

Until his death in 1564, Calvin worked to make Geneva the **City of God**. Life there was very strict. Dancing, games and gambling were forbidden. Clothes had to be black or some dark colour. No ornaments or jewellery were allowed. Everyone had to go to church on Sunday and listen to long sermons. The Calvinist churches were very bare – all statues, stained glass windows and bright paintings were removed.

☖ CALVINISM SPREADS

Reformers from all over Europe went to Geneva to see what Calvin was doing. They were impressed. An English visitor wrote:

"Geneva seems to me to be the wonderful miracle of the whole world. Many from all countries come here, not to gather riches, but to live in poverty…"

A Scotsman, **John Knox**, was just as enthusiastic about what he saw.

"Geneva is the most perfect school of Christ that was ever on the earth since the days of the apostles… Religion so sincerely reformed I have not seen in any other place."

John Knox returned to Scotland where he started the Presbyterian Church based on Calvin's teachings. It soon became the main church in that country. Later (as you will read in Section 8 on the Plantations), Scottish people came to Ireland and brought Presbyterianism here. Through the enthusiasm of men like Knox, and through the work of Calvin himself, Calvinism spread more widely than any of the other Protestant faiths.

A portrait of John Knox. What is your impression of him from this picture?

◪ QUESTIONS ◪

1. Where did Calvin come from? Why did he go to Geneva?
2. Explain in your own words the terms predestination and Presbyterianism.
3. What do you think Calvin meant by calling Geneva the "City of God"?
4. Did John Knox admire or disapprove of life in Geneva? Can you explain why he took this attitude?

CHAPTER 50

The Reformation in England and Ireland

King Henry VIII and Luther

When Luther started the Reformation in Germany, King Henry VIII of England wrote a book attacking his ideas. The pope rewarded Henry with the title of *Fidei Defensor* (**Defender of the Faith**). This title is still used by British monarchs and can be seen on all British coins as "FD".

▲ *King Henry VIII was described as "...extremely handsome... He is a good musician and a fine horseman and jouster... He is very religious and hears three Masses a day when he hunts and five on other days..."*

Anne Boleyn, the second wife of Henry VIII. Anne was both lively and fashionable, compared with the older and duller Catherine of Aragon.

The royal divorce

Henry had married his first wife, Catherine of Aragon, in 1509. They had one daughter, Mary, but no sons. In 1527, Henry wanted to divorce Catherine and marry a younger woman, Anne Boleyn. The pope refused Henry permission for a divorce.

In the early 1530s, Henry's chief minister, **Thomas Cromwell**, and the Archbishop of Canterbury, **Thomas Cranmer**, were both secret followers of Luther. They persuaded Henry that, if he made himself head of the Church in England, he would not need the pope's permission to divorce Catherine.

THE ACT OF SUPREMACY: 1534

Henry took the advice of Cromwell and Cranmer. In 1534, he got the English parliament to pass the **Act of Supremacy**. This said that Henry was now "Supreme Head on earth of the Church of England". All bishops, priests, judges and other officials had to take an **Oath of Supremacy**, saying that they accepted Henry as head of the Church. Those who refused were executed. Among them was **Sir Thomas More** who had been one of Henry's chief ministers.

▲ *Thomas Cranmer, the Archbishop of Canterbury, was a follower of Luther who persuaded Henry VIII to pass the Act of Supremacy in 1534.*

Henry now divorced Catherine and married Anne Boleyn. But they did not have a son either, only one daughter, Elizabeth. After this disappointment, Henry also grew tired of Anne. He accused her of being unfaithful and had her executed. He then married Jane Seymour, who died giving birth to his only son, Edward. Henry married three more times but had no more children.

Henry's only son, Edward VI, was a sickly boy who ruled for only six years. He was succeeded by Mary, the daughter of Henry and Catherine of Aragon. Mary was queen of England for only five years.

Thomas More refused to take the Oath of Supremacy. He bids a sorrowful farewell to his wife before his execution.

Queen Elizabeth I ruled England for forty-five years. She was a powerful woman who succeeded in making England a Protestant country.

The Reformation in England

Although he was head of the Church of England, Henry did not accept Luther's beliefs. However, he allowed Thomas Cromwell to take some steps which led towards Protestantism.

- All the monasteries were closed down. The king took over their lands and riches. Henry soon sold the land to pay for foreign wars.
- The Bible was translated from Latin into English. Ordinary people could now read the word of God for themselves.

ENGLAND BECOMES PROTESTANT

After Henry's death, the nine-year-old Edward became king. His uncle, who was a Protestant, ruled in his name. At this time, Thomas Cranmer wrote *The Book of Common Prayer* which was to be used in all churches. It contained many of the ideas of Luther and Calvin.

Edward died young. Catherine of Aragon's daughter, Mary, tried to bring back Catholic ways, but she was queen for only five years.

The next queen was Elizabeth, Anne Boleyn's daughter and a Protestant. She had a long reign, from 1558 until 1603. She appointed men as bishops who had visited Geneva and Germany and who believed in the Reformation. During the reign of Elizabeth I, England became a Protestant state.

The Reformation in Ireland

Henry VIII was also king of Ireland. He wanted Ireland to follow the religious changes which had been made in England. In 1536, the Dublin parliament passed an Act of Supremacy, just like the English one. It made Henry Supreme Head of the **Church of Ireland**. Henry also closed down the Irish monasteries and ordered the Bible and all prayers to be in English.

In Ireland at that time, most people spoke Irish. English was only spoken in the towns and in the small area around Dublin, known as the **Pale**. The Bible in English made little difference to most Irish people. The English, as we shall see in the next section, were more interested in conquering the Irish than preaching to them in their own language. For many years, only a few people in Ireland accepted the Church of Ireland.

The reformers who influenced most Irish people were Catholics, not Protestants. By the 1560s, the popes and the Catholic Church had begun their own reforms called the **Catholic Reformation** or the **Counter-Reformation**. Irishmen who were influenced by the Catholic Reformation in Europe returned to Ireland. They preached to the people in Irish, their own language, and won them for Catholicism.

◢ QUESTIONS ◣

1. Why did Henry VIII break with the pope in Rome?
2. Write a paragraph on the Reformation in England.
3. Why did Ireland not become Protestant like England?

WRITE A REPORT ON THE SIX WIVES OF HENRY VIII. LOOK FOR MORE INFORMATION IN LIBRARY BOOKS.

Finding out

Three of Henry's six wives. Jane Seymour, the mother of Edward VI, died in childbirth. Anne of Cleves was divorced in 1540 after a marriage lasting only six months. Henry's last wife, Katherine Parr, outlived Henry.

CHAPTER 51

The Counter-Reformation

The Council of Trent

In 1534, Paul III became the pope. He was the first pope who was seriously interested in reforming the Church. Paul III decided to call a Council of all the bishops to deal with abuses (page 129). It took ten years before the Council met in Trent, a small town on the border between Italy and the German Empire.

The **Council of Trent** met three times between 1545 and 1563. The last meetings were attended by bishops from all over the Catholic world.

The bishops at the Council of Trent decided what the Catholic Church's view should be on all the points which Luther, Calvin and others had argued about.

The Council of Trent was called by Pope Paul III to deal with abuses in the Catholic Church. No pope ever attended any of its meetings, however. Can you think of any reasons for this?

ATTACK ON ABUSES

The Council of Trent issued new rules about how the Church was to be run. These were intended to cure abuses.

1. No one was to pay for any office in the Church.
2. No one was to be appointed bishop unless he deserved it.
3. Every bishop was to live permanently in his own diocese.
4. A bishop was to visit every parish in his diocese at least once every three years to see that priests were doing their duty.
5. Every diocese was to have a school, called a **seminary**, where young men would be educated and trained as priests.
6. The pope was to draw up a **catechism** containing the main teachings of the Church so that Catholics could learn them.
7. A list of books, called the **Index**, which Catholics were forbidden to read, was drawn up.

Ignatius Loyola and the Jesuits

In 1540 a new order of priests, the **Society of Jesus** or the **Jesuits**, was formed by Ignatius Loyola, a former Spanish soldier.

The pope gave the Jesuits the task of spreading the Catholic faith by preaching, teaching and works of charity. In Europe, the Jesuits set out to win back people who had changed over to Protestantism. They also spread Catholicism to remote parts of the world. Some worked among the native people in America. **Francis Xavier** went as far away as Japan.

THE JESUITS IN IRELAND

Young men from Ireland went to the Jesuit schools and colleges in Europe. When trained as priests, they returned to Ireland and preached the teachings of the Council of Trent. These priests had the advantage over English Protestant reformers in Ireland because they spoke the Irish language. Because of their activities, Ireland remained largely a Catholic country.

FIND OUT MORE ABOUT IGNATIUS LOYOLA,
FRANCIS XAVIER AND THE JESUITS. CHOOSE
SOMETHING ABOUT ONE OF THEM WHICH
INTERESTS YOU AND WRITE A REPORT OF YOUR
FINDINGS.

Finding out

Heretics were burned at the stake during the Inquisition.

THE INQUISITION

In Catholic countries in Europe, the Church set up a special group to deal with heretics. It was known as the **Inquisition**. It arrested Protestants and Catholics suspected of disagreeing with the Church. Torture was often used to get them to give up their ideas. Anyone who refused was burned at the stake. One victim was the great Italian scientist, Galileo (see page 98).

A DIVIDED EUROPE

By 1600, Europe was divided into Protestant areas and Catholic areas. You can see these areas on the map.

In some countries, civil wars broke out between Catholics and Protestants. Violence caused distrust, and it was not until the twentieth century that the different Christian religions began to meet and understand each other.

QUESTIONS

1. What was done by the Council of Trent? Why was it important for the Catholic Church?
2. Look at the table of rules drawn up by the Council of Trent (page 145). In each case, say which abuse the rule was trying to correct.
3. The Jesuits were important for the success of the Counter-Reformation. Why do you think this was?
4. Why did Ireland remain a Catholic country?

Catholic
Lutheran
Calvinist
Other Protestants
Orthodox
Muslim

1. FIND OUT MORE ABOUT THE INQUISITION AND GALILEO.
2. TRY TO GUESS THE NAMES OF SOME WRITERS OF THE TIME WHOSE BOOKS WOULD HAVE APPEARED ON THE INDEX OF BANNED BOOKS. DISCUSS WHY THESE BOOKS MAY HAVE BEEN BANNED.

Finding out

Europe's main religions early in the seventeenth century. Comment on what this map tells you about the success or failure of the Reformation.

CHAPTER

🏛 The people

Around 1500 – four hundred and fifty years after the Normans came to Ireland – there were two different groups of people living in the country:

▱ The **Gaeli. Irish** were the descendants of the Celts. They spoke Irish.

▱ The **Anglo-Irish** were the descendants of the Normans. Because many of them had married into Gaelic families over the years, they spoke both Irish and English.

LOOK AT THE MAP SHOWING THE MAIN GAELIC AND ANGLO-IRISH FAMILIES. MAKE A LIST OF THE LEADING FAMILIES IN EACH GROUP.

Looking at the evidence

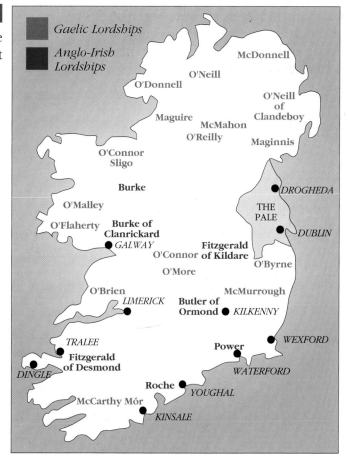

Gaelic Lordships

Anglo-Irish Lordships

McDonnell

O'Neill

O'Donnell

O'Neill of Clandeboy

Maguire

McMahon

O'Reilly

Maginnis

O'Connor Sligo

Burke

DROGHEDA

O'Malley

THE PALE

O'Flaherty

Burke of Clanrickard

DUBLIN

GALWAY

O'Connor

Fitzgerald of Kildare

O'Byrne

O'More

O'Brien

McMurrough

LIMERICK

Butler of Ormond

KILKENNY

TRALEE

WEXFORD

Power

Fitzgerald of Desmond

WATERFORD

DINGLE

Roche

YOUGHAL

McCarthy Mór

KINSALE

🔺 *Gaelic and Anglo-Irish lordships in the late fifteenth century*

Finding out

LOOK AT THE MAP ON PAGE 147. TRY TO FIND OUT WHICH FAMILIES WERE MOST IMPORTANT IN YOUR PART OF THE COUNTRY.

Looking at the evidence

LOOK AT THE MAP OF THE PALE. EXPLAIN HOW THE PALESMEN USED NATURAL FEATURES IN THE LANDSCAPE TO MAKE A STRONG BORDER BETWEEN THEM AND THE REST OF THE COUNTRY. ▼ ▼

The Pale

Ever since the arrival of the Normans in the twelfth century, kings of England claimed to rule Ireland as well. They called themselves **Lords of Ireland**. Their representative in Ireland was the **lord deputy** who lived in Dublin Castle. The area around Dublin which obeyed the lord deputy was called the **Pale**. Outside the Pale, only citizens in towns like Waterford, Wexford, Kilkenny, Galway, Limerick and Drogheda were loyal to the king and his lord deputy. In Gaelic and Anglo-Irish areas, the king's government had no control.

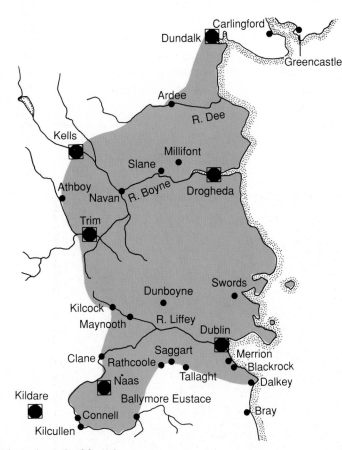

▲ *The Pale in the fifteenth century*

The Tudor conquest

In 1485, the Tudor family won the English throne. After that, Tudor kings and queens sought to gain full control of Ireland. One of them, Henry VIII, gave himself a new title in 1541 – **King of Ireland**.

◄ *In 1541, King Henry VIII proclaimed that he was King of Ireland.*

Since the Gaelic and Anglo-Irish lords would not accept being ruled by English kings and queens, Tudor monarchs sent armies to Ireland to defeat them. When English soldiers had won control of an area, English settlers were brought in to 'plant' (to live in) an area. This practice was known as **plantation**.

The **planters** spoke English, followed English laws and practised English customs. When England became a Protestant country during the Reformation, the English government hoped the planters would bring Protestantism to Ireland too. If Ireland became more like England, they believed it would be much easier to govern it.

THE PROBLEM OF LAOIS-OFFALY

During the 1540s, the Pale was raided frequently by the Gaelic families like the O'Mores, O'Connors and O'Dempseys of Laois and Offaly. These raiders stole the cattle of the Palesmen and burned their houses. When the English lord deputy tried to follow them with soldiers, they easily escaped into the mountains, bogs and forests.

This picture was drawn in 1616. It was called "Wild Irish Man". What do the picture and its title say about the artist's attitude towards the Irish?

Looking at the evidence

AN ENGLISHMAN NAMED JOHN DERRICKE CAME TO IRELAND WITH THE LORD DEPUTY IN THE 1560S. HE WROTE A BOOK CALLED *THE IMAGE OF IRELAND*. HIS WORK GIVES US THE BEST INFORMATION WE HAVE ABOUT IRELAND AT THE TIME. THE PICTURE BELOW AND THE POEM DESCRIBE AN ATTACK BY THE IRISH ON A FARMER IN THE PALE.

"THEY SPOIL AND BURN AND BEAR AWAY AS FIT
  OCCASION SERVE,
AND THINK THE GREATER ILL THEY DO, THE
  GREATER PRAISE DESERVE.
THEY PASS NOT FOR THE POOR MAN'S CRY NOR
  YET RESPECT HIS TEARS,
BUT RATHER JOY TO SEE THE FIRE TO FLASH
  ABOUT HIS EARS. . .
AND THUS BEREAVING HIM OF HOUSE, OF
  CATTLE AND OF STORE,
THEY DO RETURN TO THE WOOD FROM
  WHENCE THEY CAME BEFORE."

STUDY THE PICTURE AND THE VERSE. THEN SAY WHOSE SIDE YOU THINK DERRICKE WAS ON. GIVE REASONS FOR YOUR ANSWER. HOW DOES THIS AFFECT THE WAY YOU FEEL ABOUT THE PICTURE AND THE POEM?

🏛 THE PLANTATION OF LAOIS-OFFALY

These raids went on for many years. To defend themselves, the English built forts and manned them with soldiers, but this proved to be very costly. During the reign of Queen Mary (1553-58), the English government decided to start the policy of plantation.

The English army first drove the Irish clans out of Laois and Offaly. Laois was renamed Queen's County and its fort became Maryborough. Offaly was called King's County and its fort was named Philipstown. This was because Mary was married to King Philip II of Spain.

The government invited people from the Pale and from England to settle in (**plant**) the captured lands. Rents were low, which encouraged people to come. The government thought that these new settlers would be more peaceful than the Irish and that they would not attack the Pale.

🏛 Did the government achieve its aims in Laois and Offaly?

List A gives some of the plans the English government had laid down for the plantation of Laois and Offaly. List B sets out some of the facts we know about the results.

List A THE GOVERNMENT'S PLANS	List B WHAT ACTUALLY HAPPENED
1. 160 separate grants of land were to be made to planters.	1. Only 80 land grants were made to planters.
2. Most land was to go to Englishmen and the loyal Anglo-Irish.	2. Three sorts of people got land – Palesmen, soldiers who had served in the army (who were called **servitors**), and native Irish of the area.
3. The expelled Gaelic families were only to get land near the River Shannon.	3. The size of grants varied from 25 acres to 3,302 acres.
4. No planter was to get more than 180 acres. No Irishman was to get more than 120 acres.	4. Large grants of land went to the Gaelic Irish.
5. English language and customs were to replace Irish ones.	5. The Irish language and customs remained in use.

▨ QUESTIONS ▨

1. Look at lists A and B. Write a paragraph on the main differences between these lists.
2. Was the plantation of Laois-Offaly a success or failure? Give at least three reasons for your answer.

CHAPTER 53

The Desmond Rebellion in Munster

By the 1570s, Henry VIII's daughter, Elizabeth I was queen of England. She was a Protestant who wanted to make Ireland a Protestant country. But most Irish people were Catholics. They did not like Elizabeth's Protestant policy.

In Munster, the Fitzgeralds of Desmond were the leading Anglo-Irish family. One of the Fitzgeralds, James Fitzmaurice, went to the pope to look for help against English rule. The pope sent a small army to Ireland. When it arrived, the earl of Desmond rebelled against the queen, but he and his allies were soon defeated. English armies destroyed much of Munster. About 30,000 people died, many in the famine which followed the war.

Queen Elizabeth I was afraid that her great enemy in Europe, King Philip II of Spain, would send troops to help the Catholic Irish. She decided a plantation of English Protestant settlers would make Munster a safer and more loyal place.

▲ *Queen Elizabeth I decided to start a plantation in Munster.*
Give two reasons why she did this

Planning the Plantation of Munster

All the land of the earl of Desmond and his followers was confiscated. Surveyors and map makers were sent to Munster to draw up the very first maps we have of Ireland.

The following plan for the plantation of Munster was ready in 1586.

1. All the good land was divided into twenty estates of 12,000 acres each.
2. Men who "undertook" to follow the rules laid down by the government were given land. They were called **undertakers**. The undertakers had to follow these rules.
   (a) Undertakers had to remove all Irish people from their estates.
   (b) Undertakers had to bring to Ireland:
      ▰ 91 English tenants who would get several hundred acres each.
      ▰ 71 household servants
      ▰ carpenters, stonemasons and other craftsmen
      ▰ sheep, cattle and horses.
   (c) Each undertaker had to keep three horse soldiers and six foot soldiers. Each tenant had to equip one foot soldier.
   (d) Each undertaker had to pay a rent to the government.

WAS THE MUNSTER PLANTATION A SUCCESS?

Here are some facts about the Munster Plantation which will help you answer this question.
1. "There are 5,000 Englishmen there, besides women and children" (from a report written in 1597).
2. Undertakers took Irish tenants because it cost less than bringing over English tenants. Irish tenants would also pay higher rents.
3. Undertakers got a rent of $2\frac{1}{2}$p per acre in 1589 and $12\frac{1}{2}$p per acre in 1594.

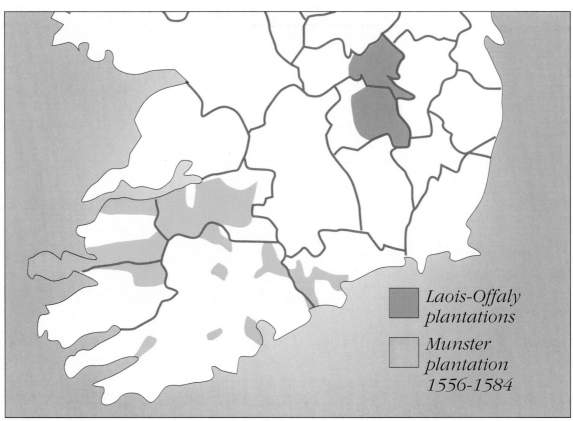

Laois-Offaly
plantations

Munster
plantation
1556-1584

◣ *The Tudor Plantations: Laois-Offaly and Munster*

◸ QUESTIONS ◹

1. Why was there a plantation in Munster in the 1580s?
2. Look at the plantation plan on page 151.
   (a) How many acres of good land were to be planted?
   (b) Explain why all Irish were to be removed.
   (c) If each tenant and servant brought his family with him (family average = 5), for how many settlers was the government hoping?
3. "On the whole, the plantation of Munster was a success." Do you agree or disagree with this statement? Write a paragraph giving reasons for your opinion.
4. Exports from Munster of wood, wool, animal hides and tallow wax to make candles increased greatly between 1589 and 1598.
5. Undertakers did not bother to keep armed men.
6. The government received rents totalling £2000 a year from Munster.

CHAPTER 54

The Beginning of the Plantation of Ulster

The conquest of Ulster

By 1590, the only part of Ireland still ruled by Gaelic lords was Ulster. The Ulster lords were headed by Hugh O'Neill, earl of Tyrone. O'Neill's struggle with the armies of Queen Elizabeth I is known as the **Nine Years' War** (1594-1603).

O'Neill asked the Spanish king for help, but when a Spanish army arrived in 1601, it landed at Kinsale in Co. Cork. O'Neill and his followers marched across Ireland in the depths of winter to join up with the Spaniards. On Christmas Eve in 1601, the army of the English lord deputy, Lord Mountjoy, defeated O'Neill at the **Battle of Kinsale**. The Spaniards surrendered and the Gaelic chiefs finally made peace with the English in 1603.

Lord Mountjoy. His victory at the Battle of Kinsale led to the Flight of the Earls.

Queen Elizabeth I died in 1603. Her cousin, the king of Scotland, became King James I of England, Scotland and Ireland. Irish lords like O'Neill did not trust his government and in 1607 they fled to the continent with their families. This is known as the **Flight of the Earls**.

Plans for a plantation

After the Flight of the Earls, King James decided on a plantation for Ulster. He confiscated the land of the earls who had fled Ireland. It amounted to six counties – Armagh, Coleraine (later renamed Derry), Cavan, Donegal, Fermanagh and Tyrone. Only land belonging to the Protestant Anglican Church was not confiscated. Surveys of the counties were made and maps were produced.

After these surveys, detailed plans for plantation were printed in London. These were known as **articles** and were given to people interested in planting land in Ulster.

THE PLANTERS

Three groups of people were to be given grants of land in Ulster – English and Scottish undertakers, servitors, and Irishmen "of good merit". The grants and duties of each group were as follows.

- **English and Scottish undertakers** – They undertook to bring English or Scottish settlers to Ulster. They were not to have Irish tenants on their land. Their rent was £5.33 per 1000 acres. An undertaker with 1000 acres or more had to build a walled enclosure called a **bawn**. An undertaker with 1500 acres or more had to build a castle or brick house as well.

▰ **Servitors** – They were soldiers who had fought against the Irish. Their conditions were almost the same as for the undertakers, but servitors were allowed to have Irish tenants. Their rent was £8 per 1000 acres.

▰ **Irishmen "of good merit"** – About 10% of confiscated land went to Irishmen who were trusted by the government. The rent was £10.66 per 1000 acres. Conditions for them were the same as for the other groups.

CONDITIONS
TO BE OBSERVED
by the *Brittiſh* Vndertakers
of the Eſcheated Lands
in Vlster,
Conſiſting in three principall
points, *Viz.*

1. What the Brittiſh Vndertakers ſhall haue of his Maieſties gift.
2. What the ſaid Vndertakers ſhall for their parts performe.
3. In what manner the ſame performance ſhall be.

¶ *Imprinted at London by* Robert Barker, Printer to the Kings moſt Excellent Maieſtie.
ANNO DOM. 1610.

◣ *This is the title page from the articles of plantation. When was it produced? Where was it printed? What three reasons are given for publishing the articles? Rewrite the title page in modern English.*

QUESTIONS

1. What events led to the Ulster Plantation?
2. Explain in your own words what is meant by these words: undertaker, servitor, bawn, Irishmen of "good merit".
3. Give two reasons why the English and Scottish undertakers had to pay lower rents than the other two groups.
4. Why did the government want the planters to build bawns and castles?

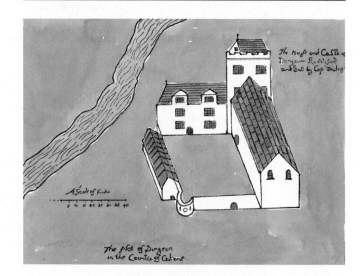

◣ *These drawings were made in 1611. Picture A is a castle and bawn built from the ruins of O'Cahan's Castle at Dungiven. Picture B is Enniskillen Castle. Study the drawings and then answer these questions.*

1. *In picture A, locate the part which was the original O'Cahan Castle. Give reasons for your choice.*
2. *Where is the bawn in picture A?*
3. *Look at picture B. Do you think this castle was newly built or adapted from an older building? Give reasons for your opinion.*
4. *Mention at least two things which these castles have in common.*

The London Guilds and the Native Irish in Ulster

🏛 The London Guilds

King James I wanted to interest rich men in "planting" Ulster. At this time, the richest men in the kingdom were the merchants of London. Some of them were already considering sending people to settle in Virginia, a new colony in North America.

King James persuaded the merchant guilds in London to plant an entire county in Ulster. The county given to them was Coleraine, which was renamed Londonderry in their honour.

The London guilds formed a new company called the **Irish Society**. It was responsible for developing the land of the guilds. It divided the land among the London companies and began to lay out a new city called Londonderry. This was on the site of an old monastery which had been established by Columcille at Derry.

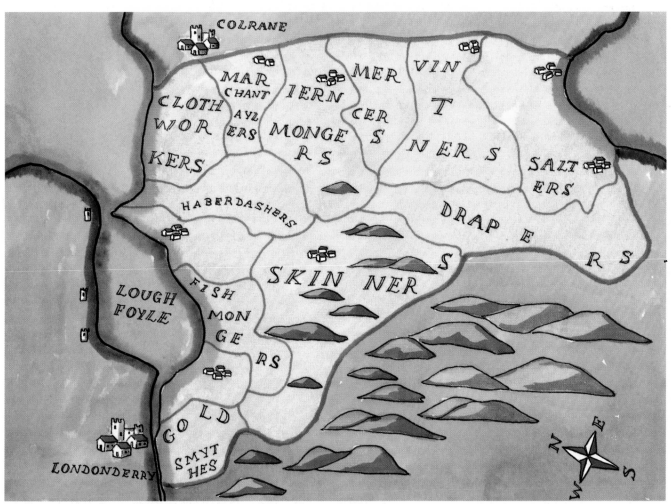

This map was made in 1622. It shows the areas given to different merchant companies. Make a list of these companies.

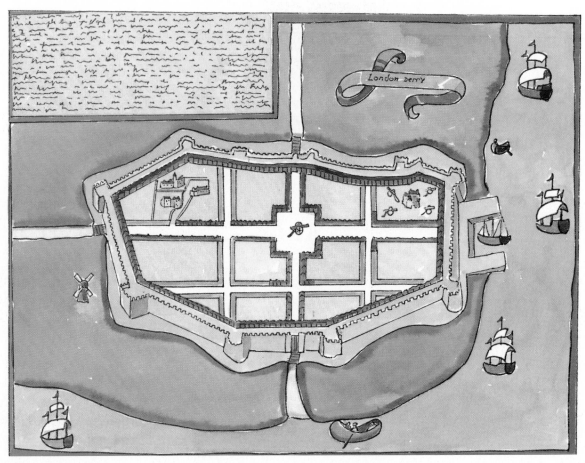

▲ *This is an early map of the newly laid-out city of Londonderry. What is the central feature of the city? Would Londonderry have been easy to defend or not? Give reasons for your answer.*

The native Irish in the plantation

All the undertakers had to drive the Gaelic Irish from their land. The Irish could remain on any other land. This meant that the Irish were expelled from large areas.

Looking at the evidence ▼
▼

WAS THE GOVERNMENT'S PLAN FOR THE REMOVAL OF THE IRISH SUCCESSFUL? READ THIS REPORT WRITTEN IN 1624, FOURTEEN YEARS AFTER THE ULSTER PLANTATION BEGAN. WHAT DOES IT TELL YOU?

"WE FIND THAT PATRICK O'CONELAN, MURTAGH O'CONELAN, DONAL O'CONELAN, PHILOMIE O'DUEIN AND EDMUND OG MCCANN DO RESIDE UPON THE TOWN OF CLONCORRE AND PASTURE THEIR COWS AT A PENNY A WEEK FOR EACH COW AND TWO PENCE A WEEK FOR EACH HORSE... FROM MR JOHN WRENCH WHO HATH THE LAND IN LEASE."

QUESTIONS

1. What two names are now given to the city founded by the London merchants?
2. Name one major change which the merchants and their settlers brought to the county they planted.

Looking at the evidence

1. WHAT IS THE NAME OF THE UNDERTAKER IN THE 1624 REPORT? HAD HE ANY IRISH ON HIS LANDS? GIVE REASONS FOR YOUR ANSWER.
2. SUGGEST TWO REASONS WHY AN UNDERTAKER MIGHT BREAK THE RULES AND ALLOW IRISH TENANTS ON HIS LAND.

The Success of the Ulster Plantation

The Plantation of Ulster started in 1610. We have a lot of evidence about how things went over the next twenty years. Our main sources are:

- ☑ **Surveys** carried out by the government
- ☑ **Letters** and **reports** sent by the settlers
- ☑ **Maps** and **drawings** made by the settlers

Let us look at some of these sources to see if the Ulster Plantation was a success.

SOURCE A

These quotations come from a survey carried out in the Strabane area in 1611.

"Sir George Hamilton... is resident there with his wife and family. He hath built a good house of timber for the present... He hath brought over some families of Scots who have built them a bawn and good timber houses. They have 80 cows among them."

"Sir John Drommond with 1000 acres... appeared in person, took possession and hath one Scotsman on his land."

"James Clapham with 2000 acres... is resident... and prepares to people his land. He hath a competent store of arms in readiness."

"Sir Claude Hamilton with 2000 acres appeared not, nor any for him. Neither is any work done."

SOURCE B

Another survey in 1613 dealt with the same settlers.

"Sir George Hamilton... set up near his house three score Irish houses or cabins...for his tenants who are estated according to the conditions. They have good stores of cattle and are well furnished with arms. Limestone and other materials are ready for the structures required by the articles of plantation."

"Sir John Drommond hath his lady with his stock and servants in the country. Nine or ten households are already settled on the land with their goods and cattle. Some quantity of limestone and timber is prepared for his building."

"James Clapham hath a sufficient house and a bawn he found ready-built. There are not yet above half his number of tenants on the land... For his backwardness in the performance of his conditions, he hath recourse to his majesty's mercy."

"Sir Claude Hamilton hath a rough portion. There are few or no tenants on his land and nothing yet built."

▲ *Here are some drawings made at the time of the plantation. They show a number of houses and other buildings. What does the writing below the pictures tell you?*

SOURCE C

In 1622, a Scottish undertaker wrote this description of his estate.

"Firstly there is a (large) stone bawn... Upon the east side of the said bawn is built a stone house..."

This seems to be very like the bawn pictured on page 154.

SOURCE D

This report comes from a survey of Strabane in 1622.

"There is a strong castle of stone and lime which stands within the town of Strabane. There are above 100 dwelling houses... 120 British families are able to make 200 able men with shot and pike. There is also a court house, a market cross... and a watermill built with stone, with a bridge over the water."

🏛 Different communities in Ulster

The Ulster Plantation was more successful than the other Irish plantations. It was the only one in which many ordinary farmers and craftsmen came from England and Scotland to settle in Ireland. Their descendants and the descendants of the native Irish live side by side in Ulster today.

In 1610, most people in England belonged to the Anglican Church, while most Scots were Presbyterians, or followers of the teachings of John Calvin. The planters who came to Ireland brought these religions with them. Today, there are more Anglicans and Presbyterians in Ulster than in any other part of Ireland. The native Irish were Catholics so religion has remained the main mark of division between different peoples in Ulster to this day.

At the same time as settlers came to Ulster, others were going to North America. A comparison between the two areas gives us the following figures.

- ◪ Settler population in Ulster in 1630 = 30,000.
- ◪ Settler population in all British areas of North America in 1630 = 5000.
- ◪ Londonderry was about the same size as Boston, but had a bigger population.
- ◪ Strabane had a population greater than New York up to the mid seventeenth century.

◪ QUESTIONS ◪

1. Which was a more important area for British settlement in 1630, Ulster or America? Give reasons for your answer.
2. In which part of Ireland were there many Protestants? Explain how this came about.

---

1. LOOK CLOSELY AT SOURCES A – D ON PAGES 157-158. NOW WRITE THREE PARAGRAPHS ON THE PROGRESS OF THE PLANTATION. WAS IT A SUCCESS? USE EVIDENCE TO BACK UP WHAT YOU WRITE.
2. THERE ARE SEVERAL REFERENCES IN THE SOURCES ABOVE TO LIME AND LIMESTONE. WHAT WAS THIS AND FOR WHAT WAS IT USED?

Looking at the evidence

CHAPTER 57

The Cromwellian Settlement

🏛 Another rebellion, another plantation

In 1641, the native Irish rose up against the planters in Ulster. Many planters were killed or driven from their estates. In 1642, a civil war broke out in Britain between King Charles I and parliament. Parliament won and King Charles I was executed in 1649. Oliver Cromwell, the leader of the parliamentary side, then led an army to Ireland and reconquered the whole country by 1653. Cromwell decided to confiscate all land still held by Catholics and give it to new Protestant landlords. This was known as the **Cromwellian Settlement**.

🏛 THE CIVIL SURVEY

Cromwell's government needed to know how much land there was in Ireland. They hired **William Petty** to survey the country and make new maps. The maps produced by Petty were the most detailed ones in existence until Ordnance Survey maps appeared in the nineteenth century. Petty also produced a detailed written report on the land, the landowners and the wealth of the country.

▶ *Oliver Cromwell*

Looking at the evidence

TRY TO DISCOVER WHETHER ANY OF THE CIVIL SURVEY FIGURES AND THE MAPS MADE BY WILLIAM PETTY ARE AVAILABLE FOR YOUR PART OF THE COUNTRY. IF THEY ARE, WHAT DO YOU LEARN FROM THEM?

🏛 Confiscation and transplantation

Cromwell ordered that the leaders of the recent revolts against the English were to lose their lands – and their lives. People who could not prove their loyalty to parliament lost up to two-thirds of their property. In theory, both Catholics and Protestants were affected, but in practice, only Catholics lost their land.

In 1652, the **Act of Settlement** ordered all those whose land had been confiscated to be **transplanted** to Connacht or to Clare. Cromwell said they could all go "to hell or to Connacht". West of the Shannon, the expelled landowners were not to get land within a mile of the sea.

After the Irish landlords had moved to Connacht,

Cromwell had six million acres of land to give to English planters. Some of them were soldiers who had fought in his armies. Others were speculators who bought up cheap land. Sir William Petty got a huge estate in Kerry in this way.

Cromwell was not able to move the ordinary farmers and labourers west of the Shannon. They continued to farm the land but now they paid their rents to the new Protestant landlords. For most of them, the change in ownership of land probably made very little difference.

LAND AND RELIGION

There are several reasons why British governments planted Ireland. One was to gain money. Planters paid more rents to the government than the Irish lords had. But religion was probably the main one.

British governments in the sixteenth and seventeenth centuries did not trust Irish Catholic landlords. They thought they would plot with Catholic rulers in Europe to overthrow Protestant rule in Ireland. Therefore in one plantation after another, they removed Catholic landlords and replaced them with Protestants whom they believed they could trust.

The chart shows how the ownership of land in Ireland changed between 1600 (before the Ulster Plantation) and 1700 (after the Cromwellian Settlement).

QUESTIONS

1. What events led to the Cromwellian Settlement in the 1650s?
2. Explain what is meant by the Civil Survey.
3. What did the Act of Settlement (1652) decide to do with the land of Ireland?

Looking at the evidence

YOU HAVE NOW STUDIED FOUR PLANTATIONS IN IRISH HISTORY – THE PLANTATION OF LAOIS-OFFALY IN THE 1550S, THE PLANTATION OF MUNSTER IN THE 1580S, THE ULSTER PLANTATION AFTER 1609, AND THE CROMWELLIAN SETTLEMENT IN THE 1650S.

1. WHICH OF THESE PLANTATIONS WAS THE MOST SUCCESSFUL? USE EVIDENCE TO SUPPORT YOUR ANSWER.
2. WHAT WERE THE MAJOR EFFECTS OF THESE PLANTATIONS ON IRELAND?

	CATHOLIC OWNERSHIP OF LAND	PROTESTANT OWNERSHIP OF LAND
1600	90%	10%
1640	60%	40%
1700	15%	85%

Land ownership in Ireland between 1600 and 1700. Comment on what this tells you about the effects of the plantations.

CHAPTER

58

Governments in the Eighteenth Century

Monarchs in Europe

Since the Middle Ages, countries in Europe had been ruled by **monarchs** – kings or queens, emperors or empresses.

King Louis XVI of France was an **absolute monarch**. He had complete power over his people and could do as he wished. He did not have to ask permission from anyone else if he wanted to appoint a government minister, pass a new law or collect a new tax. Louis believed that he had been chosen by God to rule France. This belief was known as the **divine right of kings**.

LIMITED MONARCHY

In 1760, most rulers in Europe were absolute monarchs. The only exception was Britain's King George III (see pages 164-171). Before he could raise a tax or pass a law, King George had to seek the agreement of his parliament. Parliament also chose one of its members to be **prime minister** who would help the king to run the country.

Britain's King George III (1760-1820)

THE AGE OF REVOLUTION

LORDS AND COMMONS

The British parliament was divided into two parts. The noblemen sat in the **House of Lords**. The lords were very wealthy men who owned large estates with thousands of acres of land. The members of parliament (MPs) sat in the **House of Commons**. MPs were elected by men who owned smaller estates or farms. Most of the ordinary people had no right to vote and no say in how their country was run. Women could not vote at all.

The place of religion

Ever since the Reformation (see Section 7), most governments in Europe had allowed only one official or "established" religion in their countries. All the people were supposed to belong to this official church, and those who belonged to other religions were often persecuted.

The Enlightenment

The eighteenth century is sometimes called the **Age of Reason** or the **Enlightenment**. During this time, people began to question everything. If a baby died, if an earthquake destroyed a city, or if a house was struck by lightning, they wanted to know why. They were no longer satisfied if someone said it was the will of God, or that a witch had put an evil spell on them. People now wanted a reasonable, scientific explanation for things.

During the Enlightenment, people also wondered about the best way to govern a country.

- Did kings really get their powers from God as they claimed?
- Was an absolute monarchy the best form of government, or should the laws be made by elected parliaments?
- Should people be persecuted because of their religion?

Here are some of the men who asked these questions.

JOHN LOCKE (1632-1704)

In his book, *Treatise of Civil Government*, this Englishman said that laws should be made by parliaments and then put into force by kings. By sharing power in this way, neither king nor parliament would become too powerful. The balance between them would preserve their people's freedom.

MONTESQUIEU (1689-1754)

This French thinker admired the way in which Britain was governed. In his book, The Spirit of the Laws, *he said that parliaments should make the laws of a country.*

VOLTAIRE (1694-1788)

Voltaire was also a Frenchman. He attacked the power and privileges of the established Church. He did not think that people should be persecuted for their religious beliefs. Voltaire spent most of his time in exile because his ideas annoyed the French king.

▲ ROUSSEAU (1712-78)

In his book, The Social Contract, *this French writer said that kings got their right to rule from the people, not from God. If they governed badly, the people could overthrow their rulers. Unlike the other writers, Rousseau believed that all the people, not just the rich, should take part in government.*

FIND OUT MORE ABOUT ONE OF THESE WRITERS OF THE ENLIGHTENMENT. WRITE AN ACCOUNT OF HIS LIFE AND IDEAS.

Finding out

⌂ The background to revolution

The writings of these men were read throughout Europe and the new colonies in America. They led people to question the kinds of governments they had.

At the end of the eighteenth century in both America and Europe, there were several revolutions. The questions these writers asked helped to undermine people's faith in the old governments and prepared the way for these revolutions.

◢ QUESTIONS ◢

1. Explain the terms: absolute monarchy; divine right of kings; parliament.
2. What is meant by the phrase "the established Church"?
3. The eighteenth century is often called "the Age of Reason". Explain how it got its name. What things did people stop believing in at that time?
4. What kind of government did the writers of the Enlightenment think was best? Explain why they thought this.

Britain Quarrels with her American Colonies

After Columbus discovered America (page 111), Europeans began to go to the New World to seek their fortunes and to find religious freedom. Spaniards settled in Florida and Mexico. French people settled in Canada which belonged to France. Most of those who settled on the east coast came from Britain and Ireland, although there were Dutch and Germans too. You can see this from the map.

The European settlers drove the native Indian tribes from their lands, made farms in the wilderness, and built towns like Boston, New York and Philadelphia.

Britain ruled thirteen colonies on the east coast and by 1760, two million Europeans were living there. Each of these colonies was quite separate from the others. Each had its own **governor** who

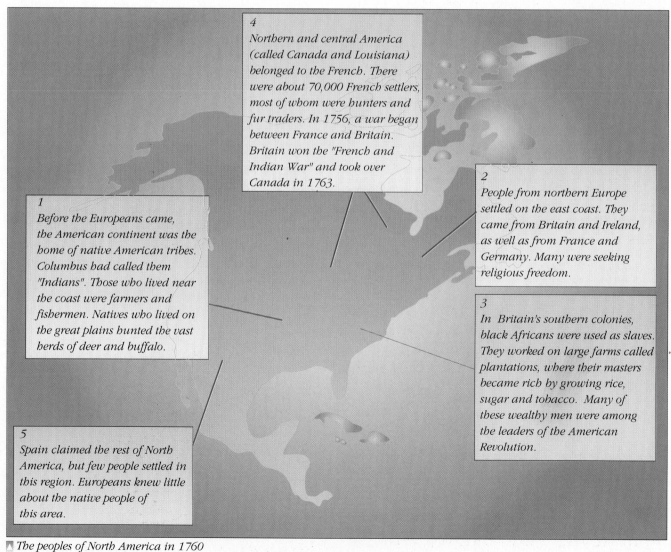

4
Northern and central America (called Canada and Louisiana) belonged to the French. There were about 70,000 French settlers, most of whom were hunters and fur traders. In 1756, a war began between France and Britain. Britain won the "French and Indian War" and took over Canada in 1763.

1
Before the Europeans came, the American continent was the home of native American tribes. Columbus had called them "Indians". Those who lived near the coast were farmers and fishermen. Natives who lived on the great plains hunted the vast herds of deer and buffalo.

2
People from northern Europe settled on the east coast. They came from Britain and Ireland, as well as from France and Germany. Many were seeking religious freedom.

3
In Britain's southern colonies, black Africans were used as slaves. They worked on large farms called plantations, where their masters became rich by growing rice, sugar and tobacco. Many of these wealthy men were among the leaders of the American Revolution.

5
Spain claimed the rest of North America, but few people settled in this region. Europeans knew little about the native people of this area.

▲ *The peoples of North America in 1760*

was appointed by King George III, and its own **assembly** (parliament) which was elected by some of the people of the colony. The assemblies made laws for the colonists and the governor enforced the laws they passed.

The Navigation Acts

The colonial assemblies had a good deal of freedom, but they were still under the overall control of King George III and the British parliament in London. Over the years, Britain passed a number of laws that regulated the way in which the Americans could carry on their trade. These laws were called the **Navigation Acts**. Here are some of the most important ones.

- Americans could not sell tobacco or rice to any country but Britain.
- Americans had to buy sugar from British colonies, where it was dear, and not from French or Spanish colonies, where it was cheap.
- Americans could not start an iron industry of their own as it would interfere with the iron industry in Britain.

For a long time, the colonists managed to get around these Navigation Acts by smuggling. But in 1763, the British government decided on a new policy. They had just driven the French out of Canada and they needed extra money to pay for the war, so they sent customs men in to stop the smuggling and to fine anyone they caught.

The Stamp Act: 1764

The arrival of customs men annoyed the Americans, but what the British did next infuriated them. In 1764, the London parliament passed the **Stamp Act** which ordered the Americans to pay new taxes called **stamp duties**. Here are some of the duties they had to pay.

- For any copy of a will – a stamp duty of six pence ($2\frac{1}{2}$p)
- For a cerificate in any degree taken in a university, academy or college – a stamp duty of two pounds (2.00)
- For every pack of playing cards – one shilling (5p)
- For every pair of dice – ten shillings (50p)

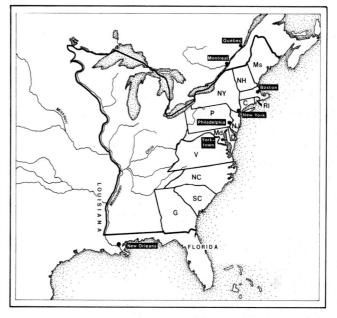

The thirteen colonies

The American colonists thought these stamp duties were most unjust. They had no votes in the British parliament, and they believed that only their own elected assemblies had the right to tell them what taxes to pay. They summed up their opinion in the slogan: "No taxation without representation".

Americans had to buy stamps like this one to pay new stamp duties.

The colonists began to resist the new taxes. Merchants refused to handle goods that came from Britain and people refused to buy them. Soon, all trade between Britain and America stopped. Mobs calling themselves the **Sons of Liberty** attacked the homes of stamp agents and burned their stamps.

British merchants found that their trade with America was suffering. They persuaded the government to drop the Stamp Act. But the British government still declared that they could tax the American colonists as they wished.

◀ *The Sons of Liberty burn some of the hated stamps.*

☖ THE BOSTON TEA PARTY: 1773

In 1773, a new row blew up when the British government gave permission to some merchants to bring tea directly from India to America. The Americans would now have to pay a tax on this tea, so they objected. When ships carrying tea entered Boston harbour, a mob disguised as native Indians went on board and dumped the tea into the water. This act was jokingly called the **Boston Tea Party**.

A man named John Andrews witnessed the incident and write about what he saw. (Look up any words you do not understand in your dictionary.)

"They say the actors were Indians from Narragansett. Whether they were or not, they appeared as such, being clothed in blankets with their heads muffled, and copper-coloured countenances, being each armed with a hatchet or axe and pair of pistols. Nor was their dialect different from what I conceive these geniuses to speak, as their jargon was unintelligible to all but themselves."

☖ *The Boston Tea Party. Describe the scene.*

In London, King George III and his ministers thought this was disgraceful behaviour. To make an example of Boston, they ordered that its port must be closed until it paid for the tea that had been destroyed. Meanwhile, the city was put under the control of the army commander, General Gage.

☖ The first Continental Congress

Other Americans rallied behind Boston. Messages of support came from the other colonies. The Americans decided to call a **Continental Congress** (a sort of American parliament) at Philadelphia to discuss the matter.

☖ THE BATTLES OF LEXINGTON AND CONCORD

Fearing a rebellion, the British government ordered General Gage to seize American arms. On 18 April 1775, Gage sent a large force of troops to the village of Concord near Boston to search for guns.

When the British reached the village of Lexington, a small group of armed colonists blocked their way. Fighting broke out and eight Americans were killed. The British then pushed on to Concord where another battle was fought.

After seizing and destroying the arms and ammunition stored at Concord, the British retreated back to Boston. All along the way, Americans hiding behind walls and trees fired on them. By the time they had reached the city, 247 of the British troops were dead or wounded. The **American War of Independence** had begun.

THOMAS PAINE AND *COMMON SENSE*

Soon after the battles of Lexington and Concord, the American Congress set up its own army. But even then, the colonists hoped they could avoid a war, since many of them were still loyal to George III.

Thomas Paine holds a copy of Common Sense. *Why was this book so important?*

Early in 1776, a small book appeared which helped them change their minds. It was called *Common Sense* and was written by Thomas Paine, an Englishman who had settled in America. Paine said that all kings were tyrants. Americans, he argued, should get rid of the monarchy and replace it with a republic where the people ruled themselves.

The Declaration of Independence: 4 July 1776

Over 150,000 copies of Paine's book were sold. Americans thought about what he said and Congress soon issued the **Declaration of Independence**. It was written by Thomas Jefferson and passed by Congress on 4 July 1776. This is part of what it said.

"We hold these truths to be *self-evident*, that all men are created equal, that they are *endowed* by their *Creator* with certain *unalienable* rights, that among these are Life, Liberty and the Pursuit of Happiness.

That to secure these rights, governments are *instituted* among men, *deriving* their just power from the consent of the *governed*. . . That whenever any form of government becomes *destructive* of these ends, it is the right of the people to *alter* or *abolish* it, and to institute a new government...

We, therefore, the Representatives of the United States of America, do solemnly publish and declare: that these United Colonies are. . . free and independent States; that they are *absolved* from all *allegiance* to the British Crown, and that all political *connection* between them and the state of Great Britain is. . . totally dissolved."

The American set up an army to fight against the British and they chose George Washington (page 168) to lead it.

Signing the Declaration of Independence on 4 July 1776 in Philadelphia

◢ QUESTIONS ◣

1. Write a paragraph explaining the Navigation Acts.
2. Explain the terms: the Stamp Act; "No taxation without representation"; Sons of Liberty.
3. What part did Thomas Paine play in the American Revolution?

Activity

WRITE AN ACCOUNT OF THE CAUSES OF THE AMERICAN REVOLUTION. REFER TO:(A) THE NAVIGATION ACTS; (B) THE STAMP ACT; (C) THE BOSTON TEA PARTY; (D) THE BATTLES OF LEXINGTON AND CONCORD; (E) THE FIRST CONTINENTAL CONGRESS. ▼ ▼ ▼

Looking at the evidence

1. LOOK AT THE ACCOUNT OF THE BOSTON TEA PARTY WRITTEN BY JOHN ANDREWS (PAGE 166). DID HE BELIEVE THAT THE DEMONSTRATORS WERE REAL INDIANS OR TOWNSPEOPLE DRESSED UP AS INDIANS? PICK OUT THE WORDS IN HIS ACCOUNT THAT SUPPORT YOUR ANSWER. ▼
2. STUDY THE QUOTATION FROM THE DECLARATION OF INDEPENDENCE AND DO THE FOLLOWING. ▼
   (A) USE A DICTIONARY TO LOOK UP THE WORDS IN ITALICS AND ANY OTHER WORDS YOU DO NOT UNDERSTAND. WRITE THE MEANING OF EACH WORD IN YOUR NOTEBOOK. ▼ ▼
   (B) THE DECLARATION OF INDEPENDENCE EXPLAINS WHAT AMERICANS FELT GOVERNMENTS WERE FOR. EXPLAIN THIS IN YOUR OWN WORDS. ▼ ▼ ▼

CHAPTER 60

George Washington and the War of Independence

🏛 Washington's early life

George Washington was born in the colony of Virginia on 22 February 1732. His father was a wealthy landowner, but he died when George was only eleven years of age.

The young George Washington was hardworking and ambitious. In 1752, he took over the family estate at Mount Vernon. In that year, Britain went to war against the French in Canada. Washington supported the British and fought with great bravery.

In 1758, Washington was elected to the Virginia Assembly. The following year, he married a young widow named Martha Dandridge. He spent most of the next fifteen years dividing his time between the Assembly and building up his tobacco plantation at Mount Vernon.

As a member of the Assembly, Washington opposed the attempts of the British government to tax the colonists. He supported the boycott of any goods which carried English taxes. Washington

George Washington. Why do you think he felt that Americans should take up arms only "as a last resort"?

men to join the army, but it had no gold or silver to pay them. It printed paper money, but this soon lost its value, so the army could not afford to buy food or weapons.

TO ALL BRAVE, HEALTHY, ABLE BODIED, AND WELL DISPOSED YOUNG MEN, IN THIS NEIGHBOURHOOD, WHO HAVE ANY INCLINATION TO JOIN THE TROOPS, NOW RAISING UNDER GENERAL WASHINGTON, FOR THE DEFENCE OF THE LIBERTIES AND INDEPENDENCE OF THE UNITED STATES, Against the hostile designs of foreign enemies,

TAKE NOTICE,

A recruiting poster encourages men to join Washington's army.

In spite of these problems, the Americans still had some important advantages. They had the support of most of the people, and they were fighting in their own countryside, which they knew well.

Washington took advantage of these things to outwit the British. He avoided big battles which the trained British soldiers were used to. Instead, he used hit-and-run tactics which the Americans had found so successful when fighting the Indians. Many colonists were crack shots who could easily pick off the British **Redcoats** in their bright uniforms while they themselves stayed hidden in the woods.

On Christmas night 1776, Washington led his forces across the frozen Delaware River and took the British garrison at Trenton by surprise. But this was a rare victory. In 1777, Washington was forced to flee when the British captured Philadelphia. He had to spend the winter at Valley Forge where his army suffered from the severe winter conditions without proper food, clothes or housing. Many died from frostbite and many more deserted.

wrote to a friend: "As a last resort, Americans should be prepared to take up arms to defend their ancestral liberties from the inroads of our lordly masters in Great Britain."

In 1774, he was elected as one of the seven Virginia delegates to the Continental Congress at Philadelphia. When the Congress decided to form its own army, they turned to Washington. On 16 June 1775, Washington accepted his appointment as commander-in-chief of the colonial army.

Washington and the American army

Washington had 17,000 troops. But they were so poorly trained and badly equipped that he had to build the American army from scratch. There were few experienced American officers and the only cannon they had were those they had captured from the British. Many soldiers were farmers who joined up for six months and then went home. They could not be relied upon to stand and fight in a battle. Congress printed recruitment posters to encourage

THE BRITISH ARMY

The British army had many advantages over the Americans. Their leaders were much more experienced. They had more money, so their soldiers were paid regularly. They also had good supplies of food and ammunition.

But the British had one big disadvantage – they were 5000km away from home. It was very difficult for them to plan and carry on a war at such a great distance.

HELP FROM FRANCE

This problem became worse for the British in 1778 when the French government decided to help the Americans. The French brought guns and soldiers and their navy. With their help, Washington was able to trap the British army at Yorktown in 1781. This defeat convinced King George III that he must end the war. After long negotiations in Paris, the British recognised the independence of the Americans in the **Treaty of Versailles** which was signed in 1783.

⬈ *The British surrender to General Washington at Yorktown in 1781.*

The Results of the American Revolution

DRAWING UP A CONSTITUTION

The Americans had got rid of British rule, but they still had a problem. What kind of government were they to have? It took them several years to work out a solution. At last a special Congress was elected in 1787 which drew up a plan for a **republic**. This plan was called the **Constitution of the United States**. It is still in operation today, over two hundred years later.

THE CONSTITUTION

The Constitution let each of the **states** (the former colonies) keep control of their own affairs, like education, local taxes and police. It also created a **federal** (or central) government to deal with things like foreign affairs, war, justice and trade.

THE BILL OF RIGHTS

The Constitution also contained the **Bill of Rights**. This guaranteed certain rights to people living in the United States. These rights included:

- the right to own property
- the right to free speech and a free press
- the right to follow any religion they wished
- the right to have a fair trial

This was the first time in history that **human rights** like these were promised to the people. But these rights applied to men only. Neither women nor slaves would have full human rights in America for many years to come.

GEORGE WASHINGTON: THE FIRST PRESIDENT OF THE UNITED STATES

The new American Constitution became law in 1789. George Washington, the hero of the American War of Independence, was chosen as the first president of the United States. He was a wise leader who set a high standard for the presidents who came after him.

George Washington – the first president of the United States

The American republic was the first modern democratic state. It was a model which many Europeans admired and wished to follow. Today, many democratic states, including Ireland, have constitutions which resemble the one drawn up by the Americans in 1787.

■ QUESTIONS ■

1. Why did the Americans pick George Washington to lead their army? Give reasons for your answer.
2. Describe the tactics used by Washington in the early part of the War of Independence. Why did he change those tactics after 1779?
3. Explain the terms: constitution; Bill of Rights; federal government; president.
4. George Washington is sometimes called the "Father of his Country". Give two reasons why he deserves this title.

Looking at the evidence

NOW LOOK AT THE RECRUITMENT POSTER ON PAGE 169. THE TERMS OFFERED ARE ATTRACTIVE, YET WASHINGTON FOUND IT DIFFICULT TO GET RECRUITS. CAN YOU EXPLAIN WHY?

Finding out

FIND OUT MORE ABOUT GEORGE WASHINGTON IN ANOTHER TEXTBOOK OR ENCYCLOPAEDIA. WRITE AN ESSAY ON HIS LIFE.

CHAPTER 61

France before the Revolution

🏛 America and France

People in Europe, particularly the French, took a great interest in the American revolution. The king of France had sent soldiers and sailors to help the Americans. He did this to get revenge on France's old enemy, Britain – not because he liked what the Americans were doing.

But many Frenchmen who had fought in America were impressed by the rights the colonists had won for themselves. How different things were in France, where not even the nobility had any say in the way their country was governed! Some French soldiers, like the Marquis de Lafayette, had read Montesquieu, Rousseau and Voltaire (page 162) who

had criticised the French monarchy. They began to think about changing the way in which France was governed.

🏛 Louis XVI and Marie Antoinette

At this time, Louis XVI was the king of France. He was a well-meaning, kindly man but a weak king. Louis hated making decisions and often changed his mind. He was easily bored with the hard work that ruling a country involved, so he left the day-to-day decisions to his ministers, most of whom were noblemen.

Louis was married to an Austrian princess, Marie Antoinette. She was pretty and extravagant, loving beautiful clothes and jewels. The French disapproved of her extravagance and distrusted her because she was a foreigner.

King Louis XVI was a weak monarch who hated making decisions.

Marie Antoinette spent a great deal of money on stylish clothes.

borrowed a great deal of money. Now they found they could not repay the loans without increasing taxes.

By 1788, peasants (farmers) in France were very poor. They had to pay taxes to the government, to the nobles and to the Church. A few years earlier, in 1778, the English traveller, Arthur Young, wrote this description of one poor French peasant woman.

"Walking up a long hill, I was joined by a poor woman who complained of the times and that France was a sad country. Demanding her reasons, she said her husband had but a morsel of land, one cow and a poor little horse, yet they had a franchar (20kg) of wheat and three chickens to pay as a rent to one seigneur (landowner) and four franchar of oats, one chicken and one sou (penny) to pay to another, besides very heavy tailles (taxes on crops) and other taxes.

It was said, at present, that something was to be done by some great folks for such poor ones. She did not know who nor how, but prayed that God send us better, for we are being crushed by the tailles and the dues."

A cartoon from the times says, "Please God, deliver us from the tax collectors".

HEAVY TAXES

After the war in America, King Louis' government was nearly bankrupt. For many years, one king after another had led France into expensive wars, and Louis himself had spent a lot helping the Americans. To pay for these wars, the French government had

The privileged groups

Not everyone in France paid the same taxes as this peasant woman. The clergy and the nobility did not have to pay taxes at all. Because of this right or privilege, the French clergy and nobility were called "the privileged groups".

Many members of the privileged groups were very wealthy. They held the top jobs in the government and the army. They also owned a great deal of land. The clergy owned about 10% of the land and the nobles about 60%. In 1788, Louis XVI suggested that the privileged groups should pay taxes too.

THE PRIVILEGED GROUPS DEMAND AN ESTATES-GENERAL

But the clergy and the nobles turned down the king's recommendation. They said that he had no right to take away their privileges without consulting them. They demanded that he call the **Estates-General** to discuss the matter.

The Estates-General was the old French parliament which had last met in 1614. It was made up of three parts, called **Estates**.

> ◪ The **First Estate** represented the clergy.
> ◪ The **Second Estate** represented the nobility.
> ◪ The **Third Estate** represented everyone else – the peasantry, workers in the towns, and the middle classes like lawyers, doctors and businessmen.

The nobility and clergy had always controlled the Estates-General. They were sure they could do so again.

Drawing up a list of grievances

King Louis hesitated, but in the end, he had no choice. In July 1788, he ordered elections for the Estates-General to be held throughout France. In every parish, peasants also drew up lists of grievances, setting out the things they wanted the Estates-General to change. This was part of the list sent by the people of the village of Longnes.

"1. We wish his majesty to abolish all the unfair taxes which have been placed on daily necessities such as food.

2. We wish his majesty to abolish all the **gabelles** *(tax on salt).*

3. We wish his majesty to ensure that the **tailles** *and other taxes we pay for the upkeep of the state are also imposed on all castles, houses, cultivated lands, meadows, woods, vineyards, moors, ponds and rivers – indeed on everything.*

4. We wish to make known the burden involved in building a road which will only be used by some lord travelling to his castle."

Hopes for the Estates-General

While elections for the Estates-General were taking place, the people's situation got worse. The 1788 harvest failed, so many peasants could barely afford food. The misery spread to the townspeople too. In Paris, the price of a loaf of bread doubled over the winter of 1788-89. This meant that poor workers were spending most of their wages on bread. Many were hungry. Everyone hoped the Estates-General would help them.

◪ QUESTIONS ◪

1. Write a paragraph explaining how the American War of Independence affected France.
2. Did Louis XVI and Marie Antoinette rule France well? Explain your answer.
3. Write a paragraph on the Estates-General. Explain: (a) what it was; (b) how it was organised; (c) when it was held; (d) what people hoped it would do.

IMAGINE THAT YOU ARE A PEASANT LIVING IN FRANCE IN 1788. WRITE A PARAGRAPH EXPLAINING WHAT YOU THINK IS WRONG WITH THE WAY YOU ARE BEING GOVERNED.

Activity ▼

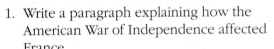

1. LOOK AT ARTHUR YOUNG'S ACCOUNT OF HIS MEETING WITH A POOR WOMAN (PAGE 172) AND THE LIST OF GRIEVANCES FROM THE VILLAGE OF LONGNES. NAME AND EXPLAIN THE VARIOUS TAXES AND RENTS THAT THE PEASANTS HAD TO PAY.
2. WRITE A NOTE EXPLAINING HOW THESE TAXES WERE AFFECTING THE PEOPLE.
3. LOOK AT THE CARTOON ON PAGE 172. DESCRIBE WHAT THE ARTIST IS TRYING TO SAY.

Looking at the evidence

CHAPTER 62

The French Revolution Begins

🏛 The meeting of the Estates-General

The Estates-General met in the king's palace at Versailles on 5 May 1789. It was a very impressive occasion.

After its first session, the king wanted the Estates-General to divide up. Each estate was to go to its own room to discuss the proposals for new taxes and vote on them. These proposals would become law if they were passed by two of the estates. Most of the clergy and the nobles were in favour of this plan, but the Third Estate disagreed. They wanted all the delegates to stay together and to vote as one assembly. This was because there were twice as many members of the Third Estate as in the other two combined.

🔺 *The Estates-General met at the magnificent palace at Versailles.*

🏛 THE THIRD ESTATE BECOMES THE NATIONAL ASSEMBLY

The delegates from Third Estate refused to leave the great hall. They said they represented the people of France and they called on the other Estates to join them. For more than a month, nothing happened.

Then at last, on 17 June 1789, the Third Estate declared that it was the now the **National Assembly** of France and that they would have to approve all new laws. Some of the nobles and the clergy joined them and they began to discuss new ways of ruling France.

🏛 The fall of the Bastille: 14 July 1789

Most French people did not trust the king to agree to any of the reforms which the National Assembly might suggest. On 12 July, a rumour went round that he had ordered troops who were loyal to him to come to Paris. Parisians began to search frantically for arms so that they could defend their city.

◄ *The storming of the Bastille, 14 July 1789*

On 14 July 1789, a large mob surrounded the Bastille, a great royal fortress that towered over Paris. It contained a large supply of gunpowder. When the governor of the Bastille refused to hand it over, the mob stormed the fortress. One man who was there described what happened.

"The first bridge had been lowered, and the chains cut. But the portcullis barred the way. People were trying to bring in some cannon.

It was decided to start the attack with musket fire. We each fired half a dozen shots. Then a paper was thrust through an oval gap a few inches across. We ceased fire. One of us went to fetch a plank which was laid on a parapet to enable us to go and collect the paper. One man started out along it, but just as he was about to take the paper, he was killed by a shot and fell into the moat."

In the fighting, ninety-eight of the attackers were killed. When the Bastille finally fell, its governor and six of the hundred soldiers who defended it were massacred by the angry mob.

KING LOUIS XVI ACCEPTS THE NATIONAL ASSEMBLY

The fall of the Bastille convinced the king that he would have to agree to the demands of the National Assembly. When he ordered the troops to withdraw from Paris, the people formed their own police force, the **National Guard**. It was put under the command of the Marquis de Lafayette who had supported the National Assembly, even though he was a nobleman. The king also agreed to accept a new flag, the **tricolour**, made up of a white stripe (the royal colour) between red and blue (the colours of Paris).

The revolution spreads throughout France

All around the country, peasants attacked their landlords' castles. In early August, the National Assembly abolished the privileges of the clergy and the nobility, as well as the feudal dues they had demanded from the peasants. Peace gradually returned to the countryside.

THE WOMEN OF PARIS MARCH ON VERSAILLES

In Paris, trouble broke out again in October. The National Assembly was still meeting in Versailles, 20km outside the city. But Parisians were worried that the king might close it down. They wanted the National Assembly to be held in Paris where they could protect it.

There was another problem. The price of bread was still very high and the poor faced starvation. On 3 October, a rumour spread that the king had given a lavish banquet for his army officers at which the new tricolour was insulted. People made angry speeches attacking these actions.

On 5 October, 7000 angry women marched out to Versailles. As they marched, they chanted: "Let us bring back the baker and the baker's wife and the baker's little boy!" The next day, they escorted Louis XVI, Marie Antoinette and their son back to Paris. The National Assembly also left Versailles. From then on, the main events of the French Revolution took place in Paris.

■ QUESTIONS ■

1. Explain why the Third Estate wanted the members of the other two Estates to join them in forming the National Assembly.
2. Write a paragraph on the fall of the Bastille. In it, refer to: (a) why it was attacked; (b) how the battle began; (c) what happened to the soldiers guarding it; (d) why the incident was so important.
3. Explain why the royal family was forced to move to Paris in October 1789.

Angry women march to Versailles to protest about the price of bread.

WHAT DID THE WOMEN MEAN WHEN THEY SHOUTED: "LET US BRING BACK THE BAKER AND THE BAKER'S WIFE AND THE BAKER'S LITTLE BOY!" ON THEIR WAY TO VERSAILLES?

Looking at the evidence

CHAPTER 63

The French Revolution: 1791-94

Reforms of the National Assembly

Over the next eighteen months, the National Assembly passed many reforms. Its most important one was the **Declaration of the Rights of Man**. This said that men were all free and equal. They were entitled to life, liberty, and freedom of speech and religion. (It did not mention women.) The National Assembly also said an elected assembly must help the king to rule France.

The flight to Varennes

King Louis was not happy with these reforms. He thought they took away too much of his power. Louis decided to leave France with his family and get help from his brother-in-law, the emperor of Austria.

On the night of 20 June 1791, the royal family escaped from their palace, disguised as the servants of a Russian baroness. They planned to flee to Belgium, which then belonged to Austria. Many nobles who had fled from France were already there. The king hoped to join them and lead them against the revolution.

▲ *The royal family is brought back to Paris. Why were so many soldiers needed to escort the king?*

Everything was going well until a postmaster recognised Louis from his portrait on a bank note. He raised the alarm and the royal family's coach was stopped at Varennes, just 50km from the Belgian border. Louis and his family were brought back to Paris.

People were angry with the king, and the National Guard had to protect his coach from the crowd. Some deputies in the National Assembly wanted Louis to abdicate (give up his throne), but most people thought he had finally learned his lesson.

> A NEW ASSEMBLY WAS ELECTED, BUT COULD IT TRUST THE KING? HERE IS PART OF A LETTER LOUIS WROTE SOME MONTHS LATER TO THE KING OF PRUSSIA. READ IT AND MAKE UP YOUR OWN MIND.
>
> *"I have just written to the Emperor of Austria, the Empress of Russia and to the kings of Spain and Sweden, and have suggested that the best method of stopping the trouble-makers here, and of ensuring that the evil which racks France does not spread to the other European states, is to set up an alliance of all the main European powers, backed up by armed force."*

Looking at the evidence

War with Austria and Prussia

The rulers of Europe did not like what was happening in France. They were afraid that the revolutionary ideas might spread to their own countries. The emperor of Austria and the king of Prussia planned on going to war to restore Louis' power.

In France, some deputies in the Assembly were also eager for a war. They did not trust the king and believed he was encouraging Austria and Prussia to attack France. However, they thought a successful war would force the king out into the open and make their revolution more popular.

France becomes a republic

In April 1792, France went to war against Austria and Prussia. But things did not go as the Assembly had hoped. Austrian and Prussian armies invaded France and were soon approaching Paris. Parisians panicked, and on 10 August, a large mob stormed the Tuileries palace where the King and his family were living. The royal family took refuge with the Assembly which imprisoned them in the Temple prison. The Assembly then declared that France was a republic.

It was the poor people of Paris who had stormed the Tuileries and brought down the French monarchy. Because they wore baggy trousers instead of the fashionable knee-breeches (culottes) and stockings worn by the nobles, they were known as the *sans-culottes* (without culottes).

The Assembly now called on the people of France to defend their new republic. From all over the country, people marched to Paris to answer the call. Those who came from the city of Marseilles sang a stirring new song, the *Marseillaise*. It became the anthem of the new republic. Singing this song, French soldiers loyal to the National Assembly defeated the armies of Austria and Prussia on 20 September 1792 and drove them out of France.

Marie Antoinette is led to the guillotine.

Later that month, the Assembly declared that Louis was not longer king and that France was a republic. It also decided to try the king for treason. A chest containing Louis' letters had been discovered in the Tuileries. These papers showed that he had been writing in secret to foreign rulers.

Louis was found guilty of treason and guillotined on 21 January 1793. In October, Queen Marie Antoinette was also beheaded on the guillotine.

Robespierre and the Committee of Public Safety

The Assembly wanted to encourage the revolutionary spirit in other countries. They promised to bring "...help to all people wishing to recover their liberty". This promise, and the execution of the French king, frightened the rulers of Europe. Britain, Spain and Holland now joined with Prussia and Austria to defeat the revolution. In 1793, their armies invaded France from every side.

To deal with this emergency, the Assembly set up the **Committee of Public Safety**. It had twelve members, but the most important was **Maximilien Robespierre**. He was a lawyer who had been elected to the Estates-General in 1789.

Robespierre spoke out in favour of freedom of the press, against capital punishment, and against the declaration of war on Austria in 1792. Because of these views, he was very popular with the *sans-culottes*. He quickly became the most powerful man in France.

Huge crowds gathered to witness the execution of King Louis XVI.

Maximilien Robespierre introduced a "reign of terror" to stop any opposition to the revolution.

ROBESPIERRE'S PROBLEMS

Robespierre and the Committee of Public Safety had to defeat their foreign enemies, but they also had problems inside France. Many people who were unhappy with the king's execution now rose in rebellion.

The Committee decided that only desperate measures could save the revolution. They set out to terrorise their opponents into submission and introduced the **law of suspects**. This stated that anyone suspected of plotting against the revolution could be put to death.

Soldiers were sent to crush the rebellions. In Lyons, nearly 2000 rebels were shot and the houses of the rich were destroyed. In the west, in an area known as the Vendée, there were too many prisoners to guillotine, so hundreds of them were put into boats which were then sunk in the River Loire. This **reign of terror** ended all internal resistance to the revolution.

RE-ORGANISING THE ARMY

To fight its foreign enemies, Robespierre and his Committee ordered all able-bodied Frenchmen to join the army. By 1793, it had a force of 650,000 men. The old officers from the nobility were gone. The army was now led by able men who were loyal to the revolution and determined to defeat its enemies. By the end of 1794, they had driven out the foreign armies and France was safe.

THE FALL OF ROBESPIERRE

The Committee of Public Safety had saved France, so most people expected that "the terror" would now come to an end. Instead, it got worse. Deputies in the Assembly who opposed Robespierre were dragged to the guillotine. Other deputies now feared

for their own safety. They decided to act.

On 27 July 1794, these deputies ordered the arrest of the members of the Committee of Public Safety. The following day, Robespierre was guillotined along with twenty-one of his close supporters. The reign of terror had come to an end.

The arrest of Robespierre

The end of the revolution

After the death of Robespierre, France was ruled by five men called the **Directors**. They did not govern France well, however. Prices rose and many people could not afford to buy food. France was still at war and the Directors became dependent on their army generals. In 1799, one of these generals, **Napoleon Bonaparte**, forced the Directors out of office and took control of the government. The French Revolution was over.

Results of the French Revolution

Although the revolution did not survive for long, it brought about many reforms, including the Declaration of the Rights of Man.

- Slavery was abolished in all lands belonging to France.
- Protestants and Jews were guaranteed religious freedom.
- A new calendar was introduced. It began on 22 September 1792, the first day of the republic. The months had new names and there was a ten-day week.
- A simple new system of weights and measures, using tens, hundreds and thousands, was introduced. This is the same **metric system** which we use today.

Many of these reforms survived the collapse of the revolution.

Stating people were entitled to liberty and equality was one of the most important achievements of the French Revolution. These ideas soon spread to other European countries and encouraged people to seek changes in the ways in which they were governed. Today, most Europeans live in democratic countries where their individual rights are guaranteed in law. This is the great legacy of the French Revolution.

FIND OUT MORE ABOUT MAXIMILIEN ROBESPIERRE USING OTHER TEXTBOOKS OR AN ENCYCLOPAEDIA. WRITE AN ESSAY ON THE PART WHICH ROBESPIERRE PLAYED IN THE FRENCH REVOLUTION.

Finding out

QUESTIONS

1. Write a paragraph on the flight to Varennes. Comment on: (a) why the king fled; (b) how he was stopped; (c) what happened when he came back to Paris.
2. Why did France go to war with Austria and Prussia in 1792?
3. Were the French right to execute Louis XVI for treason? Give reasons for your answer.
4. Explain the terms: *sans-culottes*; *Marseillaise*; reign of terror; Directors; Declaration of the Rights of Man.
5. Select what you think are the two most important achievements of the French Revolution. In each case, explain why you think so.

CHAPTER 64

Special Study: Revolutionary Movements in Ireland

Like the Americans and the French in the eighteenth century, many people in Ireland were unhappy with the way in which they were governed.

Navigation Acts

Ireland had its own parliament, but like the American assemblies, it was under the control of the British government. The British interfered with any Irish trade that might compete with British trade. They stopped the Irish from exporting cattle and wool to Britain and limited the right of Irish traders to carry goods within the Empire.

Penal Laws

In Ireland, only about 15% of the people were members of the Church of Ireland (Anglicans), yet they had all the power. Catholics and Presbyterians were not allowed to take part in politics. Catholics were not even allowed to build churches or to open schools. These restrictions were called the **Penal Laws**.

The Protestant Ascendancy

When the American Revolution began, many people in Ireland sympathised with the Americans. They demanded freedom for the Irish parliament too. The

British government was afraid that rebellion might also break out in Ireland. So in 1782, it removed the restrictions on the Irish parliament.

Although the Irish parliament was now free, it still was not democratic. It was controlled by a small group of wealthy landowners called the **Protestant Ascendancy**. These men made the laws, fixed the taxes and kept all the top jobs in the government for themselves.

When the French Revolution began, many people in Ireland also demanded changes in the way in which Ireland was governed. One of these was a young lawyer, Theobald Wolfe Tone. We can trace the growth of revolutionary movements in Ireland by looking at his story.

SPECIAL STUDY

The early life of Theobald Wolfe Tone

▲ *Theobald Wolfe Tone worked for reforms for all Irish people, regardless of their religion.*

Wolfe Tone was born in Dublin in 1763. His family were middle-class Anglicans and could afford to send him to Trinity College where he was an outstanding student.

In the summer of 1789, he began to work as a lawyer. With his ability he should have been successful, but he was not. The Ascendancy kept all the best jobs for its supporters, and a man like Tone, from a humble family, had little chance of success.

Tone soon became frustrated by this. He realised that he could only hope to change the system by reforming parliament and destroying the power of the Ascendancy.

Tone and freedom for Catholics

Tone's chance came in 1791. The French Revolution had aroused great interest in Ireland, especially among the Presbyterians in Belfast. In the summer of 1791, a group of them decided to set up a new political club in the city to work for reform. They wanted the government to change the law and allow Presbyterians to sit in parliament. However, they were unwilling to demand the same rights for Catholics.

Tone thought this was a mistake and wrote a pamphlet called *An Argument on behalf of the Catholics of Ireland*. In it, he said that "No reform can ever be obtained which shall not embrace Irishmen of all denominations (religions)." According to Tone, if Presbyterians hoped to get reform for themselves, they must also support freedom for Catholics.

The Belfast Presbyterians were won over by Tone's argument. On 14 October 1791, they set up the **Society of United Irishmen**. The society adopted three resolutions which were written by Wolfe Tone himself.

1. English influence is so great in Ireland that all the people must unite against it to protect their liberties and develop their trade.
2. The only constitutional way to overcome English influence is to change the method of electing MPs so that they would represent more people.
3. No reform is just which does not include Irishmen of every religion.

Most United Irishmen were businessmen or lawyers who disliked the power of the Ascendancy. They were not plotting a revolution. They simply wanted to persuade the Irish parliament to change the method of electing MPs and give Catholics equal rights. Tone had convinced them that only by uniting all Irishmen – Catholic, Protestant and Presbyterian – could they achieve these aims.

The Catholic Committee

Wolfe Tone's argument not only impressed the Belfast Presbyterians; it also attracted the attention of the Catholic leaders. They were members of the **Catholic Committee** which had been set up some years before to campaign against the Penal Laws. In July 1792, the Committee invited Tone to be its secretary.

The Catholic Convention: 1792

Tone helped to prepare a petition to the Irish parliament for **Catholic emancipation**. When it was turned down, the Committee decided to go directly to King George III in London. To prove that all Catholics in Ireland were behind them, they organised a **Catholic Convention** in Dublin in December 1792. The Convention drew up a petition which called for complete Catholic emancipation and for co-operation with the Presbyterians in achieving it.

SOME RIGHTS FOR CATHOLICS

The British government and the Protestant Ascendancy were frightened that Catholics and Presbyterians were getting together. They decided to enact some important reforms for Catholics, hoping these would break up the union between the two religions. When the delegates of the Catholic Committee met the king on 2 January 1793, they were promised reforms. They returned home with high hopes.

▲ *Delegates from the Catholic Committee meet King George III on 2 January 1793.*

But neither the English nor the Ascendancy was willing to give Catholics full and equal rights. In 1793, the English persuaded the Irish parliament to give Catholics the right to vote, to go to university and to hold certain state jobs. But Catholics were still not allowed to become MPs, government ministers or judges.

Wolfe Tone was very disappointed, but many Catholics felt that this was as much as they could hope for. The Catholic leaders decided it was safer to wind up the Catholic Committee. To thank Tone for his work, they gave him £1500 – a very large sum of money for that time.

War ends the hope of reform

The war between Britain and France which began in February 1793 changed everything. From then on, the government treated anyone demanding Catholic emancipation or the reform of parliament as traitors. Spies were sent to watch all United Irishmen. Several of them were arrested and imprisoned while others fled the country.

THE DEFENDERS

One reason for the government's worry was the **Defenders**. This was a secret society formed by Catholic peasant farmers. They had heard how French peasants had benefited by the revolution and wanted the same benefits for themselves. Early in 1792, the Defenders began to drill and gather arms.

A French mission to Ireland

The French knew about the discontent in Ireland. In 1794, they sent William Jackson, an Irish-born clergyman, to see if there would be any support for a rebellion against British rule.

Jackson arrived in Dublin in April 1794 with an English lawyer called John Cockayne. They were introduced to Wolfe Tone who wrote an account of the situation in Ireland for Jackson to take back to France.

This was a terrible mistake. Cockayne was actually a spy who told the British government about Jackson's mission. They arrested Jackson and found a copy of Tone's report. This gave them enough evidence to outlaw the United Irishmen and to execute Jackson for treason. But because the copy of the report was not in Tone's own handwriting, they could not arrest him. Instead, they agreed to let him leave Ireland in 1795.

TONE AND FRENCH HELP

Tone and other United Irishmen were now convinced that peaceful reform was impossible. Only a revolution would overthrow the Ascendancy. But any revolution would need outside help. Tone agreed to go to France where he would try to persuade the French government to send an army to Ireland to support a United Irish rebellion.

▧ QUESTIONS ▧

1. Why was there so much support for the French Revolution among the Presbyterians of Belfast?
2. Describe the two most important consequences of Wolfe Tone's *Argument on behalf of the Catholics of Ireland.*
3. Explain why Wolfe Tone was forced to leave Ireland in 1795.
4. Explain the following terms: Protestant Ascendancy; Penal Laws; Navigation Acts; Catholic Convention; United Irishmen; Defenders.

The United Irishmen prepare for a revolution

After Tone left Ireland, the United Irishmen began to plan a revolution. Lord Edward Fitzgerald became their military organiser. They began to form links with the Defenders.

Tone and the Directory

Tone arrived in France in February 1796. There he met the members of the Directory (page 178) and told them about the United Irishmen and the Defenders. Tone promised that if the French sent an army, most of Ireland's Catholics and Presbyterians would support it.

At this time, the Directory was also keen to defeat Britain and end the war. They decided to accept Tone's plan. This is the message which the Directory sent to General Hoche, a French army commander.

> "We intend, Citizen General, to restore to a people ripe for revolution the independence and liberty for which it clamours. Ireland has groaned under the hateful yoke of England for centuries. The Defenders... are already secretly armed... and the very hope of help from the French Republic has persuaded them to defer insurrection until its arrival.
>
> Detach Ireland from England, and she (England) will be reduced to a second-rate power and deprived of most of her superiority over the seas. The advantages to France of an independent Ireland are so manifold that they need not be listed."

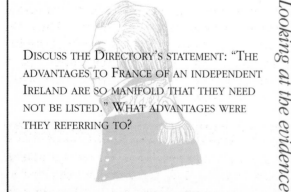

DISCUSS THE DIRECTORY'S STATEMENT: "THE ADVANTAGES TO FRANCE OF AN INDEPENDENT IRELAND ARE SO MANIFOLD THAT THEY NEED NOT BE LISTED." WHAT ADVANTAGES WERE THEY REFERRING TO?

Looking at the evidence

General Hoche's expedition to Ireland

Hoche was one of France's most brilliant military leaders. The son of a royal groom, he had reached the rank of general by the age of twenty-five. He hoped to defeat Britain and bring peace to Europe.

As soon as he had received his orders from the Directory, Hoche began to prepare an expedition to Ireland. Tone, who was made a colonel in the French army, worked with him.

On 15 December 1796, a fleet of forty-three French ships with 14,750 men on board set sail from Brest. The fleet left at night, hoping to evade the British navy. From the beginning, however, it was a very unlucky expedition. One ship foundered on rocks with the loss of nearly 1300 men. Worse still, the ship carrying Hoche and the battle plans was blown out to sea by strong winds and never reached Ireland.

BANTRY BAY: DECEMBER 1796

The remaining ships reached Bantry Bay, but the weather grew worse. On 23 December, a strong gale scattered the fleet. For days the storms continued. A despairing Tone wrote this in his journal on 26 December.

> "The morning is now come, the gale continues, and the fog is so thick that we cannot see a ship's length ahead. So here we lie in the utmost uncertainty and anxiety... Of forty-three sail, of which the expedition consisted, we can muster of all sizes but fourteen. There only wants our falling in with the English to complete our destruction...
>
> All our hopes are now reduced to getting back in safety to Brest, and I believe we will set sail for that port the instant the weather will permit...
>
> Notwithstanding all our blunders, it is the dreadful stormy weather and easterly winds, which have been blowing furiously and without intermission since we made Bantry Bay, that have ruined us. Well, England has not had such an escape since the Spanish Armada, and that expedition, like ours, was defeated by the weather."

Eventually the dispirited fleet turned for home, arriving back in Brest on 1 January 1797. Eleven ships and 5000 men were lost. The flagship, with an angry Hoche, returned to Brest on 12 January.

Hoche hoped for another invasion of Ireland, but in the following summer he became ill and died.

The government acts against the United Irishmen

The Bantry Bay expedition was an unpleasant shock for the British government. If the French had landed and gained the support of the Defenders and the United Irishmen, they might well have won, as they would have faced only 15,000 British troops. The government realised they had to bring the Defenders and the United Irishmen under control before another French expedition could arrive.

They sent the army commander, General Lake, to Ulster to disarm the province. He did so with a vengeance. His soldiers terrorised the people, burning houses and using torture to force information about the United Irishmen from them. Many leaders of Belfast's United Irishmen were arrested.

Lake's terror tactics outraged many people, but they worked. Thousands of arms were surrendered or captured, and the United Irish movement in Ulster was almost destroyed. Later, these tactics were extended into Leinster.

THE ARREST OF THE DUBLIN LEADERS

In March 1798, the British government swooped on the Dublin leaders of the United Irishmen. Lord Edward Fitzgerald and those leaders who avoided arrest now decided that a rebellion would have to take place without French help. But on 19 May, Lord Edward Fitzgerald's hiding place was discovered. Fighting against arrest, he was badly wounded and a few days later, he died in London's Newgate prison.

The Rebellion of 1798: Wexford

By 25 May, risings had broken out in much of Leinster. The most serious rebellion occurred in Wexford. It was sparked off by rumours that people were committing atrocities against Catholics.

The Wexford Rising was led by **Father John Murphy**, a curate at Boolavogue. Before long, he and his rebels were in control of Enniscorthy and Wexford. They set up a republic along French lines. A Protestant landlord called Bagenal Harvey, a member of the United Irishmen, took charge in Wexford town. The rebels were unable to capture New Ross or Arklow, so they fell back to fortified positions at Vinegar Hill and Three Rocks.

As government forces advanced against the Wexford rebels, religious hatred took over. On 20 June, ninety-seven Protestants were taken from

The Battle of Vinegar Hill, 21 June 1798

prison and savagely killed in Wexford. The following day, government forces defeated the rebels at Vinegar Hill and brought the rising to an end. Thousands were put to death as Lake sought to terrorise the county into submission.

The rebellion in Ulster

On 7 June, the rebellion spread to Ulster where **Henry Joy McCracken** led a force of 3000 rebels to Antrim town. But the British army was waiting. After a battle the rebels fled, leaving over 300 dead behind them.

A second rebel force led by **Henry Munroe** attacked Ballinahinch in Co. Down. It too was driven back. The Ulster rising was over within ten days. The two leaders were executed, but most of their followers put down their arms and were not punished.

The government began to spread stories about the massacre of Protestants in Wexford. They did this to sow distrust between the mostly Presbyterian United Irishmen and the Catholic Defenders. As a result, support for the United Irishmen soon disappeared in Ulster.

More French expeditions

News of the rising in Ireland caused great surprise in France. On 25 June 1798, the Directory decided to send help once again. There was no the time to prepare a large expedition, but the French did not think this would matter. They thought the whole country would rise to join them when their soldiers arrived. They did not realise how successful the government had been in disarming the rebels.

⌂ GENERAL HUMBERT IN CONNACHT

Two expeditions set out from France. The first had 1000 men under the command of **General Humbert**. He landed at Killala Bay in Co. Mayo at the end of August.

The United Irishmen were badly organised in Connacht, and Humbert was disappointed at the number of men who came to join him. Nonetheless, he began to march eastwards. At Castlebar, the French defeated a small British force and Humbert set up a republic in Connacht.

Humbert then led his poorly-equipped army towards Dublin. On 8 September, he met a much larger British force at Ballinamuck in Co. Longford. Badly outnumbered, Humbert had no choice but to surrender. The British treated the French as prisoners of war, but the Irish were seen as rebels. Many were killed and others, including Tone's brother, Matthew, were brought to Dublin and hanged.

⌂ The arrest of Wolfe Tone

The second French army, with 3000 men under General Hardy, did not set sail until 16 September. They did not know that Humbert's army had already surrendered. Wolfe Tone sailed on board Hardy's flagship, the *Hoche*.

Because of bad weather once again, they did not reach the Donegal coast until 12 October. There they were challenged by a British fleet. A furious battle followed, in which Wolfe Tone commanded one of the gun batteries on the *Hoche*. After a few hours, the *Hoche* was beaten. Its main mast was gone and the ship had struck rocks and was sinking. There was no choice but to surrender.

As he stepped ashore, Tone was recognised. He was immediately placed in chains and brought to Dublin. Despite French protests that he was an officer in their army, he was put on trial for treason on 10 November. The following day, Tone was found guilty and sentenced to be hanged. That night in his cell, he cut his own throat with a pen-knife. One week later, on 19 November, he died from his wounds.

⌂ Wolfe Tone: the first Irish republican

Wolfe Tone was an extraordinary man. A Protestant by birth, he had spent much of his adult life working for Irish Catholics and for unity among all religious groups in Ireland.

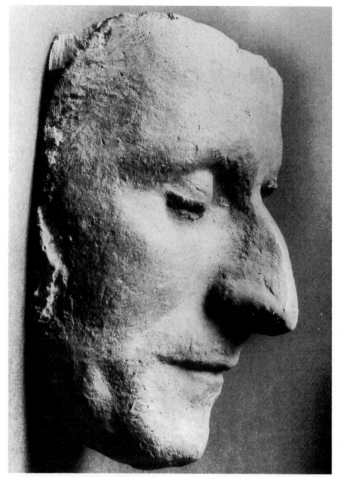

⌐ *The death mask of Wolfe Tone*

He was by nature a reformer who hoped to see his aims achieved peacefully. However, the events of 1794-5 convinced him that the British government would never allow real reform and independence for Ireland. This turned him into a revolutionary who wanted Ireland's complete separation from Britain.

Wolfe Tone's greatest achievement was in convincing the French to send three expeditions to Ireland. To the end of his life, he clung to the hope of seeing all Irishmen – whether Catholic or Protestant – unite to seek the independence of their country. For this reason, he is seen as the first Irish republican.

⌂ Results of the 1798 Rebellion

⌂ THE ACT OF UNION: 1800

By November 1798, Wolfe Tone was dead and the rising had been crushed. But the events had frightened the British prime minister, William Pitt. He feared the French might come back, and when

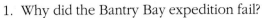

they did, they would take over Ireland. To prevent this, he decided to get rid of the Irish parliament and unite it with the British parliament in London. This, Pitt thought, would bind Ireland securely to Britain.

Some members of the Protestant Ascendancy shared Pitt's fears. They realised that only British help had saved them in 1798. Because of this, they reluctantly agreed to give up the Irish parliament.

A big debate about whether or not to agree to a Union developed in Ireland. After the debate, the Irish parliament passed the **Act of Union** in 1800.

This is what the Union meant.

- The two kingdoms of Britain and Ireland were united in a single kingdom called the **United Kingdom of Great Britain and Ireland**, with one king and one parliament.
- The parliament of the United Kingdom would meet at Westminster in London and would make laws for both Ireland and Britain.
- Irish voters would elect 100 Irish MPs to represent them in the United Kingdom parliament.
- Trade between Ireland and Britain would be completely free.

On 1 January 1801, a new flag was raised over Dublin Castle. It was the **Union Jack**, the flag of the new United Kingdom. The Union lasted until 1920.

QUESTIONS

1. Why did the Bantry Bay expedition fail?
2. What action did the government take against the Defenders and the United Irishmen after Bantry Bay?
3. 1798 is sometimes called "The Year of the French". Explain why.
4. What were the consequences for Ireland of the 1798 Rising?

Activities

1. WRITE AN ACCOUNT OF THE 1798 RISING IN WEXFORD.
2. WRITE AN ACCOUNT OF THE UNITED IRISHMEN. IN IT, REFER TO: (A) HOW IT WAS FORMED; (B) WHAT ITS AIMS WERE; (C) WHY IT BECAME A REVOLUTIONARY MOVEMENT; (D) THE PART IT PLAYED IN 1798.
3. WRITE AN ACCOUNT OF WOLFE TONE'S ROLE IN IRISH HISTORY. YOU SHOULD DEAL WITH: (A) HIS EARLY LIFE; (B) THE PART HE PLAYED IN FOUNDING THE UNITED IRISHMEN; (C) HIS INVOLVEMENT WITH THE CATHOLIC COMMITTEE; (D) WHY HE LEFT IRELAND; (E) BANTRY BAY; (F) HIS PART IN 1798.

CHAPTER

65

Causes of the Industrial Revolution

In Section 9, you read about the political revolutions in America and France at the end of the eighteenth century. These revolutions changed the ways in which those countries were run.

At around the same time, a different kind of revolution started in Britain. It was a **social revolution** which changed the way people lived.

There were several parts to this revolution.

▰ A **revolution in agriculture** changed the way in which food was grown.

▰ A **revolution in industry** changed the way in which goods were made.

▰ A **revolution in transport** changed the way in which goods and people were carried from place to place.

These things changed the way in which society was organised. This series of changes is called the **Industrial Revolution**. It began in Britain in the middle of the eighteenth century and then spread to the rest of Europe and to America.

Why did the Industrial Revolution happen?

Historians disagree about the causes of the Industrial Revolution. But they all agree that one thing was important – the growth of population in Europe after 1750. These tables show the population growth in Britain and Ireland between 1700 and 1841.

	BRITAIN		IRELAND
1700*	6,500,000	1700*	2,000,000
1750*	7,750,000	1750*	2,500,000
1801	10,500,000	1800*	5,000,000
1821	14,000,000	1821	6,800,000
1841	18,000,000	1841	8,175,000

(Numbers marked * are guesses because no accurate censuses were held in Britain until 1801 and in Ireland until 1821)

🏛 WHAT CAUSED THE POPULATION GROWTH?

Historians are not sure why this happened, but they have suggested some reasons.

BETTER FOOD AND DRINK

Famines became rare in Europe in the eighteenth century. This was partly because the explorers brought back new foods like potatoes, maize and rice from around the world. Europeans now had a more varied diet.

Up to the eighteenth century, most people in Europe drank beer or wine with their meals. They seldom drank water which was usually dirty and carried diseases. In the eighteenth and nineteenth centuries, tea and coffee became cheaper, so that most people could afford them. This improved their health since they drank less alcohol.

Better food and drink meant that fewer babies died young. Those who lived grew up and had families of their own, thus increasing the population.

EDWARD JENNER AND SMALLPOX VACCINATION

In the eighteenth century, many people still died from diseases like measles or tuberculosis (TB) which are controlled today. But doctors did find a way to stop one killer disease – smallpox.

Smallpox was especially common in children. Each year, it killed thousands and those who survived were left with terrible scars on their faces.

An English doctor, Edward Jenner, noticed that dairy maids living near him had beautiful, unscarred skin. He found that they got a mild disease called "cowpox" from their cattle. After that, they never got smallpox.

A baby is vaccinated against smallpox by Edward Jenner.

Jenner wondered if having cowpox protected the dairy maids from smallpox. He decided to test his idea. He injected a young boy with cowpox and then put him near some people who had smallpox. The boy stayed healthy. Jenner had proved that the cowpox injection – or **vaccination –** had made the boy **immune** to smallpox.

People all over Europe were vaccinated against smallpox and the disease began to disappear. Today, it has been completely eliminated. In the twentieth century, scientists have discovered ways of vaccinating people against many diseases which were once deadly killers.

🔲 QUESTIONS 🔲

1. Explain in your own words what is meant by the term "Industrial Revolution".
2. Write down three problems that might be caused by a rapidly-growing population.
3. Write a paragraph about Edward Jenner and the discovery of vaccination.

Edward Jenner developed a way of vaccinating people against smallpox.

USE THE INFORMATION IN THE TABLES ON PAGE 186. MAKE A GRAPH SHOWING HOW THE POPULATION OF BRITAIN CHANGED BETWEEN 1700 AND 1841. THEN USE A DIFFERENT COLOUR TO SHOW HOW THE IRISH POPULATION CHANGED AT THE SAME TIME. BY WHAT PERCENTAGE DID THE POPULATIONS OF THE TWO COUNTRIES CHANGE DURING THAT TIME?

Activity ▼ ▼ ▼ ▼ ▼

CHAPTER 66

The Agricultural Revolution

Farming in 1750

In the eighteenth century, most people in Europe were farmers. Their methods of farming had changed little since the Middle Ages. Many still lived in villages like the one you studied in Section 4.

The land of the village belonged to the landlord who was called the **squire** in England. In 1750, the squire still lived in an old medieval-style manor house. The villagers paid him a rent for the land.

The land around the village looked much the same as it had in the Middle Ages. There was a wood where the villagers gathered firewood, a marsh where nothing would grow, and the big common where all the village animals were grazed.

Each family in the village had the right to put animals on the common, where they all grazed side by side. Sick animals often infected healthy ones. There was seldom enough hay to feed the animals during the winter. So each autumn, most were killed and their meat salted down to preserve it for the winter. Because of this, people seldom had fresh meat or milk.

The rest of the land consisted of three huge open fields. They are called East Field, West Field and North Field. Each field was divided into long, ploughed strips.

CROP ROTATION

The villagers grew crops on the three ploughed fields. They kept the land fertile by rotating crops in the medieval way. It worked like this.

PLOUGHING, SOWING AND REAPING

The whole village worked together in the fields as a team. First they ploughed with heavy wooden ploughs. Then they took bags of seed and scattered it by hand as they walked along. A lot of the seed was lost in the ditches or eaten by birds. When the crop was ripe, it was cut with a curved knife called a sickle.

WEAKNESSES IN THE OLD SYSTEM

This kind of farming was not efficient. The villagers grew enough to feed themselves and pay a small rent to the squire, but they did not grow enough to feed the growing population. And it was hard for any one farmer to try out new ways of growing crops or raising better animals because everyone worked together.

▲ *The rich farmer*

The small farmer

The labourer

	WEST FIELD	EAST FIELD	NORTH FIELD
Year 1	wheat	barley & beans	fallow
Year 2	fallow	wheat	barley & beans
Year 3	barley & beans	fallow	wheat

THE PEOPLE OF THE VILLAGE

The villagers worked together, but they were not all equal. Here is an account of three families living in one village.

THE RICH FARMER

The rich farmer had many acres of land which were scattered throughout the three open fields. He also grazed many cows on the common. He paid a big rent to the squire, but he had so much land that he could afford to pay his rent and still have plenty left over. His family lived in the biggest house in the village.

THE SMALL FARMER

Most villagers were not so rich. The small farmer had only ten acres or so. He had a cow, several sheep and a small flock of geese grazing on the common. But his animals were thin and sickly and did not earn much for him.

Like the rich farmer, he had to pay rent to the squire, but with so little land, he had to struggle to find the money. When the rent was paid, he had very little left to feed and clothe his family. They lived in a two-room cottage and in winter they were often hungry and cold.

THE LABOURERS

But the small farmer was better off than the labourers. They had no land of their own but depended on what they could earn by working for the squire and the big farmers. They lived in one-roomed huts in the village. They kept a few geese on the common and sold eggs in the nearby town. On the poorest land at the edge of the marsh, they dug out small gardens where they grew potatoes and vegetables.

TIME FOR A CHANGE?

Many villages were like this in the middle of the eighteenth century. But things were starting to change. The growing population needed more food, and landlords and big farmers realised that they could become rich if they could find a way to grow it. Their efforts resulted in the **agricultural revolution**.

QUESTIONS

1. Look up the meaning of the following words: crop rotation; fallow. Write two sentences explaining why crop rotation is necessary.
2. Look at the diagram of crop rotation on page 188 and say what percentage of the land was fallow each year. What grows in a field when it is fallow? Is this a good way of using land? Give reasons for your answer.

Activity

IMAGINE YOU ARE THE SQUIRE OF THE VILLAGE DESCRIBED IN THIS CHAPTER. WRITE A LETTER TO ANOTHER SQUIRE AND INCLUDE THE FOLLOWING POINTS:
- ☑ TWO THINGS YOU THINK ARE WRONG WITH THE PRESENT METHODS OF FARMING
- ☑ TWO REASONS WHY YOU WOULD LIKE TO CHANGE FARMING METHODS
- ☑ TWO REASONS WHY THAT WOULD BE DIFFICULT.

Important people

At the start of the agricultural revolution, some people began to experiment with new ways of farming. Here are some of them.

"TURNIP" TOWNSHEND AND THE NORFOLK ROTATION SYSTEM

In Norfolk on the east coast of England, farmers experimented with new crops like turnips and clover. They found that turnips kept the soil clear of weeds and that clover returned a chemical called nitrogen to the soil which is used up by growing wheat. If they grew these crops, they did not have to "rest" the soil by leaving it fallow.

This led to a new rotation system called the **Norfolk four-course rotation**. It went like this.

	North Field	South Field	East Field	West Field
Year 1	wheat	turnip	barley/oats	clover/grass
Year 2	turnip	barley/oats	clover/grass	wheat
Year 3	barley/oats	clover/grass	wheat	turnip
Year 4	clover/grass	wheat	turnip	barley/oats

Compare this rotation with the old one shown on page 188. As you can see, there is no fallow land in the new system. All the land produced crops every year, and farmers could now get nearly three times as much wheat as before.

There was another advantage to this plan for crop rotation. The extra grass and the turnips were fed to cattle and sheep during the winter. This gave people fresh meat and milk all year round.

A wealthy landlord named **Charles Townshend** heard about these ideas. He became so enthusiastic about them that his friends called him "Turnip Townshend". He helped to spread the idea of new crops and new rotations all over Britain and Ireland.

Charles "Turnip" Townshend was enthusiastic about new farming ideas.

ROBERT BAKEWELL AND SELECTIVE BREEDING

At this time, it took five years for a sheep to be ready for the butcher. **Robert Bakewell** wanted to breed sheep that would fatten more quickly. He watched his sheep carefully. He kept those which grew fat quickly and slaughtered the rest. Bakewell bred only those animals which he thought were the fastest growers. His system was called **selective breeding**.

Bakewell did not make money from his new breeds of sheep and cattle. People said his huge animals were "too dear to buy and too fat to eat". He went bankrupt, but other farmers took up selective breeding. The figures below show how the average weight of animals on sale in London changed as a result.

Robert Bakewell developed new breeds of sheep and cattle through selective breeding.

	1710	1795
Ox	800kg	1750kg
Calf	115kg	340kg
Sheep	85kg	180kg

NEW TOOLS AND MACHINES

Some people experimented with new tools and machines.

- Farmers began to cut their corn with a **scythe** instead of a sickle because it was quicker.
- Others replaced the heavy wooden ploughs with stronger and lighter **iron** ones.
- In 1701, a man named **Jethro Tull** invented a **seed drill** which buried the seed in the soil so birds could not get at it. But Tull's machine was clumsy and expensive and few farmers used it.

IMPROVING LANDLORDS

Some landlords realised that they could make more money with these new farming methods, so they urged their tenants to take them up. These men were known as **improving landlords**.

THOMAS COKE

One improving landlord was Thomas Coke. In 1776, he inherited a big estate in Norfolk where he got his tenants to try the new methods by giving them advice and holding competitions.

Thomas Coke encouraged his tenants to try new farming methods.

Coke was very successful. When he began his improvements, he earned £12,000 in rents from his estate. By 1816, this had gone up to £34,700.

ARTHUR YOUNG (1741-1820)

Arthur Young also helped to spread these new ideas. He toured all over England, Ireland and France, writing books about the kind of farming he found. A Frenchman who travelled with Young, François de Rochefoucauld, described how Young worked.

"We met a stout farmer mounted on a good horse who had been inspecting his crops. He had an air

of prosperity about him... He told us that... the land never lies fallow and that they divide their crops on a four-year rotation – in the first year, turnips; in the second, barley sown with clover; in the third, clover by itself; in the fourth, wheat. What astonished me was the way in which all those whom Mr Young questioned replied with more intelligence than one would expect from peasants..."

READ DE ROCHEFOUCAULD'S ACCOUNT OF HIS TRIP WITH ARTHUR YOUNG. WHICH FARMING METHOD WAS THE FARMER THEY SPOKE TO USING? WAS HE DOING WELL OR BADLY AS A RESULT? GIVE REASONS FOR YOUR ANSWER.

Looking at the evidence

▲ *Arthur Young's writings are a valuable source of information about farming in England, Ireland and France.*

Young's books inspired many landlords and farmers to try the new methods he described. Today, they are some of the most important sources of information we have about farming in his time.

▲ *This picture of ploughs and other implements appeared in a magazine in 1745. Pictures like this helped to spread the new farming methods to a wider audience.*

Enclosure and the results of the agricultural revolution

THE NEED FOR ENCLOSURE

By 1780, many landlords had heard of the new ways of farming and wanted to try them out. But this was impossible in the medieval open field village you read about at the beginning of this chapter.

So landlords decided to get rid of the open fields and **enclose** all the land. This would give each farmer his own farm, all in one piece. He could enclose it with hedges to cut it off from the neighbouring farms. He would then be free to try any kind of farming he wished.

ENCLOSURE ACTS

Many landlords asked parliament to pass **enclosure acts** which would allow them to enclose their land. Between 1750 and 1850, over 4000 enclosure acts were passed for England.

QUESTION

What improvement in farming do you associate with (a) Robert Bakewell and (b) Jethro Tull?

DRAW TWO DIAGRAMS, ONE SHOWING THE MEDIEVAL CROP ROTATION, THE OTHER THE NORFOLK FOUR-COURSE ROTATION. LIST THREE WAYS IN WHICH THE NEW ROTATION WAS BETTER THAN THE OLD ONE.

Activity

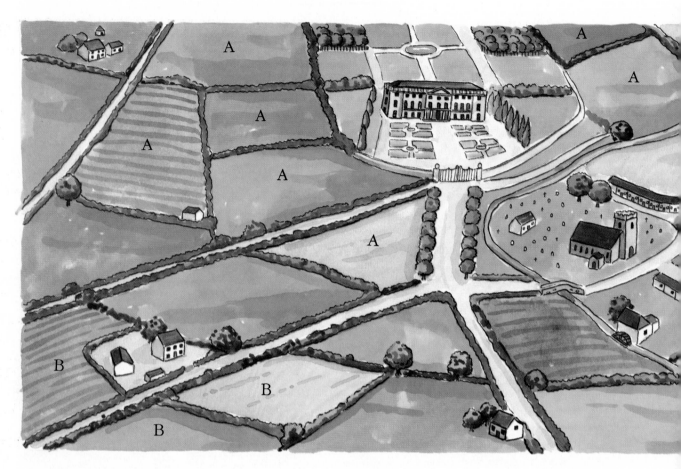

A village after enclosure. Compare it with the medieval village on pages 56-57.

ASKING FOR AN ENCLOSURE ACT

Let us return to the village we read about on pages 55-58 and see how enclosure worked there.

The squire wanted to build a new house. He read Arthur Young's books and realised he could get higher rents from his tenant farmers if he enclosed the open fields. He called a meeting to suggest this to the villagers.

A MIXED RESPONSE

- The big farmers liked the idea. They had heard of the money to be made if they had extra crops to sell.
- The small farmers were more doubtful. On their small farms, they could not grow very much, so what would they have to sell? After enclosure, would they still have other rights, like grazing animals on the common and collecting firewood?
- The labourers were even more worried. If the common was enclosed, where would they keep their geese? And what was to happen to the land near the marsh where they had planted their vegetable gardens?

But the objections of the small farmers and labourers did not count. Voting was based on the amount of land a man had, not on the number of people involved. So the squire and the big farmers won easily. The village asked parliament to pass an enclosure act.

ENCLOSING THE VILLAGE

An enclosure act appointed surveyors to measure the land and decide how much each villager was entitled to. They interviewed everyone and mapped out the land. Anyone who claimed land or rights had to have documents to prove that his claim was true. The squire and most of the big farmers easily proved they were entitled to land. But the small farmer could not prove his right to keep animals on the common.

The surveyors also decided that the marsh belonged to the squire and that the labourers must give up their little gardens.

All of this planning took three years. When it was completed, the surveyors were ready to divide the land into separate farms.

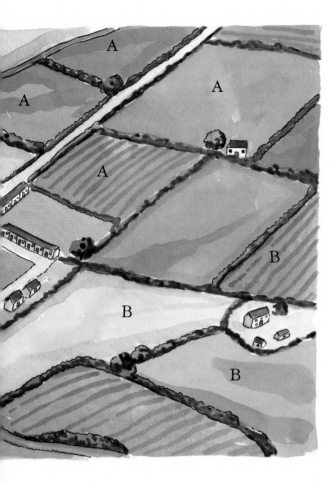

The results of enclosure

Arthur Young was in favour of enclosure. Here is what he said about it in one English county.

"I found (land) which formerly... yielded little or no produce, converted by enclosure into profitable farms... The effects of these enclosures have been very great, for while rents have risen... farmers are in much better circumstances, cattle and sheep are increased and the poor employed."

But was enclosure all good? Here is how enclosure affected the inhabitants of our typical village. Read it and see if you agree with Young about the results of enclosure.

ENCLOSURE AND THE BIG FARMER

When the surveyors enclosed the village, they gave the big farmer 100 acres in a solid block. He made an agreement, called a **lease**, with the squire. The terms of the lease were:

- Every year, the farmer would pay the squire £1 for each acre.
- The squire would not increase this rent for thirty years.
- The farmer would divide his land into fields and plant hedges.
- He would use the new farming methods.

The big farmer had to spend a lot of money on fencing and draining his new farm. He employed many labourers to do the work. At first, he had to borrow to pay for the changes, but soon he had more wheat and cattle to sell and he began making money. Within a few years, he was a rich man, living in a fine new farmhouse. After thirty years, the squire doubled his rent. The big farmer may have grumbled a lot, but he was able to pay easily.

ENCLOSURE AND THE SMALL FARMER

The surveyors decided that the small farmer was only entitled to ten acres (marked B in the picture). He got nothing to make up for losing his free grazing on the common. He too got a lease from the squire on condition that he enclose his new farm. But this cost money, which he had to borrow. With only ten acres, he could not grow enough to pay off his debts or buy turnip seed or better breeds of cattle.

For a few years he struggled on, falling deeper and deeper into debt. At last he was unable to pay

Activities

THE ENCLOSED VILLAGE

THE PICTURE ON THESE TWO PAGES SHOWS THE MEDIEVAL VILLAGE AFTER IT WAS ENCLOSED. COMPARE IT WITH THE DRAWING ON PAGES 56-57 AND ANSWER THESE QUESTIONS.

1. WHAT HAPPENED TO (A) THE MARSH, (B) THE WOOD AND (C) THE COMMON?
2. FIND THE LAND BELONGING TO THE BIG FARMER (A). CAN YOU SUGGEST ANY ADVANTAGES HE GAINED BY ENCLOSURE?
3. FIND THE LAND BELONGING TO THE SMALL FARMER (B). WAS IT EASIER OR HARDER FOR HIM TO FARM IT AFTER ENCLOSURE? GIVE REASONS FOR YOUR ANSWER.
4. HOW DID ENCLOSURE AFFECT THE LIVES OF THE LABOURERS?
5. IN ENGLAND, ENCLOSURE CREATED THE MODERN LANDSCAPE — THE WAY THE COUNTRYSIDE LOOKS TODAY. WHICH PICTURE (THIS ONE OR THE ONE ON PAGES 56-57) LOOKS MORE LIKE THE IRISH COUNTRYSIDE TODAY? BASED ON YOUR ANSWER, SAY WHETHER YOU THINK WE HAD ENCLOSURE IN IRELAND.

his rent, so the squire put him off his farm and gave it to the big farmer. The small farmer ended up working as a labourer.

This picture is called "Leaving the country due to enclosure". Which group of villagers do you think it shows? Was the artist sympathetic or unsympathetic to them? Explain your answer.

ENCLOSURE AND THE LABOURERS

The labourers did worst of all after enclosure. They lost the right to keep geese on the common and to have gardens near the marsh. They had hoped to get cottage gardens, but the surveyors decided against this. The labourers still had their cottages in the village, and part of the woodland was left standing so they could get fuel, but that was all.

At first there was plenty of work for these people in planting hedges and digging drains. But their wages were too low to buy enough food for a family, much less clothes or other things.

A man called William Cobbet rode around England in 1820 and described some of the labourers he met.

"Three poor fellows, digging stone for the roads, told me they never had anything but bread to eat and water to wash it down. One of them was a widower with three children and his pay was 18d (7½p) a day, that is to say (enough to buy) about 3½ pounds of bread each day for six days a week; nothing for Sunday or for lodging, washing, clothes or fuel."

As a result, many labourers were forced to depend on charity to survive. Some labourers expressed their anger about enclosure in this bitter verse:

*"They hang the man and flog the woman
Who steals the goose from off the common,
But leave the greater criminal loose
Who steals the common from the goose."*

QUESTIONS

1. Explain what is meant by "enclosure". Who wanted it and why?
2. (a) Some people in a village gained from enclosure. Who were they? List three ways in which they gained.
   (b) Some people lost by enclosure. Who were they? Explain what they lost.
3. On balance, do you think the agricultural revolution was good or bad? Give reasons for your answer.

SELECT ONE OF THE FOLLOWING: SQUIRE, BIG FARMER, SMALL FARMER OR LABOURER. WRITE AN ACCOUNT OF HIS LIFE DURING THE AGRICULTURAL REVOLUTION. REFER TO THE FOLLOWING POINTS: (A) LIFE BEFORE THE CHANGES; (B) HOW THE CHANGES CAME ABOUT; (C) THE EFFECTS ON HIS LIFE; (D) WHETHER HE WAS BETTER OR WORSE OFF AS A RESULT.

Activity

A Revolution in Industry

The domestic system

In the eighteenth century, country people still made their own clothes at home, just as they had for thousands of years. They made two kinds of cloth – wool and linen. Wool came from the sheep raised by the farmers. Linen was made from flax which they grew in their fields.

Women spun the wool or flax into yarn (thread), and then the men wove the yarn into cloth. The cloth which they produced was made into coats, dresses, trousers and so on.

By the 1760s, more and more people were living in cities. They had no way of making their own cloth, so they had to buy it. To supply these needs, country people began making cloth to sell to city-dwellers. This was known as the **domestic system** of manufacturing.

Flax fibres were bleached outside in the open air.

The Irish linen industry

In Ireland, people made both woollen and linen cloth. Wool was made mainly in the south and linen in the north.

BLEACHING AND COMBING THE FLAX

Linen was made from flax which farmers grew. After the flax was harvested it was rotted down until only the fibres were left. The fibres were then bleached outside in the open air. The flax was then combed before it was spun. Parents and children all worked together to prepare the flax.

SPINNING AND DYING

Women did the spinning and dying. In this picture, two women are working with spinning wheels. The large bundles above the wheels are the combed flax fibres which the spinning wheels are twisting into yarn (thread). The woman on the right is winding the finished yarn onto a reel, while the woman by the fire is stirring dye in a big pot.

Spinning and dying

WEAVING

The men did the weaving. They got the yarn from the women and wound it onto bobbins. The man in this picture is weaving the yarn into cloth. The machine he is using is called a **loom**. The horizontal threads are set up on the loom to form the **warp**. Another thread is passed through them to form the **weft**. The weaver uses a **shuttle** to pass the weft back and forth across the warp. Can you see the shuttle in the weaver's hand and the roll of cloth that is forming at his feet?

At this stage, the linen cloth was a dirty-grey colour. The weavers left it out in the sun and rain to bleach it white. They then took it to the nearest market to sell it.

THE PROSPERITY OF THE WEAVING FAMILY

As the population grew in the eighteenth century, there was an increased demand for cloth. So weaving families prospered.

QUESTION

Explain the phrase "the domestic system of manufacturing" in your own words.

Looking at the evidence

IMAGINE YOU WERE A MEMBER OF A LINEN-MAKING FAMILY IN THE EIGHTEENTH CENTURY. USING THE EVIDENCE IN THE LAST SECTION, DESCRIBE A DAY IN YOUR LIFE.

The start of the cotton industry

The first Europeans to reach India found an unfamiliar cloth called **cotton**. Like linen, it was smooth against the skin, but it was much lighter and cooler. Wealthy merchants imported cotton to Britain and Ireland where it became fashionable.

Spinners and weavers started to make cotton cloth, but they could not keep up with the demand. This encouraged people to invent new machines to speed up the making of cotton. Here are some of the main inventions.

NEW INVENTIONS FOR THE COTTON INDUSTRY

JOHN KAY'S "FLYING SHUTTLE": 1733

Looms were big and clumsy and it took two men to push the shuttle from side to side. In 1733, **John Kay** put his shuttle on wheels so he could pass it back and forth more quickly, and without help. He called his invention a **flying shuttle**. It made weaving more efficient.

JAMES HARGREAVES AND THE "SPINNING JENNY": 1765

James Hargreaves' "spinning jenny" Compare it with the spinning wheel on page 195.

In 1765, **James Hargreaves** invented a spinning machine that spun seven threads at once. He called it a **jenny** after his wife (who may have thought of the idea herself). Others improved on this innovation and soon there were jennies that could spin eighty threads at once.

RICHARD ARKWRIGHT'S "WATER FRAME": 1769

Richard Arkwright was a poor barber who wanted to be rich. He invented a better spinning machine in 1769 which was so big that it had to be turned by water. It was called the **water frame**. For centuries, people had used water power to turn heavy mill stones to grind the corn. Arkwright was the first person to use water power to turn a spinning machine.

THE FIRST FACTORIES

Arkwright found a fast-flowing stream and built a large building beside it. He filled it with water frames and paid people to work on them. This was a big change from the domestic system where people worked in their own homes. Arkwright built many more spinning mills (or factories) and became a millionaire.

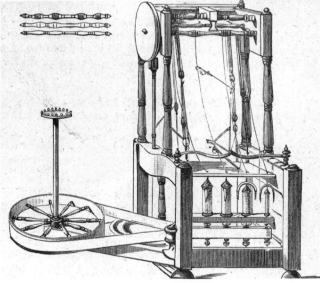

▲ Richard Arkwright invented a better spinning machine called the water frame. How did this invention lead to large factories being set up throughout England?

SAMUEL CROMPTON AND THE "MULE": 1779

The jennies and the water frames made a rough yarn. In 1779, a spinner named **Samuel Crompton** invented a machine which he called a **mule**. It spun a very fine yarn and was easy to work. Factory owners put mules in their factories and employed women and children to operate them because they worked for lower wages than men.

▲ Samuel Crompton. How did his "mule" lead to more women and children being employed in factories?

JAMES WATT AND THE STEAM ENGINE: 1782

The first factories ran on water power, which had its disadvantages. There were not many suitable rivers in Britain. Rivers sometimes dried up in the summer, so factory owners wanted a different way to power their machines.

▲ James Watt studies Newcomen's steam engine

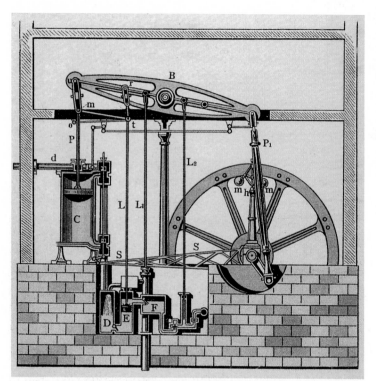

James Watt's steam engine

An early factory, with power looms being used to weave cloth. Who were the main workers? Why?

The domestic system of making cloth had ended and the Industrial Revolution had begun.

THE SPREAD OF INDUSTRIALISATION

The Industrial Revolution soon spread to other industries.

- Iron was needed for new machines, so the **iron industry** prospered. **Abraham Darby** discovered a way to melt iron using coal instead of charcoal. People also found out how to mould iron into shapes and how to make it flexible so that it did not break so easily.
- The growing iron industry created an increased demand for **coal**. New coal mines were opened up. Miners discovered how to pump water out of deep mines and how to keep the roofs from caving in.

The Industrial Revolution began in Britain where it changed people's lives completely. We will look at some results of these changes in the Special Study part of this section.

In 1709, a man named **Newcomen** had invented a steam engine to pump water out of coal mines. But Newcomen's steam pump was not very efficient.

James Watt, a Scottish engineer, began to experiment with new kinds of steam engines, and in 1782, he built one which could turn a wheel. Now steam power could be used to drive the spinning machines in the factories. This meant that factories no longer had to be built beside running water.

EDWARD CARTWRIGHT AND THE POWER LOOM

Edward Cartwright

Up to this, weaving was done at home and skilled weavers earned very high wages. One day a clergyman, **Edward Cartwright**, heard some cotton manufacturers complaining about this. He asked why they did not invent a power-driven loom. They told him that this was impossible because weaving was more complicated than spinning.

Cartwright decided to make a power loom himself. It took him a year. His power looms were not very good, but others improved on Cartwright's design. By 1820, power looms were working in factories.

Activities

1. MAKE A TIME LINE SHOWING THE MAIN INVENTIONS IN THE SPINNING OF COTTON YARN AND THE YEAR IN WHICH EACH ONE WAS MADE. BEGIN LIKE THIS:
   1733: JOHN KAY'S _____
   IN EACH CASE, SAY WHAT THE INVENTION DID.
2. IN THE LAST CHAPTER YOU WROTE ABOUT A FAMILY ENGAGED IN DOMESTIC INDUSTRY. NOW FINISH THEIR STORY BY TELLING HOW THEIR LIVES WERE CHANGED BY THE INDUSTRIAL REVOLUTION.

A Transport Revolution

As the Agricultural and Industrial Revolutions developed, heavy goods like wheat or coal had to be moved from place to place. Businessmen looked for cheap and quick ways of doing this. This led to the building of canals, the improvement of roads and the invention of the railways.

Canals

The cheapest way to carry heavy goods was by water. The seas around Britain and Ireland were full of sailing ships carrying goods such as coal, iron, wheat, tea and cotton. Inland, barges carried these products along the rivers.

But many places were not near the sea or on a suitable river, so people began to build **canals**. The first modern canal in Britain or Ireland was built in Ulster. It carried coal from Coalisland in Co. Tyrone to the sea at Newry. The coal was then shipped to Dublin where the people bought it to heat their houses.

🔺 *A viaduct on the Bridgewater Canal*

JAMES BRINDLEY AND THE BRIDGEWATER CANAL

🔺 *James Brindley designed Britain's first big canal.*

The first big British canal was built in 1759 by **James Brindley**. At that time, Manchester was growing fast and its people needed coal. But coal was dear because it cost so much to carry it by road.

The Duke of Bridgewater had coal mines on his land. He thought he could make more money if he could find a cheap way to bring his coal to Manchester. He asked Brindley to build him a canal.

The main problem facing Brindley was a deep valley between the duke's land and the city. Brindley solved the problem by building a **viaduct**, a bridge which carried the water of the canal across the valley.

The canal was an immediate success. The price of coal in Manchester fell from 7d (3p) to 4d (1.7p) per hundredweight (51 kg). Demand for coal soared and the Bridgewater Canal earned £80,000 in its first year.

After this, more canals were built. In Ireland, the Grand Canal linked Dublin with the Shannon. It is still in use today. Because Ireland had so few big industries, the Grand Canal carried mainly passengers.

Travel by road

Most travel in the eighteenth century was by road. But they were full of potholes, and in winter they were so muddy that nothing could travel on them.

Heavy goods were carried in huge wagons pulled

by teams of horses. They went at two or three miles an hour.

Carriages were not much quicker. A blind engineer, James Metcalf, made a bet that he could walk from London to York (about 320km) faster than another man could go in his carriage. He made the journey in six days; the carriage took eight.

IMPROVING THE ROADS

Three engineers showed how to improve roads.

- **James Metcalf** built roads on firm foundations.
- **Thomas Telford** built roads with good drainage and took his roads around steep hills rather than up and over them.
- **John McAdam** used rough stone chippings to make his roads. This material let the water drain through so roads were less muddy. Today, we add tar to the chippings to produce the **tarmacadam** from which modern roads are made.

TURNPIKE ROADS

Businessmen who wanted good roads built private roads called **turnpike roads**. They charged people tolls to travel on the turnpikes. The best engineers were hired to build their roads, so turnpikes were wide and well made. Coaches could travel much more quickly on them.

This table shows how the journey time between London and Manchester (250km) changed as the roads improved.

| 1736 | 4½ days |
| 1836 | 18 hours |

STAGE COACHES AND MAIL COACHES

With improved roads, public **stage coaches** began to operate. They were pulled by four horses, with passengers sitting both inside and on top. Like buses, they stopped at stages along the road to change horses and pick up passengers.

Mail coaches, which carried letters, were the fastest. The post had to arrive on time, so nothing was allowed to delay them. Toll gates were opened when the coachman blew his horn and all other carriages had to get out of the way.

The Irish Mail between London and Holyhead was one of the best services. The government got Telford to improve the road. As a result, the journey time fell

A mail coach travels between London and Bath around 1830.

from 44 hours in 1815 to 27 hours by 1830. That was an average of 10 miles an hour.

In 1828, when coaches were at their best, a Frenchman called Gustave d'Eichthal wrote this account of a coach journey.

"On Monday we took our seats on the coach for York... Each coach carries eight passengers outside and only four inside. When...you take the precaution of equipping yourself with 2 or 3 overcoats, and kerchiefs (scarves) to wrap around your face, there is no hardship in travelling outside. We reached York in 25 hours, an average of 8 miles per hour, a very good speed, one reached only on good roads. If the road was not paved, the outside passengers would not stay in their seats for long. We only stopped half an hour for dinner and half an hour for lunch."

CHARLES BIANCONI

Mail coaches and stage coaches travelled between the main towns in Ireland too. In 1815 an Italian, Charles Bianconi, set up a coaching service between the smaller towns of Munster. On Bianconi's **long car**, passengers sat facing sideways, with their luggage in the centre.

Charles Bianconi's long car. How is it different from the mail coach?

QUESTIONS

1. Why did people build canals in the eighteenth century?
2. List three ways in which roads improved in the eighteenth century.

Looking at the evidence

1. READ D'EICHTHAL'S ACCOUNT OF HIS JOURNEY (PAGE 200). DID HE TRAVEL OUTSIDE OR INSIDE THE COACH? HOW CAN YOU TELL? WHAT PRECAUTIONS DID HE TAKE TO MAKE HIS JOURNEY MORE COMFORTABLE? DID HE THINK THE COACH WAS FAST OR SLOW? HOW DO YOU KNOW?
2. USING THE PICTURE AND D'EICHTHAL'S ACCOUNT, WRITE A PARAGRAPH DESCRIBING A JOURNEY IN A MAIL COACH.

The invention of the railways

Roads and canals were much improved by 1820, but travel on them was still very slow. Business people wanted a means of transport which was even faster.

One idea they considered was **railways**. Railways were first used in coal mines where carts loaded with coal were put on rails. In this way, horses could pull far heavier loads than when the carts were on ordinary roads.

LOCOMOTIVES

Another idea was a steam-driven coach called a **locomotive**. The first locomotive was invented in 1784. It ran on the road and was very slow.

In 1804, a man named **Trevithick** put a steam locomotive on rails. He called it the *Catch-me-who-can*. It went well, but it was slow and the rails broke if the load was too heavy. It could only be used as an entertainment.

Other engineers improved on Trevithick's idea. They wanted to make a locomotive which was **reliable** (early ones often broke down), **cheap** to run (early ones used so much coal they could only be used near coal mines) and **fast**.

▲ *Richard Trevithick's* Catch-me-who-can, *giving rides to the public in 1809.*

GEORGE STEPHENSON

George Stephenson solved the problems of reliability, cost and speed. He had little schooling and always had difficulty in writing, but he was a brilliant engineer. He improved the rails and increased the amount they could carry. He built several locomotives for coal mines, improving his design each time.

George Stephenson improved the design of railway locomotives.

In 1821, some businessmen asked Stephenson to build a railway from Stockton to Darlington in the north of England. Some wagons on it were pulled by horses, others by a locomotive which Stephenson built. Called the *Locomotion*, it was slow and very heavy – but it worked.

▲ *The opening of the Stockton to Darlington railway. What kind of scene is shown in the painting?*

THE LIVERPOOL-MANCHESTER RAILWAY

In 1824, businessmen in Liverpool decided to build a railway to carry cotton from Liverpool to Manchester. They put Stephenson in charge. He had to tunnel through rocks, lay rails across a bog, and build a viaduct to carry the rails over a deep valley. After five years, in 1829, it was finished.

▲ *Crowds gather to cheer Stephenson's new locomotive, the* Rocket

The question then was: how would the railway wagons be pulled? Stephenson wanted a locomotive. But the owners were doubtful, since they felt that locomotives were slow and unreliable. To settle the question, they announced a competition for the best locomotive. The winning locomotive must have three things: speed, economy of fuel and reliability. The prize was £500.

On the race day, five locomotives entered – but only two had a real chance. One was the *Novelty*. The other was Stephenson's new locomotive, the *Rocket*. The *Novelty* reached 28 miles per hour without a load but it broke down on the second day. The *Rocket* reached 25 mph without a load, 12 mph pulling 1½ tons and it never broke down. Stephenson had won.

The first modern railway

The railway between Liverpool and Manchester opened in 1830. It was the first modern railway in which all wagons were pulled by steam locomotives. Everyone wanted to ride on them. Here is a description of a trip taken by an elderly gentleman named Thomas Creevy.

"I had the satisfaction, for I cannot call it pleasure, of taking a trip of 5 miles, which it did in just a quarter of an hour – that's 20 miles an hour.... The quickest motion is to me frightful; it is really flying and it is impossible to divest myself of the notion of instant death to all, upon the least accident happening. It gave me a headache which has not left me yet. The smoke is very inconsiderable but sparks of fire are about... One burned Miss de Ros's cheek and another a hole in someone's gown. Altogether, I am glad to have seen this miracle and to have travelled on it, but having done so, I am quite satisfied with my first achievement being my last."

The spread of railways

Fortunately, not many passengers were as nervous as Mr Creevy. Within weeks, 1200 people were travelling by rail every day.

This success inspired others to build new railways. In Ireland, the first railway was built in 1834 between **Dublin and Kingstown** (Dun Laoghaire).

By 1850, the main cities in Britain and Ireland were linked by rail. The time taken on journeys and the cost of transporting goods fell. Stage coach companies closed down and the roads were neglected until the motor car became common early in the twentieth century.

A tunnel along the Dublin-Kingstown railway

◤ QUESTIONS ◥

1. What is the real meaning of the word "railway"? Where were railways first used? Explain why.
2. What is a "locomotive"? Who first put a steam locomotive on railways?

Activity ▼ ▼

GEORGE STEPHENSON WAS THE ENGINEER WHO MADE THE FIRST PRACTICAL LOCOMOTIVE. FIND OUT MORE ABOUT HIM IN AN ENCYCLOPAEDIA AND WRITE AN ACCOUNT OF HIS LIFE AND WORK.

Looking at the evidence

1. READ THOMAS CREEVY'S ACCOUNT OF HIS RAILWAY JOURNEY (PAGE 202). DID HE ENJOY IT? POINT TO THREE SENTENCES IN HIS ACCOUNT TO SUPPORT YOUR ANSWER.
2. IMAGINE YOU WERE A PASSENGER ON THE LIVERPOOL-MANCHESTER RAILWAY IN ITS EARLY DAYS. WRITE AN ACCOUNT OF YOUR JOURNEY, USING WHAT CREEVY.

3. THIS TABLE SHOWS HOW LONG A JOURNEY FROM LONDON TO EDINBURGH TOOK IN DIFFERENT YEARS.

1750	12 DAYS
1796	2 ½ DAYS
1830	1 ½ DAYS
1850	10 HOURS

(A) DRAW A GRAPH SHOWING HOW THE JOURNEY TIME HAD CHANGED IN 100 YEARS.
(B) IN THE CASE OF EACH OF THE ABOVE DATES, SAY WHAT NEW DEVELOPMENT IN

CHAPTER

69

Britain and Ireland in the 1840s

🏛 Britain in the 1840s

By 1840, the Industrial Revolution had had a great influence on life in Britain and Ireland. It affected the two countries in very different ways, however. Britain was the world's first industrial country. This changed the lives of people there. Here are some of the positive (good) changes.

▣ Clothes and food became **cheaper**, so many people were better clothed and fed.

▣ People could **travel** more easily and quickly from place to place.

▣ Many people connected with the new industries became **rich.** They wanted the landowners to let them into parliament. The landowners were afraid that, if they said no, Britain might have a revolution like the one in France. So in 1832, they let the **middle class** (the group of people between the rich landowners and the poor workers) share power with them. This started the move towards a more **democratic government** in Britain.

▣ Workers formed **trade unions** to campaign for better wages and working conditions. Some of them also wanted the right to vote for their MPs, but this did not come for many years.

Other changes were much less pleasant. We will look at some of them.

🏛 Children at work

🏛 FACTORY CHILDREN

During the Industrial Revolution, employers set up great steam-powered factories. Most of the workers in these factories were women and children. Factory owners liked this because they only had to pay women half as much as men and children only one-third, even though women and children did just as much work.

In the old domestic system, children worked beside their parents. When the parents went into the factories, they brought their children with them because they needed the money their children could earn. Many factory children were orphans. When their parents died, they were put into workhouses which they left every day to go to work in the factories.

▲ *Children being paid for their work. Do you think they were well paid? Explain your answer.*

SOURCE A

A Manchester doctor described what happened to the children.

"Children of a very tender age are collected from workhouses in London and transported in crowds to masters many hundreds of miles distant where they serve, unknown, unprotected and forgotten..."

SOURCE B

A boy who was sent to work in a factory at the age of seven described what his life was like.

"I had to rise early and work late. My orders were never to sit down during the hours of work. Once I was fifteen minutes late. For this I was beaten, kicked and scourged. I could hardly stand when my tormentor gave over, but was instantly driven to my work."

⌂ CHILDREN IN THE MINES

SOURCE C

Women and children also worked down the mines, helping to bring up coal. Some pushed heavy trucks along rails underground, while others carried large baskets of coal on their backs up steep ladders. Very young children worked as "trappers". They opened and shut the trap doors which kept the mines ventilated.

⌂ *A child working as a trapper. Comment on what you see.*

SOURCE D

In 1842, the government set up an enquiry into the work of women and children in the mines. The enquiry team talked to some of the children. Sarah Gooder was a trapper. She was only eight years old. She said:

"It does not tire me, but I have to trap without a light and I'm scared. Sometimes I sing when I have a light, but not in the dark. I dare not sing then. I do not like being in the pit."

SOURCE E

Another girl, Margaret Higgs, said this to the enquiry.

"I work from eight in the morning till six at night. Occasionally we work all night. I fill a bagie (cart) with two to three hundredweight (120-150 kg) and drag it a good distance, 200-400 yards (150-300 metres). The pavement I drag it over is wet and I have to crawl on my hands and knees."

⌂ *Children had to crawl on their hands and knees to pull the carts.*

⌂ *Children being lowered into a mine. What dangers would these children face?*

ROBERT OWEN

Robert Owen was a factory owner who tried to improve conditions for his workers. He would not employ children below the age of ten and set up a school for the younger ones. He built decent houses for his workers and started a shop where they could buy food at a reasonable price. But even so, he still expected ten-year-olds to work a $12\frac{1}{2}$ hour day for six days a week.

FACTORY REFORM

People like Owen and the factory workers themselves wanted the government to pass laws protecting workers. The government investigated factory conditions. What they found was so shocking that various **factory acts** were passed which controlled what factory owners could do. Here are the main factory acts.

> ☑ 1833: Children between 9 and 13 could only work 8 hours a day and were to go to school for 2 hours.
> ☑ 1842: Women as well as boys under 10 were not to work underground in mines.
> ☑ 1847: Women and children were only to work for 10 hours a day in factories.
> ☑ 1850: Factories were only to work between 6.00 am and 6.00 pm, with $1\frac{1}{2}$ hours for meals. Now even men were only working $10\frac{1}{2}$ hours a day.

◪ QUESTIONS ◪

1. Why did factory owners like to employ women and children?
2. What was a "factory act"? Name one person who campaigned for factory acts.
3. Describe the contents of one factory act. Tell why this was necessary.

1. USING THE EVIDENCE IN SOURCES A AND B, WRITE A PARAGRAPH ABOUT FACTORY CHILDREN.
2. USING THE EVIDENCE IN SOURCES C, D, AND E, WRITE A PARAGRAPH ABOUT CHILDREN IN THE MINES.

Looking at the evidence

Industrial Cities in Britain

URBANISATION

During the Industrial Revolution, workers left the countryside and crowded into the towns and cities to get work in the new factories. In 1750 (before the Industrial Revolution), about 70% of British people lived in the countryside. By 1850 (after the Industrial Revolution), 50% lived in cities. This move to the cities is called **urbanisation**.

BRITISH CITIES

The greatest city in Britain was London. In 1801, there were 975,000 people living there. By 1850, London had a population of 2,362,000. The other big cities were in the north, near the coal fields.

▲ *Urbanisation began to create situations like this.*

THIS TABLE SHOWS HOW INDUSTRIAL CITIES GREW BETWEEN 1801 AND 1851.

	1801	1811	1821	1831	1841	1851
GLASGOW	77,000	101,000	147,000	202,000	275,000	345,000
LEEDS	53,000	63,000	84,000	123,000	152,000	172,000
MANCHESTER	75,000	89,000	126,000	182,000	235,000	303,000
BIRMINGHAM	71,000	83,000	102,000	145,000	183,000	233,000
LIVERPOOL	82,000	104,000	138,000	202,000	286,000	376,000

MAKE A GRAPH SHOWING HOW THE POPULATION IN EACH CITY CHANGED BETWEEN 1801 AND 1851. IN WHICH DECADES DID THE POPULATION GROW FASTEST? LOOK BACK TO THE ACCOUNT OF THE INDUSTRIAL REVOLUTION (PAGES 195-198) TO FIND REASONS TO EXPLAIN THIS RAPID GROWTH.

OVERCROWDING

Urbanisation led to overcrowding. There were not enough houses, so workers moved into old houses near the centre of the cities. The novelist, Charles Dickens, described these **tenement houses** in London in the 1830s.

"Wretched houses with broken windows patched with rags and paper. Every room let out to a different family and in many instances to two or even three. Filth everywhere, a gutter before the house and a drain behind, clothes drying and slops emptying from every window."

Workers were badly paid, so they could only afford to rent a single room for the whole family. They had only one bed and slept in their clothes because they had no blankets to cover them. Their main foods were bread, cheese and beer.

One small tenement room was the home for this family.

Outside a London tenement. Why were such conditions so unhealthy?

WASTE DISPOSAL AND WATER SUPPLY

Overcrowding led to dirt and unhealthy conditions. There were no sewers, so people emptied their waste and sewage into open drains in the streets. The drains in turn emptied into streams and rivers from which people got their drinking water.

This is an account of water supplies in Liverpool in the 1840s. (Find out what "culinary" means before you read it.)

"In some of the districts there are pits. The water accumulates in those pits into which have been thrown dead dogs and cats and a good many other offensive articles. The water is nevertheless used for culinary purposes. I could not believe this at first. I thought it was used only for washing, but I found it was used by the poorer inhabitants for culinary purposes."

HEALTH HAZARDS

Overcrowding and dirt made cities very unhealthy places. People suffered from diseases like typhoid (spread by dirty water) and TB (spread by living in damp, overcrowded conditions). At that time, doctors could do little to cure these diseases. The wealthy people who controlled the government did not live in the crowded cities or suffer from these diseases, so they ignored the plight of the city poor.

CHOLERA

In 1831, a disease called **cholera** appeared. In one year, 31,000 died of it in Britain and 25,000 in Ireland. No one knew what caused it or how to treat it. Unlike other diseases, cholera killed rich and poor alike. The government grew very

▲ *This picture is called "A court for King Cholera". Explain what the artist meant.*

worried.

EDWIN CHADWICK

In 1842, Edwin Chadwick wrote a book called *The Sanitary Conditions of the Labouring Population*. He had worked among the poor and knew about their living conditions. He suggested that diseases like cholera were caused by dirty water. Every town, he said, should have a sewerage system and a constant supply of clean water.

▲ *Edwin Chadwick campaigned for better conditions for working people.*

◄ *The title of this cartoon from the 1830s is "Death's Dispensary". The caption reads: "Open to the poor. Gratis. By permission of the parish". What do you think this means?*

Chadwick backed up his ideas with descriptions of life in the big cities. His book shocked all who read it. Most well-off people had no idea of how bad conditions were. But even so, some of them opposed Chadwick's solution. Known as the "Dirty Party", these people did not like the idea of the government interfering in their lives, even to improve their health.

THE PUBLIC HEALTH ACT OF 1848

In 1848, cholera appeared once again. This time it was worse, with 200,000 people dying. Parliament passed the **Public Health Act**. It said that all cities must deal with drainage, water supply and street cleaning. Where these things were improved, the death rate fell. But it was many years before there was a supply of fresh water and a flush toilet in most houses. When these were installed, many of the diseases that had been so common in the new industrial cities began to disappear.

The caption of this cartoon says: "Oh, Mabel, is it not dreadful? What a miserable place to bring up such a lovely dog!" What point do you think the cartoonist wanted to make?

◤ QUESTIONS ◤

1. Explain what "urbanisation" means. Set out two ways in which urbanisation affected the lives of city dwellers.
2. Name two diseases caused by poor living conditions. Which disease appeared in Britain in 1831? Why did it attract more attention than other diseases?
3. What book did Edwin Chadwick write in 1842? Explain in your own words what Chadwick had to say.
4. Why did parliament pass the Public Health Act in 1848? What did it do?

SELECT ONE OF THE FOLLOWING PEOPLE LIVING IN BRITAIN IN THE 1840s: A CHILD WORKING IN A MINE; A FACTORY OWNER; A WOMAN LIVING IN MANCHESTER. WRITE AN ACCOUNT OF HIS/HER LIFE.
YOU SHOULD INCLUDE: (A) BACKGROUND; (B) WAY OF MAKING A LIVING; (C) HOURS OF WORK; (D) LIVING CONDITIONS; (E) HEALTH.
LOOK IN YOUR LIBRARY FOR ADDITIONAL INFORMATION ON YOUR SUBJECT.

Finding out

Life in Ireland in the 1840s

Ireland and the Industrial Revolution

The Industrial Revolution affected Ireland too, but the results here were very different from those in Britain.

In the eighteenth century, before the Industrial Revolution, many Irish people worked in domestic industry as well as in farming. But the new factories in Britain could make cloth more cheaply than Irish weavers could. As a result, Irish domestic industry declined.

Because Ireland had so little coal, few factories were built here. By the 1840s, the only industrial city was Belfast where there were linen factories. Elsewhere, 80% of Irish people lived in country areas and worked on the land.

Landlords in Ireland

Although so many Irish people worked on the land, it did not belong to them. Instead, it belonged to 20,000 **landlords**. Each landlord had a big estate with thousands of acres. He divided his land into farms and rented them out to tenant-farmers who paid him a rent of between £1.50 and £3 per acre each year.

Like the squires in England, Irish landlords lived in big houses. Their lives were comfortable, with servants to wait on them and horses to draw their coaches. They had plenty of food, fine clothes and lots of entertainment.

DIFFERENT CLASSES OF PEOPLE

Most Irish people were not landlords, but farmers who grew crops and raised animals. But it would be wrong to think that all Irish farmers were the same. A farmer's standard of living depended on how much land he had.

- A farmer with a lot of land was well off.
- A farmer with a some land was comfortable.
- Most farmers had very little or no land and they were very poor.

Irish landlords had fine houses, like Bantry House in Co. Cork.

Looking at the evidence

THIS TABLE FROM THE 1841 CENSUS SHOWS HOW MANY IRISH FARMERS THERE WERE IN THE DIFFERENT CATEGORIES.

FARMERS WITH OVER 30 ACRES	277,000
FARMERS WITH UNDER 15 ACRES	310,000
LANDLESS COTTIERS AND LABOURERS	1,000,000

REMEMBER: THESE ARE **FARMING FAMILIES**, NOT INDIVIDUAL PEOPLE. ASSUMING THERE WERE ABOUT FIVE PEOPLE IN EACH FAMILY, WORK OUT THE NUMBER OF PEOPLE IN EACH GROUP.

One of the beautiful rooms in Bantry House

Others were two-storey buildings with slated roofs. Big farmers could afford to send their sons to school so they would be able to get work in offices or shops. Very few sent their daughters to school, since they did not think education was necessary for girls.

SUB-DIVISION

Some big farmers tried to help their sons by dividing the farm land among them. For example, a farmer with thirty acres and five sons would give each of them six acres. This is called **sub-division**. It was very common along the west coast where there were few jobs outside farming.

Sub-division created many small farms in Ireland. But by the 1840s, farmers realised that sub-division was bad because it was very hard to make a living on a small farm.

THIS IS AN ACCOUNT OF LIFE ON A FARM IN SWORDS, CO. DUBLIN, IN THE 1840S. IT WAS WRITTEN BY ANDREW KETTLE AND TELLS HOW HE REMEMBERED LIFE ON THE FARM WHEN HE WAS A BOY OF SEVEN.

"Our 30-acre farm supported grandfather, grandmother, father, mother and six children, a carter, ploughman, servant boy, servant girl and thrasher. Our settlement would have felt lonely indeed without a lodger or two, and sometimes there were as many as ten or twelve. Most commonly they were broken-down labourers in search of employment.

The food and clothing of our family were nearly all made on the premises. I have often seen in the house on a winter's night a woman carding wool, a girl spinning yarn, an old woman knitting, the carter mending harness, the thrasher soling his brogues (shoes), the servant boy plaiting a straw hat, my grandfather telling stories.

The food was nearly all home-made – wholemeal bread, oaten meal grown on the farm and made into stirabout, potatoes all floury, first-quality butter, bacon raised and cured on the farm, milk freely for all, and honey bees in almost every garden."

1. "FARMERS WITH 30 ACRES HAD A GOOD STANDARD OF LIVING." LIST FIVE POINTS IN ANDREW KETTLE'S ACCOUNT WHICH SUPPORT THIS STATEMENT.

2. DESCRIBE THE TYPE OF FOOD WHICH KETTLE'S FAMILY HAD. WERE THEY WELL FED?

3. HOW MANY WORKERS WERE USUALLY PART OF THE KETTLE FARM? WHAT JOBS WOULD THEY HAVE DONE? WHAT DOES THE PRESENCE OF THESE WORKERS TELL YOU ABOUT THE KETTLE FAMILY?

Looking at the evidence ▼▼▼▼▼▼

BIG FARMERS

A farmer who rented a lot of land was well off. With thirty acres or more, he could grow wheat, oats, barley and potatoes and rear cattle, pigs and horses. When he sold these, he could pay his rent and still have enough left over to pay for a decent house, buy clothes for his family and feed them well on potatoes, vegetables, meat, milk and tea.

His house usually had four or five rooms. Some farmers' houses were long, low and thatched.

THE LIFE OF A SMALL FARMER

In the 1830s and 1840s, the government became worried about the number of poor farmers in Ireland. In 1844, they set up a committee to enquire into their situation. It was called the **Devon Commission**. The members of the commission went around the country, asking people about their lives.

Looking at the evidence ▼

HERE IS PART OF THE DEVON COMMISSION'S INTERVIEW WITH JOHN CONNOLLY, A SMALL FARMER FROM CARRICKMACROSS, CO. MONAGHAN. READ IT AND SEE WHAT IT TELLS US ABOUT THE LIFE OF A SMALL FARMER. DISCUSS YOUR OBSERVATIONS WITH THE CLASS.

ANSWER THE QUESTIONS AT THE RIGHT.

How many acres of land do you hold?
Three.
What rent do you pay?
I pay £3-10s-6d (£3.52½) a year.
What family have you?
Seven.
Do you earn anything by weaving?
No, I gave it up. It was no good at all.
Does your wife keep fowl?
Only for that, it would go very ill paying the rent. Only for that and England. I go over every year to England.
How much do you earn there?
Sometimes I have £4 and sometimes not a shilling.
How do you put together the money to pay the rent?
I put the wages and the fowls together and make up my rent with a great struggle. It is a great thing to do, to maintain ten in a family, my wife, seven children and an old woman.
What is your food?
Potatoes mostly, and a sup of milk betimes.
How do you and your family provide for clothing?
When I go to England, they try to get some money for that. They do as well as they can.

QUESTIONS

1. Where did John Connolly live? How much land did he farm?
2. What rent did he pay? List two ways in which he raised the money for his rent.
3. Why did he give up weaving?
4. List three things, besides rent, that the Connolly family needed money for.
5. Did the Connolly family have a good standard of living? Pick out the points in the interview that support your answer.
6. Write a paragraph on the life of a small farmer, using information from this passage.
7. Here is a list of clothes and what they would have cost around 1840. Make a list of the clothing which the Connolly family would need in a year. Then work out the cost. Do you think John Connolly could afford to clothe his family? Give reasons for your answer.

Men's clothes
hat   15p
coat   84p
waistcoat   8p
trousers   37p
stockings   5p
shirt   10p

Women's clothes
cloak   47p
gown   30p
petticoat   13p
shift   6p
cap   2p
apron   5p
(Women seldom wore shoes.)

COTTIERS AND LABOURERS

Small farmers like John Connolly may have been poor, but cottiers and labourers were poorer still. They had no land of their own and earned their livings by working for farmers or landlords. A cottier had a regular job with a big farmer, while a labourer had no regular employment and took any work that was going.

A COTTIER'S LIFE

When a cottier went to work for a farmer, he was given a plot of land instead of a wage. He paid the farmer by working for him. The cottier's wife and children also worked for the farmer during harvest time.

The cottier built a tiny one-roomed cottage on his land. It had a thatched roof, mud walls and a mud floor. On the rest of the plot, he grew potatoes. In a good year, he grew enough to feed his family and a few pigs as well. He sold the pigs to earn money for clothes and other needs.

A LABOURER'S LIFE

A labourer took any job that was going. Sometimes he had to walk many miles from one job to another. In harvest time, gangs of labourers from Connacht went to work for big farmers in Leinster. They were called **spailpíns**.

Labourers lived in great poverty. They built simple mud cabins along the sides of the road near big towns. Often, when they could not get work, they had to beg from the townspeople.

Sometimes, labourers hired a plot of land to grow potatoes. A good crop lasted from September until June, but once the old crop was finished, they went hungry.

Spailpíns went from place to place looking for work. They carried their tools with them.

Labourers built huts of mud and branches at the side of the road.

Here are three documents from which we can learn about the living conditions of labourers. Read them and answer the questions that follow.

SOURCE A

THIS IS PART OF THE INTERVIEW GIVEN TO THE DEVON COMMISSION BY MICHAEL SULLIVAN WHO LIVED NEAR SKIBBEREEN.

What quantity of ground do you hold?
I have no ground. I am a poor man. I have nothing but my labour.

Under whom do you hold your house?
Under a farmer called Daniel Regan – just a house and an acre of ground.

Have you constant employment?
No, but whenever he wishes to call me, he (Regan) gives me 6d (2½p) a day and a meal. Then at other times, I go down the country and earn £1 or 30 shillings (£1.50), according to the wages there.

Where do you go to?
I may work in Tipperary or Limerick, digging potatoes.

What children have you?
Seven

What is your food for the family?
Nothing but dry potatoes.

Have you fish?
If my poor wife sells her eggs or spins a skein of thread for the market, she may take home with her a penny worth of something to nourish the children, but in general I do not use 5 shillings (25p) worth of kitchen* in a year, except what I may get at Christmas.

Do you have milk with your potatoes?
Not a drop. I have no means of getting it. I would think myself middling happy if I could get the children that, and if they were near a National School**, I could give them schooling.

Have you a pig?
Yes.

Have you a pig sty?
No. He must be kept in some part of the house, in a corner.

What bedding do you have?
I have a bed that would do myself; but I am in want of a second. I cannot afford to have it.

* "Kitchen" meant fish or bacon used to give potatoes a flavour.
**National Schools were started in 1831 to give free education to children in Ireland.

SOURCE B

THESE TABLES FROM 1840 SHOW THE NORMAL DIET OF LABOURERS IN ENNIS AND CLONMEL.

	ENNIS	CLONMEL
BREAKFAST	4 to 5 lbs. of potatoes 1 pint of skimmed milk.	$4\frac{1}{2}$ lbs of potatoes. Milk only in harvest time.
DINNER	The same. And in winter, a herring and water instead of milk	The same; herring occasionally.
SUPPER	The same. Supper is seldom eaten in the months of Nov., Dec. and Jan.	Supper is not always eaten. When it is, the same quantity of food is taken.

Looking at the evidence

QUESTIONS

1. Read Source A. How much rent did Michael Sullivan pay for his cottage and acre of ground? Write down three of the ways in which he earned the rent.
2. Sullivan says his family only ate "dry potatoes". From Source B, work out the weight of potatoes he might eat every day. Weigh out this amount in class and look at it. Would you eat so many potatoes every day? Why not?
3. What else did the Sullivans eat?
4. Can you find anything in Michael Sullivan's answers to support the opinion that "labourers walked many miles for a job"? Explain your answer.
5. Using the evidence from sources A, B and C, write two paragraphs describing a visit to Michael Sullivan's house. Include a description of the house, both outside and in, what the people were doing, what they had to eat. Be sure to include only points for which you have evidence.

SOURCE C

THIS IS A DESCRIPTION OF LABOURERS' CABINS IN CO. WICKLOW.

Looking at the evidence

"The cabins are usually 14 feet by 10. The height of the walls, which are made of mud or clay, is about 7 feet. They never have a second storey or ceiling. They are thatched, generally with straw, but sometimes the people use heather, reeds or potato stalks. The roofing is wretched, letting in the wet in twenty places when it rains.

The floors are merely the natural earth. They are usually damp in wet weather. The best cabins have large open chimneys, while the rest have only a hole in the roof. The window is usually 16 inches by 10. More often, it is just a hole with a wooden shutter which is closed at night and in bad weather."

▲ *Michael Sullivan would have lived in a house life this.*

The Poor Law and the Workhouses

THE POOR LAW

Families like the Sullivans were very poor. In the 1830s, the government decided to bring in a **poor law** to help them. The poor law divided the country into 130 areas called **unions**. Farmers and landlords in each union had to pay a tax to build a big workhouse so that poor people who needed help would have a place to go.

WORKHOUSE LIFE

Life in a workhouse was grim. When a poor family went to the workhouse, they were separated. The boys were sent to the boys' part, the girls to the girls' part. The mother went to the women's part and the father had to stay with the men. As long as they stayed in the workhouse, the family was not allowed to meet.

People in the workhouse were supposed to work for their keep. Young children got a little schooling. Women had to spin and sew and help with the cleaning and cooking. Men had to weave or break stones for road-building.

Workhouse food was bad. There were only two meals a day which were eaten in total silence. For breakfast, adults got 200g (7 ounces) of oatmeal made into porridge and a pint of buttermilk. For dinner, they got 7kg of potatoes and a pint of buttermilk. They were not allowed tea, tobacco or whiskey.

This harsh life and poor diet meant that people did not go into a workhouses unless they were almost starving.

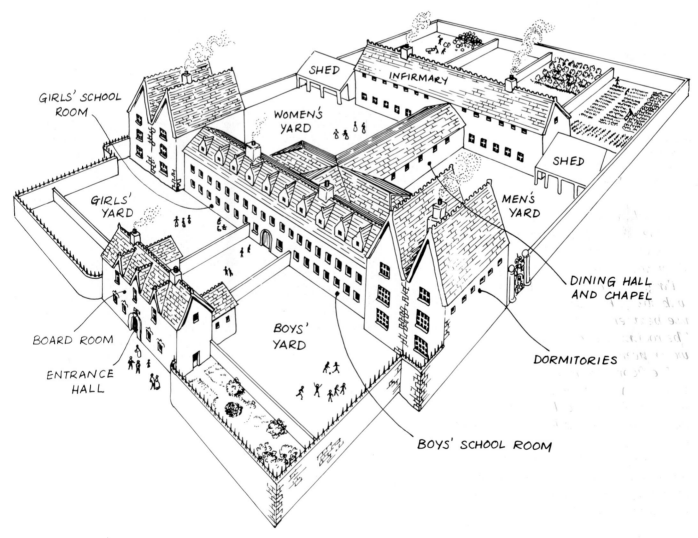

The plan of a workhouse

HERE IS WHAT A POOR OLD MAN HAD TO SAY WHEN ASKED WHY HE DID NOT GO INTO A WORKHOUSE.

"I'd rather share the fox's hole and lie down to die with the open air of heaven above me than be put alive into that poor man's jail and be looked at once a month by the quality for a show."

1. THE OLD MAN CALLED THE WORKHOUSE "A POOR MAN'S JAIL". DO YOU THINK THIS IS A FAIR DESCRIPTION? GIVE REASONS FOR YOUR ANSWER.
2. WHAT DID THE OLD MAN MEAN WHEN HE SAID HE DID NOT WANT TO "BE LOOKED AT ONCE A MONTH BY THE QUALITY FOR A SHOW"?

◼ QUESTION ◼

What was the Irish Poor Law? What was it supposed to do?

IMAGINE YOU ARE THE CHILD OF A POOR LABOURER WHO HAS JUST BEEN ADMITTED TO THE WORKHOUSE. WRITE A LETTER DESCRIBING YOUR IMPRESSIONS AND EXPERIENCES ON THE FIRST DAY. YOU SHOULD INCLUDE: (A) WHY YOUR FAMILY WENT INTO THE WORKHOUSE; (B) WHAT HAPPENED TO THE REST OF THE FAMILY; (C) WHAT THE PLACE LOOKS LIKE; (D) THE FOOD; (E) THE WORK.
YOU MAY WANT TO FIND MORE INFORMATION IN LIBRARY BOOKS.

THIS IS HOW A POOR LABOURER, PATRICK HEGARTY, DESCRIBED HIS LIFE IN WEST CORK IN 1841.

"I am fifty years old. I have a wife and five children. The eldest is only nine. I went out to beg last summer. It was the first time I had no employment. My wife went out every summer. In winter, I used to gather little twigs for making baskets for gathering potatoes. The neighbours used to give us potatoes in the plentiful season. I was obliged to go and beg as well last May. We had another child, and I had to carry it."

1. HOW DO PATRICK HEGARTY AND HIS FAMILY GET FOOD?
2. IF THERE IS A BAD HARVEST, WHAT COULD HAPPEN TO THE HEGARTYS?
3. ARE THE HEGARTYS WORSE OFF OR BETTER OF THAN THE SULLIVANS (PAGE 213)? GIVE REASONS FOR YOUR ANSWER.
4. DESCRIBE WHAT WOULD HAPPEN TO THE HEGARTYS IF THEY HAD TO GO TO A WORKHOUSE.

SOME OF THE WORKHOUSES WHICH WERE BUILT AT THIS TIME ARE STILL STANDING TODAY. IS THERE AN OLD WORKHOUSE NEAR YOU? PERHAPS YOU COULD VISIT IT AND FIND OUT WHAT YOU CAN ABOUT THE HISTORY OF THE PLACE.

The Great Famine

Potatoes: the main food of the people

In the accounts which you have read about life in Ireland in the 1840s, one kind of food is mentioned over and over again – potatoes. Spaniards brought them to Europe from South America in the sixteenth century, but we do not know when or how they reached Ireland. One legend says that Sir Walter Raleigh planted them on his land near Youghal in Co. Cork, but we have no proof of this.

What we do know is that, by 1800, potatoes were the main food of most Irish people. There were two reasons for this.

- The Irish climate suits potatoes.
- Potatoes grow in greater quantities than other crops. An acre of potatoes will feed a family of five for a year; while an acre of wheat will feed only one or two people. Small farmers and labourers could feed a whole family on one acre of potatoes and still have space to grow other crops to pay the rent.

A DANGEROUS DIET

Potatoes are a good, nutritious food. People who ate large quantities of them stayed strong and healthy, especially if they had milk as well. An Irish labourer like Michael Sullivan, working in the fresh air and eating his fill of potatoes, would be healthier than a factory worker or a miner in Britain.

But it is dangerous for anyone to depend on only one food crop. In a wet, cold year, that crop could fail. Then small farmers and labourers were forced to sell their pigs and chickens, and to beg from their neighbours. In this way, they got just enough food to stay alive until the next potato crop was ready. This is what happened five or six times between 1800 and 1845.

The potato blight of 1845

In 1844, a strange disease destroyed the potato crop in Canada. Today, it is called **potato blight**. It is caused by a fungus which spreads easily in warm, moist weather. Now we have sprays which control blight, but in 1844 it was something new. No one knew what it was or how to treat it.

The blight reached Ireland in September 1845. At first, people noticed a strange smell from the potato fields. Then the stalks withered. When people dug them up, they found the potatoes were rotten. About one-third of the crop was destroyed in that year.

This was a hard blow for the small farmers and labourers, but they were used to such difficulties. They sold their animals and pawned their furniture to pay their bills. The government set up road-building schemes where people were able to earn a few pence. The people were then able to buy oats

This drawing is called "Breakfast time". What are the people eating?

and "Indian meal" (maize) to make porridge. They were always hungry during the months that followed, but they survived.

In the spring of 1846, they planted seed potatoes. They had never known the potato crop to fail for two years in a row. Throughout the mild, wet summer they waited, full of hope, for the harvest.

> ### ◪ QUESTIONS ◪
>
> 1. Write two sentences describing what an attack of potato blight was like.
> 2. How much of the potato crop was destroyed in 1845? List three things the labourers and small farmers did to cope with that loss. Why did they hope things would be better in 1846?

A drawing from 1846 shows peasants in despair at the failure of the potato crop.

The same thing happened in every county in Ireland. This time, the entire potato crop was destroyed.

The blight in 1846 meant that people like those you have read about, John Connolly and Michael Sullivan, had lost their only source of food. They had already sold or pawned everything they owned the year before, so they had nothing left. In 1845 they were hungry. Now, in the autumn of 1846, they faced famine.

A woman and her children realise that their potato crop is ruined. Talk about how they would have felt.

🏛 The blight returns: 1846

On 11 August 1846, a priest in Clifden, Co. Galway, wrote to *The Nation* newspaper.

> *"As to the potatoes, they are gone, clean gone. If travelling in the dark, you would know when a potato field was near by the smell. The fields present one space of withered stalks; in some places, the stalks themselves have melted away. Mine, which were safe a few days since, are all going – some gone – though I had none of the disease last year. But if the wheat and other crops take the disease, the world must end."*

> 1. THE PRIEST WHO WROTE FROM CLIFDEN WAS CLEARLY IN DESPAIR. PICK OUT TWO SENTENCES IN HIS LETTER WHICH SHOW THIS.
> 2. LOOK BACK AT THE INTERVIEW WITH MICHAEL SULLIVAN (PAGE 213). NOW WRITE TWO PARAGRAPHS SETTING OUT HIS FAMILY'S EXPERIENCE AT THIS TIME. INCLUDE THEIR REACTION TO THE BLIGHT OF 1845, HOW THEY SURVIVED THE WINTER, THEIR HOPES FOR THE HARVEST, AND THEIR FEELINGS IN AUGUST 1846.

Looking at the evidence

The Famine gets worse

PACKED WORKHOUSES

In 1846, three million small farmers, cottiers and labourers in Ireland faced famine. In their desperation, they flocked into workhouses which were soon overflowing with starving people. Late in 1846, a group of English Quakers visited Ireland to see the situation for themselves. They sent back this report on what they had witnessed.

"In the first cabin, the mistress said they had pawned almost every article of furniture to purchase food. In the next cabin were seven persons who had eaten nothing the previous day except one meal of turnips and a small ration of oatmeal.

At Carrick-on-Shannon, our first visit was to the workhouse. A most heart-rending sight presented itself. Poor wretches in the last stages of famine, imploring to be received into the house. Women who had 6 or 7 children begged that 2 or 3 be taken in, as their husbands were earning but 8d (3p) a day, which, with the present high prices, is totally inadequate to feed them. Some of the children were worn to skeletons, their faces sharpened with hunger."

SOUP KITCHENS

The Quakers gave money to local people to set up **soup kitchens** where free or cheap food was given to hungry people. Soup kitchens run by such charities saved many lives during the famine.

Here is a description of one soup kitchen in Dublin. It comes from a modern book on the Irish famine by Cecil Woodham-Smith called *The Great Hunger*.

"Soyer's new model soup kitchen ... was a wooden building... with a door at each end. In the centre was a 300-gallon soup boiler and a hundred bowls, to which spoons were attached with chains. The people assembled outside the building and were first admitted to a narrow passage, a hundred at a time. A bell rang, they were let in, drank their soup, received a portion of bread and left by the other door. The bowls were rinsed, the bell rang again and another hundred were admitted... The people of Dublin were starving and they crowded to the kitchen; 5000 rations were considered the probable maximum, but 8750 were supplied daily..."

Destitute peasants gather outside a workhouse

FAMINE FEVER

A disease called **famine fever** soon broke out among the people who were weakened by hunger. A Cork priest, Father Matthew, described how this changed people's attitudes to the famine victims.

"At first the sympathy of the citizens was awakened, but when fever began to spread, they became alarmed for themselves and anxious to get rid of the wretched creatures. The lodging housekeepers always turned them out when they became sick. Many perished in rooms and cellars without receiving aid from outside. One Sunday, a person told me: 'There is a house that has been locked for two or three days'. It was a cabin in a narrow alley. We went in and saw 17 persons lying on the floor, all ill with fever. We got them to hospital but they all died."

Many people died of diseases such as famine fever.

During the famine, about ten times more people died from diseases such as famine fever than from starvation. But brave people of all kinds went on helping as much as possible. Many doctors, landlords, clergy and others died from fever themselves while they worked among the poor.

⚜ COLD KILLS

Clothes were as badly needed as food, because the winter of 1846-47 was very cold. This is shown in a report from a man who was working on behalf of a London charity in Belmullet, Co. Mayo.

10 February 1847

"Since my arrival, I have seen the days alternating only with snow, rain, hail, frost and thaw. The state of the weather is rendering the misery of the poor worse... Among the thousands I meet, I have not seen one who had clothing corresponding to the bitter cold. On the contrary, what I see is the emaciated, pale, shivering and worn-out country people, wrapped in the most wretched of rags, standing or crawling in the snow, bare-footed."

came to tell me that in a cabin close to the town, a woman was lying dead, a live infant in her arms, and the other child drowned in a ditch close by."

▲ *The story that went with this drawing from 1847 reads: "Mullins dying, his wife already dead, children starving, vicar powerless to help." What do the picture and the story tell you about the misery of the people during the famine?*

▲ *This drawing is called "Bridget O'Connell and her children". Describe their clothing and appearance.*

13 April 1847

"The weather has continued so bad that our operations have been sadly impeded. All day yesterday, I was employed getting seed and clothes landed, and every package had to be introduced at the point of a bayonet. Both police and soldiers are very much harassed. The people are not dangerous, but they fall on the meal, cut open the sacks and scramble for the contents. This is done chiefly by the women and sick creatures who are much more difficult to repel than able-bodied men with whom we could deal harshly. . .

I have been distributing turnip and parsnip seed all morning. While I was thus employed, a police sergeant

THE EXTRACT TELLS US THAT TURNIP AND PARSNIP SEED WAS BEING DISTRIBUTED. COMMENT ON WHETHER YOU THINK THIS WAS HELPFUL OR NOT TO THE STARVING PEOPLE.

Looking at the evidence

⚜ Evictions

When poor tenants could no longer pay their rent, some landlords **evicted** them from their land. These **evictions** led to further suffering among the poor and starving people.

A visitor to Mayo in 1848 described what he saw.

"From Tiraun to Mullaroghe there was a scene of devastation beyond belief. It was literally a heap of ruins. I tried to count the roofless houses and after proceeding as far as seventy, I gave up in despair. All around were scattered the broken remains of looms, bed frames, stools, straw mats, crockery and rafters.

Landlords evicted poor tenants who could not pay their rent. Describe the scene.

A few miserable people still lingered around this desolate village, imploring relief. They told us that a week before Christmas, the landlord's son, with two drivers, had come and pulled down the roofs of their houses and forced them to leave the place. It was a night of high wind and storm. They implored the drivers to allow them to remain a short time as it was so near the festival, but they would not and all were scattered up and down the country."

WHAT DID THE GOVERNMENT DO?

The government in London was slow to act about the famine. At first, they bought Indian meal (maize) and sold it cheaply to the people. They also set up **public works** which gave grants to build roads or dig drains. The idea was to enable poor people to earn money so that they could then buy food.

This scheme was a failure. People were so weak from hunger that they could not work, so they were unable to earn enough to feed themselves or their families.

CHANGING THE POOR LAW

Irish leaders urged the government to change the poor law so that workhouses could set up soup kitchens and feed the poor for nothing. But it was only in the spring of 1847, when many people had already died, that this was done. And even then, the government would not pay for these things. They insisted that Irish taxpayers must carry the cost of the workhouse soup kitchens.

IMAGINE YOU WERE A CHARITY WORKER WHO CAME TO IRELAND DURING THE FAMINE (LIKE SOMEONE FROM CONCERN OR TROCAIRE HELPING FAMINE VICTIMS TODAY).

WRITE A LETTER HOME DESCRIBING WHAT YOU HAVE SEEN AND DONE. USE THE INFORMATION IN THIS CHAPTER AND IN ANY OTHER SOURCE YOU HAVE STUDIED. YOU SHOULD:

- ☑ EXPLAIN WHAT CAUSED THE FAMINE
- ☑ DESCRIBE THE PLIGHT OF THE PEOPLE
- ☑ MENTION SOME OF THE THINGS YOU HAVE DONE TO HELP THEM
- ☑ SAY WHAT THE GOVERNMENT HAD DONE TO HELP AND WHETHER YOU THINK THIS WAS ENOUGH
- ☑ COMMENT ON WHETHER YOU THINK THE THINGS YOU HAVE BEEN DOING HAVE BEEN OF ASSISTANCE
- ☑ SAY WHAT YOU THINK SHOULD BE DONE

Looking at the evidence ▼▼▼▼▼▼

The results of the Famine

THE POPULATION FALLS

The most obvious result of the famine was a fall in the population. This table shows the population of Ireland before and after the famine.

1841	8,175,000
1851	6,550,000

As you can see, there were nearly two million fewer people in Ireland in 1851 than in 1841.

What became of all the people? Historians think that about a million died, either from hunger or disease, during the famine. The rest emigrated.

THE POPULATION DID NOT FALL AT THE SAME RATE IN ALL PARTS OF THE COUNTRY. THE MAP SHOWS HOW THE POPULATION CHANGED IN EACH COUNTY DURING THE TEN YEARS BETWEEN 1841 AND 1851. LOOK AT IT CLOSELY AND SAY (A) WHERE THE POPULATION FELL MOST; (B) WHERE THE POPULATION FELL LEAST; AND (C) WHERE IT ACTUALLY GREW. CAN YOU THINK OF ANYTHING TO EXPLAIN THESE DIFFERENCES?

Looking at the evidence

TRACE A MAP OF IRELAND, WITH THE COUNTIES, INTO YOUR COPYBOOK. COLOUR THE COUNTIES ACCORDING TO THE AMOUNT OF POPULATION THEY LOST DURING THE FAMINE. USE ONE COLOUR FOR 30% AND OVER, A SECOND ONE FOR 20% TO 29%, AND SO ON. TRY TO EXPLAIN THE DIFFERENCES YOU NOTICE.

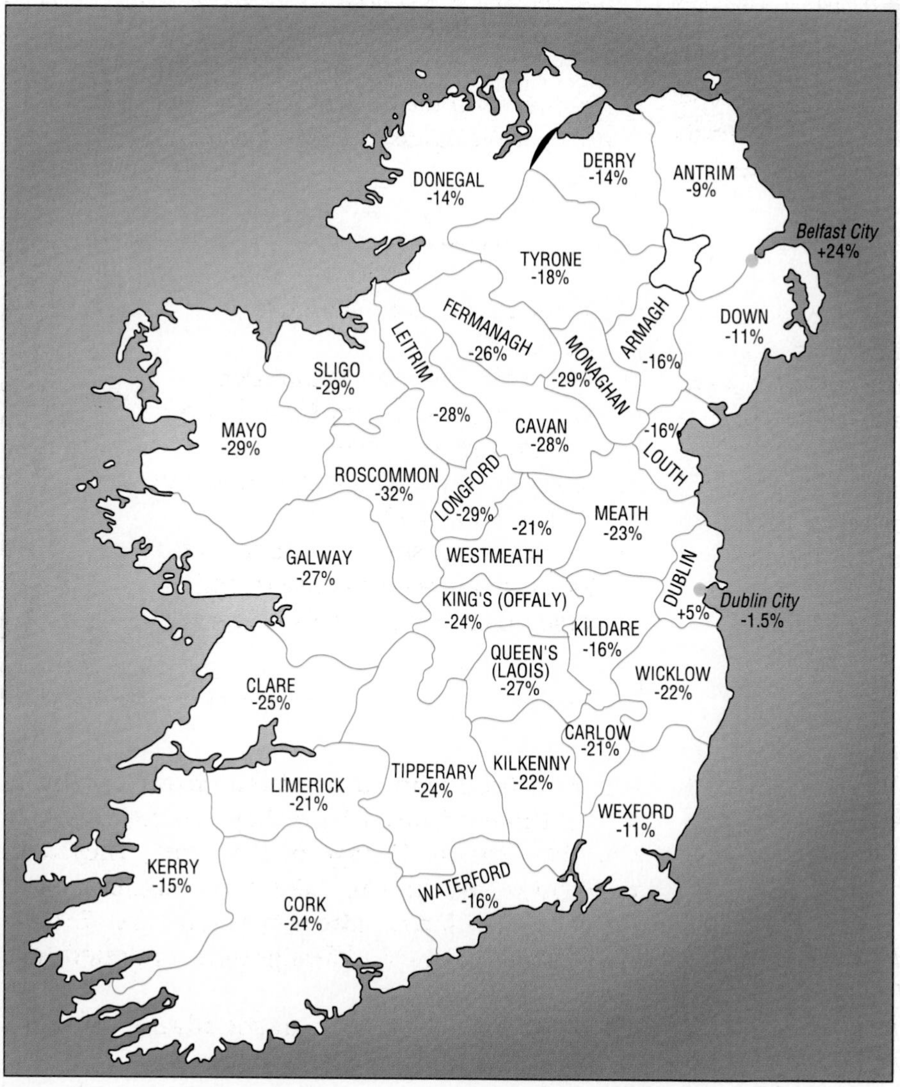

Activity

EMIGRATION

Most Irish emigrants went to Britain. At the time, it was possible to cross the Irish Sea for as little as one shilling (5p), so the poorest could afford to go there. By June 1847, 300,000 Irish people had landed in Liverpool and many thousands more flooded into other ports. The local people hated them because they carried disease and begged.

A drawing from 1851 shows emigrants crowding the quays in Cork before boarding ships bound for Liverpool.

Poor Irish people were often evicted from their lodgings in Britain. Explain why.

Others went to North America. The United States closed their ports when they realised that many of the Irish had fever. As a result, most of them went to Canada. They were put in **quarantine** before they were allowed to land.

Here is a letter written by an emigrant from Sligo, whose landlord, Henry Gore-Booth, had paid the fare (about £5) to send many of his tenants to Canada.

15 February 1848

Dear Father and Mother,

I take the present opportunity of letteing you know that I am in good health. We cast anchor at Partridge island after 5 weeks. There were 4 deaths on the passage, but the second day after we arrived here the Sickness commenced. We were put on the Island for three weeks (in quarantine), at the end of which time my dear little Biddy died. Thank God I got safe off and continue to enjoy good health since.

Dear Father, pen could not write the distress of the Irish Passengers which arrive here. Through sickness and death and distress of every kind, the

Irish I know have suffered much and is still suffering. There are thousands of them buried on the Island and those that could not go to the States are in the Poorhouse or begging through the streets. Do not neglect but write as soon as you can I will be uneasy till I hear from you.

No more at present But remains your affectionate Daughter till Death.

Catherine Hennagan

READ THE LETTER FROM CATHERINE HENNAGAN.

1. HOW LONG DID HER VOYAGE TAKE?
2. WERE MANY PEOPLE SICK (A) AT SEA OR (B) AFTER THEY LANDED?
3. WHAT DOES SHE SAY ABOUT OTHER IRISH PEOPLE IN CANADA?
4. DO YOU THINK SHE WAS WELL EDUCATED? PICK OUT THE POINTS IN HER LETTER WHICH LEAD YOU TO THAT CONCLUSION.

Looking at the evidence

Many of those who survived the crossing went on to the United States where they settled mainly in cities like Boston, Chicago or New York. They were very poor and had to take the toughest, most poorly-paid jobs. They blamed the British government for their sufferings and supported Irish demands for freedom.

As time passed, some descendants of Irish emigrants became wealthy and successful. In 1960, one of them, John F. Kennedy, was elected president of the United States.

SOURCE A

THE CHART SHOWS THE NUMBERS OF PEOPLE WHO EMIGRATED FROM IRELAND BETWEEN 1841 AND 1855. STUDY THE CHART, THEN ANSWER THE QUESTIONS.

1841	16,400
1842	89,700
1843	37,500
1844	54,300
1845	75,000
1846	105,960
1847	215,400
1848	178, 159
1849	214,400
1850	209,000
1851	152,000
1852	190,300
1853	173,000
1854	140,000
1855	91,900

1. DRAW A BAR CHART IN YOUR COPY BOOK TO ILLUSTRATE THESE FIGURES.
2. THE BLIGHT FIRST HIT THE POTATO CROP IN 1845, SO YOU WOULD EXPECT EMIGRATION TO RISE IN THE FOLLOWING YEAR. DID IT? BY HOW MANY? BY WHAT PERCENTAGE?
3. WHY WAS THERE A FURTHER JUMP IN EMIGRATION IN 1847? USE EVIDENCE FROM THE TEXT TO SUPPORT YOUR ANSWER.
4. THE "FAMINE YEARS" LASTED FROM 1846 TO 1852. WHAT IS THE TOTAL NUMBER OF PEOPLE WHO LEFT IRELAND DURING THESE YEARS?
5. WHY WAS THERE A DROP IN EMIGRATION NUMBERS IN 1855? TRY TO THINK OF TWO REASONS FOR THIS.

SOURCE B

DEATH AND EMIGRATION REDUCED THE POPULATION OF IRELAND. HOWEVER, THIS DID NOT STOP WITH THE END OF THE FAMINE.
LOOK AT THESE POPULATION FIGURES OVER SEVENTY YEARS, BETWEEN 1821 AND 1891.

1821	6,800,000
1831	7,760,000
1841	8,175,000
1851	6,550,000
1861	5,800,000
1871	5,410,000
1881	5,170,000
1891	4,700,000

1. DRAW A GRAPH SHOWING HOW THE POPULATION OF IRELAND CHANGED BETWEEN 1821 AND 1891.
2. IN WHICH DECADE DOES YOUR GRAPH CHANGE DIRECTION? EXPLAIN WHY.
3. DID THE POPULATION RISE OR FALL AFTER THE "FAMINE YEARS"? SUPPORT YOUR ANSWER WITH FIGURES. THEN TRY TO COME UP WITH AT LEAST ONE REASON FOR WHAT YOU HAVE DISCOVERED.

Looking at the evidence

The Famine changes Ireland

The famine changed Ireland greatly.
- The cottiers and labourers, who were already the poorest people before the famine, suffered most. Many of them died or emigrated, so that after the famine, few of them were left.
- Emigration continued as people left the country to find work. As a result, the population continued to fall. Today, the population of Ireland is still less than five million, compared with eight million before the famine.
- Parents who expected their children to emigrate thought that the schools should teach them in English, not Irish. As a result, the Irish language began to disappear.

QUESTIONS

1. Where did most people emigrate to during the famine? Explain why they did so.
2. List three changes that took place in Ireland as a result of the famine.

INDEX